S

THE LAST
TOURIST
IN IRAN

From Persepolis to Nuclear Natanz

First published by O Books, 2008
O Books is an imprint of John Hunt Publishing
Ltd., The Bothy, Deershot Lodge, Park Lane,
Ropley, Hants, SO24 0BE, UK
office1@o-books.net
www.o-books.net

Distribution in:

UK and Europe
Orca Book Services
orders@orcabookservices.co.uk
Tel: 01202 665432 Fax: 01202 666219 Int. code
(44)

USA and Canada
NBN
custserv@nbnbooks.com
Tel: 1 800 462 6420 Fax: 1 800 338 4550

Australia and New Zealand
Brumby Books
sales@brumbybooks.com.au
Tel: 61 3 9761 5535 Fax: 61 3 9761 7095

Far East (offices in Singapore, Thailand, Hong
Kong, Taiwan)
Pansing Distribution Pte Ltd
kemal@pansing.com
Tel: 65 6319 9939 Fax: 65 6462 5761

South Africa
Alternative Books
altbook@peterhyde.co.za
Tel: 021 447 5300 Fax: 021 447 1430

Text copyright Nicholas Hagger 2008

Design: Stuart Davies

ISBN-13: 978 1 84694 076 7

A CIP catalogue record for this book is available
from the British Library.

Printed in the US by Maple Vail

O Books operates a distinctive and ethical publishing philosophy in
all areas of its business, from its global network of authors to
production and worldwide distribution.

No trees were cut down to print this particular book. The paper is
100% recycled, with 50% of that being post-consumer. It's processed
chlorine-free, and has no fibre from ancient or endangered forests.

This production method on this print run saved approximately
thirteen trees, 4,000 gallons of water, 600 pounds of solid waste,
990 pounds of greenhouse gases and 8 million BTU of energy. On its
publication a tree was planted in a new forest that O Books is
sponsoring at The Village www.thefourgates.com

THE LAST
TOURIST
IN IRAN

From Persepolis to Nuclear Natanz

Nicholas Hagger

BOOKS

Winchester, UK
Washington, USA

BOOKS PUBLISHED BY NICHOLAS HAGGER

A Mystic Way
A Smell of Leaves and Summer
A Spade Fresh with Mud
Awakening to the Light
A White Radiance
Classical Odes
Collected Poems 1958 – 2005
Collected Stories
Collected Verse Plays
The Light of Civilization
Overlord
Overlord, one-volume edition
Selected Poems
The Fire and the Stones
The Last Tourist in Iran
The Light of Civilization
The One and the Many
The Rise and fall of Civilizations
The Secret History of the West
The Secret Founding of America
The Syndicate
The Tragedy of Prince Tudor
The Universe and the Light
The Warlords
The Warm Glow of the Monastery Courtyard
Wheeling bats and a Harvest Moon

CONTENTS

To John Hunt, who suggested it; to Farhad, with gratitude; to Ann who saw it was important I should take the risk and go; and to the memory of T. E. Lawrence, sometime owner of land at Pole Hill, Chingford, who would have appreciated my quest into Persian and Shia Islamic culture and my attempt to reveal the Iranian soul through its holy places.

1

BEHIND THE NEGATIVE IMAGE

Persia. The country had loomed large in my imagination ever since, as a schoolboy studying Greek literature, I had read of the mighty invader that threatened to crush Greece. Herodotus referred to the Persians as "the barbarians". Their awesome power gathered in 492 BC under Darius I, King of kings, who was incensed at the burning of Sardis by Athenians, and was miraculously repulsed by Greek heroism at Marathon. They came again in 480 BC in a revenge attack under Xerxes I, Darius's successor, crossing the Hellespont on a bridge of boats with 180,000 men. They were held up at Thermopylae but burned Athens. Then, with Xerxes watching on high from a throne of rock, they were thrown at Salamis. After further battles during the next two years including the battle of Plataea of 479 BC the civilized Greeks were saved from an implacable foe, Ionian cities became independent and the Athenian Empire was born. That led to Rome, to Christendom, Western culture and the world we know today. In my boyhood the Persians were the enemy. Reviled, they stood for barbarism and everything bad.

Now I was standing in Persepolis, "city of the Persians", among the superlative Achaemenian carvings there. I had the massive 33-acre site all to myself. I had been looking at meticulously realistic carvings on the Apadana platform, and I had a startling – indeed, stunning – revelation that sent a shiver up my spine, a thrilling moment that seemed to turn my boyhood – indeed, the West's – understanding of ancient history on its head. All the carvings had been executed around, or soon after, 515 BC. This was *before* the Persian expeditions to Greece, *before* Greek philosophy rose in Persian-ruled Ionia, long before Greek art flourished and reached its highest achievement in Pheidias's carvings on the Athenian Parthenon.

The Persians believed that Ahura Mazda – who may have been shown as the winged soul (*Faravahar* or *Fravahar*) displayed on early Persian monuments although this may merely be the Achaemenian crest – was the supreme, if not sole, god and that the universe was "One" within him. The vision of an ordered and whole universe, inspired by a single spirit, which was at the source of Greek – and then Western – philosophy, had arisen from this developing Persian monotheism. It had travelled from Persia to Ionia, been taken to Elea in Southern Italy by Xenophanes of Colophon, who passed it on to Parmenides, the grandfather of Western philosophy. But it was originally *Persian*. Therefore in c.515 BC the idol-worshipping Greeks, not the nearly monotheistic Persians, were the true barbarians; and Persia, which had been behind Greece, not Greece, was the true source of our Western civilization.

And now we, the beneficiaries of early Persian culture, were as mighty in our time under the leadership of Bush II as Persia had been in the time of Darius I and Xerxes I. We had this troublesome, backward country of Iran to deal with, full of people who dressed oddly, behaved strangely, and seemed to go their own way irrespective of our strategic interests. Obligingly, we had destroyed their enemies on either side, removing the threats from Iraq and Afghanistan. By some miscalculation we had let it become, by default, the main force in the region. Even worse, the Iranian President Ahmadinejad had threatened to wipe Israel off the map and was defiantly developing nuclear energy, a policy felt by many to be a cover for a nuclear bomb, as if he was the spiritual descendant of Xerxes rather than ourselves. So we in turn we were proposing to crush terrorist-supporting Iran and with it, no doubt, some of the early Persian culture that had inspired our civilization's Greek precursor, just as the "barbarian" Persians had tried to crush early, pre-imperial Greece. Who were the barbarians now?

*

"Please don't say you're an author on this form," the travel agent said. "It'll take forever to obtain a visa. Just put down retired teacher." And so that was how I went in (Tehran – "Teheran" with an "e" is an incorrect, French spelling – having authorised my visa in a fortnight and the Iranian Embassy in London having issued it a week later).

Why Iran? I had long had an interest in the Middle East. I had spent eight months lecturing in English Literature at the University of Baghdad back in 1961 and had visited the cradle of civilization in Mesopotamia: the ancient site of Paradise where the Tigris joined the Euphrates, out of which had grown the Sumerian, Akkadian, Babylonian and Assyrian empires in lands around nearby Babylon. In Iraq I had encountered young men who spoke enthusiastically about Iran, and I had been offered a job there in 1968 but had gone to Libya instead to be closer to ancient Egypt.

Iran was as much a cradle of civilization as Iraq. Although, influenced from Mesopotamia, the Elamites were progressing between c.3000 and c.2500 BC. The Iranian civilization was the result of two migrations: of Indo-European Aryans through Mesopotamian Akad c.2250 BC and of Indo-Iranian Aryans from the east c.1500 BC. It was unified by Cyrus the Great and his Achaemenian dynasty. It then expanded with the Sasanians before being conquered by Arab Muslims by AD 640. It eventually passed into the Arab civilization when the Safavids completed their subjugation of Iran and made Shiite Islam Iran's official religion in 1511.

For me, a student of the rise and fall of civilizations, going to Iran would be an opportunity to study a civilization that had passed through all the stages in a civilization's life cycle, and which boasted a great tradition. In 1971 the last Shah had proudly honoured 2,500 years of kingship, which began with Cyrus the Great. He had planted 2,500 trees at Persepolis to symbolise the antiquity and continuity of Iranian kingship, and had famously and grandly proclaimed before the tomb of Cyrus, the first Iranian king, at Pasargadae: "O Cyrus, sleep calm and peaceful for *I* am here."

I had always been fascinated by early religions as well as civilizations, and had been particularly interested in Zoroaster, founder of the earliest religion based on revealed scripture, the *Avesta*, which probably originated c.600 BC (although there are claims that it was much earlier). He proclaimed Ahura Mazda as the god of the early Persians. Ahura Mazda was transmitted to the Jews held in exile in Persian-ruled Babylon. In the seven generations or so that they lived in Persia they assimilated many of the Persian beliefs – the idea of a holy, just God who all men should worship, with evil embodied separately in Satan, rather than the local tribal god of the Hebrews; the immortality of the soul, along with life after death, resurrection, heaven and hell, and the judgement of the dead; and the final prophet, the world saviour, the Holy Spirit (the Persian Spenta Mainyu), down to the details of the seven archangels, the seven-branched candlestick (*menorah*) and the Sabbath, the full moon day. When Cyrus liberated Babylonia in 539 BC and permitted the Jews to return home the following year, the Jews took back with them the concept of Ahura Mazda as supreme god. Zoroastrianism had influenced Jewish monotheism and is therefore perhaps the most influential religion of all time. I knew that Ahura Mazda is still worshipped in Iran, particularly in remoter areas.

I was interested in Iran's ethnic diversity. In 1935 Reza Shah, the father of the last Shah, called on the world to refer to his country not as Persia but as Iran ("land of the Aryans"), a name first used by Ardashir I, founder of the Sasanian dynasty, to reflect all ethnic groups, Persian and non-Persian, which now include the Kurds, the Turkmen, the Baluchis and the Lurs. The Sasanian "Iranshahr" (or "Eranshahr") meant "Empire of the Aryans".

I also appreciated Iran's modern significance in international politics. The story had been a turbulent one. The rise of Ayatollah Khomeini ("*Ayatollah*" means "sign of God") and his replacement of the last Shah in a Cromwell-style (but civil-warless), puritanical revolution in 1979 marked the highest point of the Islamic movement and inspired bin Laden to attempt to replace the House of Saud. 9/11 struck at the House of Saud's main ally. More recently President Ahmadinejad's determination to make Iran nuclear in defiance of US wishes and a UN Security Council resolution (1737) has made military action against Iran by the new Coalition a very real possibility. Indeed, given the uncompromising stance of both sides at the time it seemed unavoidable. Iranian intransigence was now a byword, and could have profound implications for the supply of the world's oil.

I wanted to see Iran's cultural heritage before the country became impenetrable and before its monuments were destroyed. Not much, alas, has been left of Iraq's cultural treasures after five years of relentless war and civil war. I was fortunate enough to see Iraq's early Islamic caliphate buildings in conditions of relative peace and security under the military dictatorship of Abdul Karim Kassem, and this might be my last chance to absorb early Iranian culture in similarly peaceful conditions.

So what is the aim of this book? My immediate personal reason was that I was planning a long poem on the Middle East, and, as in the case of my poetic epic *Overlord*, which I researched on the

Second World War's battlefields, I wanted to do some on-the-spot research and absorb some local colour for this new work before Iran became a no-go area. More broadly, I thought my traveller's notes might help a wider audience appreciate the sheer wealth of Iran's cultural and spiritual heritage. Iran was richly diverse, and in its tourist sites and ruins Achaemenian, Sasanian, Islamic, Safavid and modern motifs were woven together into a fine pattern, like the pattern on an exquisite Persian carpet. Its awe-inspiring mix of culture, history, politics and spirituality could not fail to impress the most casual observer and nourish all personal quests for universality, the philosophy of embracing the "whole" whilst retaining our individual distinctiveness which I see as the only way forward for our troubled world. It was lamentable that some of its beauty might be about to be lost in war. Maybe in tracing its history and culture I could see how we came to this impasse, and how it might be negotiated.

No country had been the recipient of a more negative image than Iran. President Ahmadinejad had been identified by one of the hostages as one of the student leaders who held 66 American diplomats and citizens hostage in their own Embassy in Tehran for 444 days in 1979-81. An AP picture of this particular student leader can be found in Mark Bowden's *Guests of the Ayatollah*, and he certainly looks like a younger version of Ahmadinejad. It was suggested that a "fanatic" who allegedly climbed the gates to the US Embassy and paraded the blindfolded Jerry Miele on 11 November 1979 was now on the verge of acquiring, allegedly with Pakistani and perhaps North Korean help, a nuclear weapon that can be used against the United States.

To the US, if true this was a preposterous state of affairs and was a possible factor in the US's decision to urge the UN to introduce targeted sanctions against Iran under resolution 1737, which banned the export of nuclear technology to Iran, and to call on a reluctant Europe to implement an economic squeeze against Iran to foment internal dissent. Iran had been given 60 days to comply with a list of demands, and had so far ignored them. Tehran had just turned down applications for visas from 38 UN nuclear inspectors. The situation looked potentially more dangerous than the situation in Iraq, which had 1,200 UN inspectors looking unsuccessfully for nuclear weapons in 2003, and the US and Britain still went to war.

Furthermore, there had been allegations that the Supreme Leader has been host to al-Qaeda and has funded Hamas in Palestine, Shiites in Iraq and Nasrallah in the Lebanon, all of whom were anti-US. It is hard to know how much of this is true, but there does seem more evidence of substantial involvement with these groups than was produced for similar involvement by Saddam Hussein. There had been claims in the press that Iran had been responsible for the insurgency in Iraq, through the 31,690 Iranian agents (named by an opposition group, the National Council of Resistance) allegedly working in Iraq, paid in Iranian *rials* and supplying Shia militias with money, bomb-making equipment and expertise. To the US this was unacceptable, and according to press reports, Bush had authorised American troops to kill these agents. Put all this together and it is easy to see why word was out that Iran was a pariah state and was not a safe place to visit, and why a country that should be in the top ten destinations in terms of its attractions has not been in the top one hundred over the last couple of years.

Tour operators confirmed this image. "I'd like to go to Susa," I told the travel agent, "which was the Elamite capital and also one of Cyrus's and Darius's capitals in the south-west; to the tomb of Daniel, the *Old Testament* prophet; and to the two ziggurats, Choqa Zanbil and Haft Tappeh, nearby."

The answer came back from the ground handlers that the area

was not safe for Westerners. "It's just across the Shatt al-Arab from Basra. It's a strongly Arab area, there are al-Qaeda present. The tour company can't guarantee your safety in the south-west. They don't allow any tourists to go to the Ahwaz area, they may be kidnapped on the sites."

And Bam in the south-east, where there was a terrible earthquake on 27 December 2003?

"There are still many homeless camping round the ruins. Visitors are discouraged from going there. It's also not safe. Visitors can be attacked."

The UK's Foreign-and-Commonwealth-Office website reflected this concern. Iran was listed as a second-category country, meaning a country "the FCO advises against all travel to parts of ". "There is a threat from terrorism in Iran. Attacks could be indiscriminate and against civilian targets." The FCO website continued, "We strongly advise against all travel to the border areas with Afghanistan, Pakistan and Iraq. Westerners have been the target of kidnaps by armed gangs in south-east Iran.... We cannot rule out the possibility of further kidnaps." (The Lonely-Planet website said that one should only go overland to Iran if one has a death-wish.)

The week before I went Bush Jr announced that 21,500 more US troops would be sent to Iraq. A front-page *Sunday Times* article about Israel also appeared, claiming that Israeli planes were rehearsing sorties to Iran by flying to Gibraltar and back, the distances being comparable. Israeli pilots were being trained to bomb the nuclear sites near Isfahan and Arak with conventional bunker-busters and the nuclear site near Natanz with nuclear-tipped tactical nuclear weapons one-fifteenth of the size of the Hiroshima bomb. If this happened, Natanz would soon be as well-known as Hiroshima.

With all these considerations in mind I chose my itinerary by looking at books and maps and aiming to be compact. The main principle was to see as much as possible, operate out of a car and keep moving, and to sleep in a different place each night so that if any ill-disposed "terrorists" heard of my presence I would be gone before they could locate me. I was clear that it was too risky on several counts to take my wife, who had been my travelling companion to so many places that feature in my literary works. This was a journey I should undertake alone. I designed a tailor-made itinerary in conjunction with a tour company who liaised with their "ground handlers" in Iran. The itinerary was agreed before I left the UK. I consulted my doctor's surgery and was deemed to be covered for typhoid. I was given tetanus, diphtheria and polio in one arm and hepatitis A in the other. I made sure I had good travel and medical insurance.

The tourist season in Iran is from March to December. Few tourists go in January and February because of possible snow and hazardous ice. I had originally planned to go in December but my visit was delayed until mid-January as it became clear that my visa would not be through in time. The compensation for this was that the "nuclear crisis" had caused the hardy souls who might otherwise have braved the anticipated winter weather in January to cancel, and I seemed to be the only tourist in Iran. I pretty much had Iran to myself. I was the last tourist in Iran before the bombing was expected to begin.

2

IN EARLY IRANIAN AND REVOLUTIONARY TEHRAN

On the plane I had a foretaste of the extraordinary charm and kindness of the Iranian people. I had begun to read a guidebook on Iran when I was spoken to by a matronly lady wearing a black headscarf sitting two seats away. (The plane was not full, and the seat between us was unoccupied.)

She asked, "Are you going to Iran on business?"

I explained I would be touring.

"Oh, you must ask for guides I know."

She opened a pocketbook and wrote out the names of two guides in Tehran. I explained I was with a tour company and was being met by a car.

"You may need this if they don't turn up. There's been snow in Tehran."

I explained I would be going on to Shiraz later that afternoon.

"Oh, I know a guide in Shiraz. I am from Yazd."

I said I would be going to Yazd.

"Oh, I know a guide in Yazd as well."

She insisted on writing out all their names, and I was greatly impressed by her sheer kindness and eagerness to help.

She told me, "I've lived in England for eighteen years. I used to teach at the University of Tehran, yes, English. I live in Barnes, my two children went to Imperial College."

I asked what her husband did.

"We export to Iran. Electrical parts."

I asked if they had been affected by UN sanctions.

"Yes, because our bank has been blacklisted, it has affected us. I'm going to be in Tehran until Wednesday, a short business visit."

I asked where she felt safer, London or Tehran?

"Tehran, I can get in a taxi in Tehran and go to my address. I don't feel safe in London."

I asked if her religion was Shiite.

"Oh yes. We believe the Hidden *Imam* helps us. He was the twelfth and according to our Shia belief he is still alive because of his occultation."

I knew the Hidden *Imam*, Muhammad al-Mahdi, had descended down the Jamkaran well near Qom on a Wednesday in AD 874 and had been in occultation – hidden by Allah and alive – ever since, and that he was due to return soon to establish absolute justice throughout the world. Iraqi Shias believe that he descended down a well in Samarra in Iraq, but both Iraqi and Iranian Shias see Him coming on a white mule – some believe horse – accompanied by Jesus on a Friday. Jesus is also waiting, presumably also hidden by Allah, awaiting the moment.

But the Hidden *Imam* would only return when there was chaos, when mankind realised the futility of trying to organise its own affairs and was ready to receive him. President Ahmadinejad is reputed to be a member of the *Hojjateieh*s, a sect who believe that chaos should be caused in the Middle East, notably in bordering Iraq, in order to speed up the return. (In the same way some Rapture-believing Christians in the West eagerly search the news for more earthquakes, wars and famines for evidence that Christ will soon take them up to heaven.) According to one website President Ahmadinejad reckoned the return would be in 2008.

"All the *imam*s are important, particularly the first and the eighth," she said. "Mashad in Iran is holy because the eighth *Imam* is buried there. But the twelfth is especially important. I have a friend who went to Mecca. She got lost. She told me, 'I felt lost. I prayed to the Hidden *Imam*, "Help me, I'm lost." And then suddenly I saw my nephew. I didn't know he was in Mecca. He helped me. It was the Hidden *Imam*'s doing."' She said, "Christianity and Islam are so close. Jesus and the Hidden *Imam* will pray together when the Hidden *Imam* returns."

I asked if she thought of the Hidden *Imam* as being in a particular location.

"He's everywhere, not in one particular place."

I asked if there were many tourists in Iran.

"No, not many tourists."

"Americans?"

"No, no Americans come."

I spoke of the wonderful history of Iran, of Cyrus, Darius and Xerxes. I said Iran used to have a very close connection with England in the 1930s – hence the Anglo-Iranian Oil Company. The Americans entered Iran following the 1953 *coup* against Mossadeq, the Iranian Prime Minister who was too radical for the Shah, and sixteen years later there was a reaction against the Americans which resulted in the Revolution.

"We were very anxious during the Revolution. My father was ill and could not go abroad for the treatment he needed. But he still loved Ayatollah Khomeini."

I mentioned President Ahmadinejad.

"The West don't like him. He was a university lecturer before he became Mayor of Tehran."

I said he had an engaging smile on television and was clearly very intelligent.

"Yes, he is. But the West don't like him."

*

The driver who had taken me to Heathrow airport in London, an ex-soldier who had served in Northern Ireland and fought in the Falklands, had asked "Are you mad?" His words came back when, after the night flight and little sleep, and seemingly the only Westerner on the plane, I landed at Mehrabad airport in Tehran in the dark, queued at passport control among women in black *chador*s and was promptly separated from my passport.

"VIP lounge," the uniformed passport inspector said in English, leaving his booth and pointing towards an open door twenty yards away, and I had to walk and sit on my own in a comfortably furnished room with four easy chairs and a computer while portraits of Ayatollah Khomeini and the current Supreme Leader Ali Khamenei glared accusingly at me from a wall.

Eventually an Iranian came in with three passports and sat at the computer. He examined my passport and called my name. "Yes," I said. He handed me my passport and I was free to go. I walked up a flight of stairs and encountered a small crowd behind a barrier, where a youngish man dressed in brown held my name on a placard. I waved in acknowledgement and found myself shaking hands with a courteous, softly-spoken man who said, "Welcome to Iran. I am your guide."

"For Tehran?"

"No, for the whole of your tour. I will be with you for all your time in Iran. My name is Farhad. I was watching you from above. I was getting worried. Was there a problem with your passport?"

I identified my green suitcase and he lifted it on to a trolley and trundled it to an Exchange counter where he took my passport.

"A hundred dollars will be enough for the whole time. I will be covering all entrances on our travels."

He changed a $100 note I gave him into *rials*. The rate was 9,130 *rials* per dollar, down from 8,800 in 2005 for the *rial* was a declining currency. Then he took me out to our car, where I met our driver "just for Tehran", a tall, smiling thin man who spoke no English.

Dawn had broken, and it was now light at 7 am It had snowed

heavily the previous day but there was no trace of snow now, though it was faintly misty. The temperature was a few degrees above freezing. The driver put my luggage in the car boot and I seat-belted myself at the back, behind Farhad. We set off through early morning traffic for Rey (or Rayy), driving on the right, and I fixed my eyes on the diversity of dress: women in black headscarves called *maghwae*s, Farhad told me, or long black *chador*s that left their faces uncovered, men in open-necked shirts walking among *mullah*s wearing white or black turbans, the black ones indicating that they were descendants of the Prophet, Farhad said.

All round me was a honking and mesmerizing crowding-forward of cars. "In your country, pedestrians have priority on crossings," Farhad said. "Here, cars have priority." And we bore down on pedestrians trying to cross a crossing, missing them by inches, and maintained our forward progress while cars surged alongside on either side, attempting to cut in front of us from left and right. When we stopped at a red traffic light there was a board alongside it with a countdown from 60 seconds, the red number descending every second to let us know how much longer we had before we could move off. And every so often there would be posters on public buildings of the grimly unsmiling duo: Khomeini and Khamenei.

"You don't mind if I write some of my impressions down?" I asked. "I shall forget them if I don't write them down." And I suddenly realised I was not holding my mint reporter's book which I had ordered specially in England so that I would not be taking in any of my past notes. I asked if we could pull over and stop so I could remove my shoulder-bag from the top of my suitcase, in which I had packed my camera and reporter's book.

The driver pulled over and opened the boot, and as I went to unlock the padlock on my suitcase, for the first time I realised that it was open, hanging at right angles to its brass arm which I lifted off. I unzipped my case and removed my shoulder-bag and felt inside it. The camera was there, but there was no reporter's book. I rummaged in my suitcase and in my hand luggage while cars nosed up behind and swerved out to overtake, sometimes hooting. But no, the reporter's book which I had so carefully placed inside my shoulder-bag at the top of the suitcase had not fallen out or been placed elsewhere. It was definitely missing.

Now it dawned on me that my case had been deliberately opened, perhaps while I was in the VIP room, and that my mint reporter's book had been taken. Had someone wondered if it contained writing that needed to be examined? Or had someone decided to test my mint book with chemicals in case it contained writing in invisible ink? Or did someone not want me to write my impressions down? What other explanation could there be?

"I'll have a good look later," I said, playing the incident down. "I'll use paper until then. It was here, but it must have fallen out when my bag burst open during the unloading."

I was impatient to make contact with old Persia, and we resumed our tour through long traffic-filled streets. Misty mountains occasionally showed on the northern horizon under a faint blue sky.

We reached Rey, the ancient Rhaga or Rhages which had been settled since the third millennium BC, now a suburb ten kilometres south of Tehran and not far from the airport on the west. It was at the very start at the Iranian civilization and preceded the coming of the first Aryans from Oxus and the Jaxartes before 2000 BC. It featured as a sacred place in the Zoroastrian *Avesta* – where it was the twelfth city of the world to be created by Ahura Mazda – and in the Apocryphal book of *Tobit* as the place ("Rages of Media") where Tobias and the angel stopped after the wedding in Ecbatana (Hamadan). It had been burned by Alexander and rebuilt by the

Seleucids, and was the main Median city under the Parthians and Sasanians.

Later, it was captured by the Muslim Arabs in 641, and in the 8th century, as the birthplace of the Abbasid *caliph* Harun al-Rashid, it rivalled Damascus and Baghdad. In the 10th and 11th centuries it was governed by the Samanids, Ziyadids (or Ziyarids), Buyids and Ghaznavids, names I had encountered in my study in the rise and fall of civilizations. Under the Seljuq sultanate from 1038 it was known as "the most beautiful city in the East" and was second only to the city of Baghdad, the Abbasid centre of the Islamic empire. It was more important than Tehran, which was merely a suburb of Rey, and it was destroyed by the Mongols in 1220.

Hardly anything remained of the ancient city, which was now occupied by two-and-a-half million Afghan refugees, but we went straight to the old Sasanian walls of the Ghal-e Tabarak fortress, ruined sandstone on sloping sandy rock under a blue sky. A stretch of wall had been restored with crenellations and doorways to show what it originally looked like. Cut into the base of the sloping rock was a relief above a mountain spring, Cheshmeh Ali ("Spring Water of Ali"), a 19th-century Qajar monument. The relief showed the Qajar Shah Nasir al-Din and his ten sons, and an earlier panel shows Fath Ali Shah, who died in 1934 and had about 200 wives and at least 170 – some say 189 – children. I was more interested in the ancient Sasanian fort.

We saw the outside of a shrine built for descendants of the second and fourth *Imam*s and the brother of the eighth *Imam*: the shrine of Shah Abd al-Azim, a mausoleum with a 14th-century tomb under a golden dome and beautiful tiles. Farhad said, "I am a Shiite, and so is the driver. The Prophet Mohammad died in 632, and there was a debate about his successor. One group, the Shia ('party, supporters') held that he had designated his son-in-law Ali as successor. Another group, the Sunnis ('people of the *Sunna*, the Assembly'), argued that he had not designated anybody and that his successor should be chosen from a group of elder companions of Mohammad, and they chose his father-in-law Abu Bakr as the first *caliph* ('successor') while Ali was attending to Mohammad's funeral rites.

"So the Sunnis and the Shias split and the Shias followed an *Imam* ('leader' of Islam, 'successor' to Mohammad). The Shiite minority was persecuted by the Sunni majority and I will be telling you about the suffering and martyrdom of Husayn (or Hossein and other variants), the third *Imam*, in 680 AD, which Shiites relive every year with tears and sometimes self-flagellation. Of the eleven *Imam*s, only one is buried in Iran, the eighth *Imam*, in Mashad. Of the rest, number one (Ali) is buried in Najaf in Iraq, number three (Husayn) is buried in Kerbala, Iraq; numbers two, four, five, six and nine are buried in Medina, Saudi Arabia; and numbers ten and eleven are buried in Khadimain, Iraq." The other Islamic monument, the Seljuq-period mausoleum, Toghril Beg, named after a sultan – the Turkish conqueror who founded the Seljuq dynasty – who died in 1063 but built sixty years later, was closed.

We headed back and soon passed a procession and band. A drum was beating and Farhad said that those marching were raising money for *Moharram* (or *Muharram*). He explained that *Moharram* would begin on January 20 and would last ten days, during which local communities would put on playlets with a religious theme. The tenth day was like Christmas Day, no one would go to work. It celebrated the martyrdom of Husayn, the younger son of Ali and Fatima, the third *Imam* who was murdered in heroic circumstances. When the Ummayad *caliph* Muawiya died in 680, Husayn was invited by the Medina governor to swear an oath in support of Yazid, his successor. Advised not to swear the oath in support of the Sunnis, Husayn went to Mecca and then to Kufa in Iraq. He was pursued by the Ummayad army. He told his 72 supporters to save themselves but they refused. The Ummayad forces poisoned the water-holes and his relative Abbas Abu'l Fazl volunteered to find drinking-water. He was captured and both his hands were cut off. Husayn again urged his followers to save themselves and to flee, but they refused. During the battle that followed Husayn and his 72 supporters were all killed on 10 *Moharram* AD 680. Many car windows carried pictures of Husayn and Abbas on their back windows.

I asked Farhad if, as a Shia, he believed the story actually happened.

"Of course," Farhad said. "All Shias believe it."

*

Now we headed for Tehran, which began as a suburb of Rey and was probably founded in the 11th century. It was established by the 15th century, but not surrounded by a fortified wall until the 16th century when the bazaar was rebuilt and a citadel (*arg*) was added, of which nothing is left. It became the capital of Iran in 1789. We passed the Azadi (Freedom) Tower, an arch that was completed for the Shah's 1971 celebration of the 2,500th anniversary of the monarchy. It is 45 metres high and echoes Seljuq and Timurid architecture.

We drove up Valiasr Avenue, a long street that slopes slightly up towards the snow-capped Alborz mountains that had now emerged from the early-morning mist and hung under a clear blue sky. "It used to be called Pahlavi Avenue, after the family of the Shah," Farhad said. We passed *façades* of Iranian houses. "In the West great houses are extroverted, turned outwards. The outside tells you something about the grandeur inside." I thought of the traditional houses at the Hyde-Park end of Piccadilly and how imposing they looked from outside. "But Persian houses are introverted, turned inwards. They do not look important outside, but once you are through the entrance and down a corridor to the reception lobby, surprises begin. There may be several courtyards. These houses do not look grand from the outside."

Now we were passing banks and Farhad told me, "The Persians are more cultured than the Arabs. Many Arab states had little before the beginning of the 20th century, they were uncivilized then. The Persians have a long-established civilization and are more cultured." Now we turned right into the financial quarter, where there are many banks, ministries, government offices, embassies and airline buildings that are taller than those in the surrounding streets.

I took in faces of martyrs of the Iran-Iraq war. Each poster had a close-up of the face of one of the Iranians who had given their lives to repelling Saddam Hussein's invasion of Iran in 1980. He had struck soon after the Revolution, attempting to seize the rich oil-producing Iranian border province of Khuzestan and in particular the oil refinery at Abadan. Taken by surprise, Iran found the city of Khorramshah occupied by Iraqi troops and many Iranian cities, including Tehran, suffered air-raid bombing similar to that experienced by London during the wartime *Blitz*. Within two years Iraq had been pushed back to within its borders but for a further six years Khomeini pursued the war, attempting to overthrow Saddam Hussein. There was a stalemate, but wave upon wave of Iranians launched infantry attacks that were doomed to fail, a generation of young men believing Khomeini's promise that they would go to Paradise if killed. A million young men were killed on both sides by 1988 until, exhausted and facing new Iraqi gains in the battle-field, and a deteriorating economy, Iran accepted a UN-brokered cease-fire it had previously rejected.

In towns and cities across Iran these martyrs' faces were remembered from 1980-1988, several faces together on advertising hoardings by roads or on boards individually supported by stakes in the central reservation so that motorists passed one after another. On these boards throughout Iran, the leadership proclaimed the perennial importance of martyrdom and reminded citizens that martyrdom today could lead to Paradise just as readily as it had led the local young men, remembered from twenty or more years previously, to Paradise.

We turned right into Khomeini Avenue and left into Ferdowsi Street (named after the author of the *Shahnameh*, the national epic of Persia). Many of its buildings were in Western style. We turned right and later left and left again into the tree-lined Ayatollah Taleghani Boulevard, and on the left Farhad pointed out the US Embassy, where the US hostages were held: a long low building set back from high railings with a columned entrance in the middle, a sand-coloured wall on either side with many windows. There were a few trees inside the railings.

In front of part of the railings was an enormous blue hoarding

Tehran. US Embassy.

Tehran. Anti-US banner on railings.

on which there was a red Persian inscription and beneath it in English: "We will make America face a severe defeat." In smaller letters in English was the author of these words: "*Imam Khomeini.*" (Ayatollah Khomeini had taken the title of *Imam* after the Revolution. Farhad said that he did not have the standing or the status of the twelve *Imam*s, who according to Shiite belief, had the authority to interpret the *Koran* and give rulings.)

"May I take a photo?" I asked.

"Strictly, no," said Farhad, "as there are soldiers present. But if we stop here and you can take it from inside the car, it will be all right."

This building had played a major part in contemporary Iranian and American history. The Shah had let the Americans into Iran after meeting Kermit Roosevelt, a CIA agent based in this Embassy, in his White Palace at midnight one night during 1953. He plotted with him the CIA overthrow of his Prime Minister Dr Mossadeq for his radical nationalisation of the Anglo-Iranian Oil Company, an anti-British move that anticipated Col. Nasser's nationalisation of the Suez Canal Company in Egypt in 1956. The

Shah sent Mossadeq a letter ordering him to resign, but Mossadeq brought out demonstrators against the Shah, who had to flee to Rome for a week. He returned when the situation was under control and Mossadeq was jailed.

Then soon after the beginning of the 1979 Revolution students believed that the CIA were planning to restore the Shah and the throne, and they seized the US Embassy. They branded it "a den of spies" or "a nest of spies" (or "a den of espionage"). This building acted as a prison for 66 American diplomats and citizens. Outside this gate a man suspected of being the present President paraded a blindfolded American hostage. It is claimed that the students had originated the idea of taking over the US Embassy, that Ayatollah Khomeini did not order the seizure but went along with it and supported the students once it had happened. The students held the building for nearly a year and a quarter to deter the Shah from returning. Their action signalled a reversal of Iranian policy towards the US.

The incarceration of the 66 Americans in their own embassy building led to President Carter's failed attempt to rescue them. In confused circumstances three of eight helicopters crashed in the desert outside Tehran and charred bodies of US Special Forces killed in the mission were displayed in Tehran, an incident that ended Carter's presidency in failure. (In February 1981, in a show of strength, the SAS ended a siege at London's Iranian Embassy, sending a powerful message to those holding the Americans hostage in Tehran.) The American hostages were released after the Shah died, but Democrats – who were officially opposed to military action against Iran – might want to get even with Iran for the humiliation of 1979-81.

After his welcome by a million people in the streets of Tehran and after ordering the execution of many members of the ex-regime, Khomeini had held a referendum to secure the people's approval for an "Islamic Republic". This he had obtained, and a constitution had been drawn up in 1979 recognising Twelver Shiism (ie Shiism which acknowledged twelve *Imam*s) as the State religion. Sovereignty was in the hands of Allah but delegated to the Supreme Leader, President (officially the Head of State) and elected representatives of the *Majlis* (Parliament).

Khomeini created for himself the position of Supreme Spiritual Leader, *valiy-e faqih,* who should be chosen for his knowledge of Islamic theology and to act as the representative of the Twelfth *Imam*, to be the final authority in all executive, legislative and judicial matters and to approve of the President's appointment of his prime minister and cabinet. (It is like the Queen being the supreme spiritual leader and representative of God and Christ, as in a sense she is for those who believe in the Divine Right of Kings, while as the Crown in theory having final authority in all government matters and being able to approve a new government, as she does when she receives a new Prime Minister – but possessing the spiritual authority of the Archbishop of Canterbury.) When the Supreme Leader died, a Council of Experts (jurists) elected by the people was to choose his successor.

A Guardian Council – the "guardianship of the jurists", a concept the Islamic Khomeini drew from the Western Plato's Guardians in *The Republic*, an educated Guardian *élite* or "class" (Plato's word) living in austere simplicity and led by a "Philosopher Ruler" or "Philosopher King" who knew transcendent truth and could deliver perfect government (which in the event turned out to be violent) – was to make sure that bills conformed to the *Shariah* (religious law). However, this Guardian Council was to be appointed and was to include, at Khomeini's insistence, the most learned jurists who in the absence of the Hidden *Imam* would interpret and decree laws.

Khomeini as the foremost "juriconsult" gave himself the

greatest powers: supreme command over army, security, declaration of war and the election of the president, while the clergy took command of the legal system. The Guardian Council was to have six Muslim clerics, appointed by the Supreme Leader, and six Islamic jurists appointed by the head of the judiciary, who was to be appointed by the Supreme Leader. It was conservative and anti-reformist: it blocked 111 out of 295 pieces of legislation passed by the *Majlis* up to 2004. The Supreme Leader had all the authority, the President did his bidding and the democratically elected representatives in Parliament had little power. In this sense Iran was a theocracy rather than a democracy.

And what of Ayatollah Khomeini's successor, the Supreme Leader and representative of the Twelfth *Imam* now? Did he have the same outlook as Khomeini? "He did not support President Khatami in his dialogue of civilizations. Khatami tried to set up a dialogue with America and things improved, but the present Supreme Leader was hard-line and close to the present President's position – conservative rather than reformist. As I see it, the Supreme Leader provides spiritual authority, and the President and Cabinet implement his ideas in action."

*

As we drove on to the (National) Archaeological Museum, Farhad explained Persian architecture. "The *iwan* in a mosque – the rectangular hall opening onto a courtyard – is barrel-vaulted without columns. It comes from the Sasanian arch at Ctesiphon in Iraq." (My Baghdad University students took me for a picnic under this arch soon after my arrival in Baghdad.) "Ctesiphon was the winter capital of the Parthian Empire and later of the Sasanian Empire, and the style has influenced many buildings in Persia. The Archaeological Museum was built in this neo-Sasanian style. The vaulted brick entrance was designed in 1936 to recall the Sasanian audience hall at Ctesiphon."

The Archaeological Museum was in Shahid Yarjani Street, parallel to Khomeini Avenue. Exhibits were in relatively tiny glass cases or standing free in vast high-ceilinged halls. They started in the 5th millennium BC: Neolithic pottery made by coiling clay. By the 4th millennium the pottery was wheel-mounted, and decorated with ostriches and olive trees, and in one case a pre-Indo-European cross. From the 3rd millennium there were basket-patterned pots from Elamite Susa. There was a copy of Hammurabi's code, which was brought from Babylon to Susa by an Elamite king, the presence of Shamash conferring legitimacy on Hammurabi. These rules were set out in cuneiform regarding property, marriage and being a good citizen. There was a realistic cow from Choqa Zanbil, near Susa, c.1250 BC.

I homed in on an Achaemenian polished *bas*-relief from Persepolis, which showed how the Persepolis carvings originally looked before they became pitted by exposure to weather, and on an Achaemenian frieze of glazed tiles with lotus and mountain motifs. There was an Achaemenian tablet of a respectful messenger approaching a seated, bearded Darius I with a bearded Xerxes standing behind him. I gazed at the lower half of a stone statue of Darius I in ankle-length Elamite dress, a tunic with folds over his boots. It was carved in Egypt – Darius I's predecessor, Cambyses II, had conquered Egypt and incorporated it into the Persian Empire – and had stood in Egypt by the gate of Heliopolis, City of the Sun. It had been brought back to Susa by his son, Xerxes I, and was discovered in Susa in 1972.

The inscription on the top of the pedestal in Old Persian, Elamite and Babylonian records Darius's campaigns in Egypt and proclaims (Farhad translated): "This stone statue Darius ordered to be made in Egypt so that in the future anyone who looks on it will know that the Persian man ruled Egypt."

There was a gold-and-silver inscription by Darius found in a stone box in the foundations of his Hall of Audience (Apadana) at Persepolis, which says: "Darius the great King, the King of kings, the King of countries, the son of Hystaspes, an Achaemenian. Darius the King says: This (is) the kingdom , which I hold – from the Scythians, who (are) beyond Sogdiana, thence as far as Ethiopia – from India, thence as far as Sardis, which Ahura Mazda (*Auramazdaha*), the greatest of the gods, bestowed on me. Me may Ahura Mazda preserve and my (royal) house!" "The greatest of the gods" – Ahura Mazda was the supreme god but as there were still other gods, monotheism had only partly arrived. There was also a cuneiform inscription from Talar-e Bar proclaiming Xerxes' connection with Ahura Mazda.

There was an Achaemenian column on a plinth, the capital at the top being a palm with an Ionic scrolled top. And, standing before it I sensed with mounting excitement that the conventional perception of Ionic columns would have to be turned on its head. I intuitively sensed that the concept of the Ionic column was actually Persian, it had been exported to Persian-ruled Ionia from Persian Persepolis. The first Doric columns in Greek temples could be dated to the late 7th- and early 6th-centuries, the first Ionic columns with scroll-shapes on either side of the capital were after c.550 BC. This Persian Ionic column was near the origin of the Ionic style. On top was a double bull.

We passed to the later exhibits. There was a small statue of Zeus which reflected Alexander's conquest of Persepolis in 330 BC, and a bronze statue of a Parthian prince found at Shami in 1934, mournfully moustached, from the 1st-2nd century AD. The Parthians, who harried the Romans, were nomads who moved about on horseback, had no fixed capital and left little art. Their pottery was simple and utilitarian, not ceremonial. There was a

Sasanian "Salt Man" from Zanjan, who died in the 3rd or 4th century AD. He was buried in salt, and his head, which had white hair and a white beard, and one of his legs wearing a leather boot, were well-preserved.

I came away in awe of the range of Iranian archaeological finds from the 5th millennium to the Sasanian period, my appetite whetted to see the Achaemenian ruins of Persepolis and Pasargadae. In my mind the history of the Achaemenians had now been superimposed on the history of the Revolution, which I had glimpsed while driving past the US Embassy.

*

We went on to the Abgineh Museum of Glass and Ceramics, which is housed in a traditional white-and-grey brick-and-tile building dating back to the 19th century. Originally the home of a prominent Persian family, in the 1920s it was the house of Reza Shah's Prime Minister, and it was the Egyptian Embassy from 1953 to 1960 (during the Suez Crisis). The rooms retained many traditional features and contained Persian ceramics and glass going back to the 2nd millennium BC.

There was much to admire: angular Kufic calligraphy, lustreware (ceramics with an iridescent glaze) and octagonal star-shapes. Apart from a wonderful Achaemenian glass bowl, I was especially interested in wine-flasks, water-jugs, glasses and cups from Nishapur, Omar Khayyam's hometown. I recalled lines from the 4th (1879) edition of Edward Fitzgerald's translation of *The Rubaiyat of Omar Khayyam:*

"A Book of Verses underneath the Bough,
A Jug of Wine, a Loaf of Bread – and Thou
Beside me singing in the Wilderness –

Oh, Wilderness were Paradise enow!"

And also the last stanza (which has an upper-case O in "One") on how Omar's death should be marked by Saki, the water-pourer or wine-pourer:

"And when like her, oh Saki, you shall pass
Among the Guests Star-scatter'd on the Grass,
    And in your joyous errand reach the spot
Where I made One – turn down an empty Glass!"

Before me in a glass case were 11th- and 12th-century wine-jugs and glasses from Nishapur, exactly the kind of wine-jug to be taken on a picnic (intoxication in a Sufi poem reflecting spiritual ecstasy) and kind of glass to be turned down when the Sufi Omar returned to the One.

In the shop downstairs I bought a set of coins from the Shah's time, a book on Persian ceramics and – after deliberation – a book entitled *The Inscriptions in Old Persian Cuneiform of the Achaemenian Emperors*, a translation of most of the stone-carved Achaemenian inscriptions in Iran by the Rev. Ralph Norman Sharp, which I consulted after visiting many of the 20 inscriptions translated in the book. The English translations in this book would take me to deep into an experience of the Achaemenian time.

We came out and resumed our drive up to Jomhuriye Islami Street, past the closely guarded 19th-century British Embassy building in Ferdowsi Street, "the Oxford Street of Tehran" (Farhad called it). It reminded me of Shanghai because its Shopping Mall resembled China's shopping malls. We passed writers' coffee-houses where writers met in the past, and, Farhad said, still do.

*

We stopped for lunch in the Ferdowsi Grand Hotel. The car pulled up at the entrance, leaving me two paces to walk inside. A table with six chairs had been reserved for us, and the driver joined us. I furtively squirted anti-bacterial gel on my fingers and "washed" them dry. We ordered chicken (two kinds) and lamb kebabs and rice, and it came with soup and yoghurt which we ate first, in that order. Diet coke was available here. Otherwise I would have had bottled water; there has been no alcohol in Iran since the Khomeini Revolution. We could help ourselves to salad from more than a dozen dishes, but I chose carefully, declining anything that could have been washed in impure water or handled by staff. I meant to avoid being ill and therefore missing any part of my compact tour. There were many plates on the table – I understood we were only stopping for ten minutes and Farhad said, "This is the Iranian way, to order more than we can all eat. We are having a feast in honour of your arrival." Later I found out that after my visit he had no bookings for the next two months.

We returned to the car and turned right into Inqelab Boulevard and right again down Sadi Avenue (named after the Shiraz poet) and on to *Imam* Khomeini Square, where a statue to the Shah had been pulled down in the early days of the Revolution. We passed the Ministry of Finance and proceeding down Davar Street, reached 15 Khordad Square, which was named after the date of Khomeini's 1963 speech to his theological school in Qom when he attacked the Shah and was consequently exiled. We drove into 15 Khordad Avenue and stopped at the main entrance to the bazaar – the Tehran market which has more than 10 kilometres of covered stores.

Farhad and I left the car and immediately plunged down a steeply-sloping narrow street, or rather alley-way under cover. On either side there were open "shops" or bays, or more truly stalls, stacked with carpets and between them flowed a slow tide of people perhaps six wide, the women in *chador*s, the men in Western shirts or *mullah*s' robes, and up and down this street through the people men bent and pushed or dragged carts laden with merchandise for one of the stalls. "Mind your feet," Farhad said as we walked, "mind your back." And we had to step aside, rubbing shoulders with Iranians who could not proceed until we stepped back out of their way. I kept a hand firmly on my wallet in my trouser pocket, wondering how safe it was as we went deeper and deeper in, farther and farther from the road.

Farhad explained that each corridor specialised in a particular commodity, for example, carpets (where we were), spices, paper, copper and gold. Here could be found groups of shoemakers, knife makers, tinsmiths and saddlers. I was the only Westerner and a lot of the hundreds of people I rubbed shoulders with looked at me and one or two called out "Hello", but I did not feel under threat. Though I was subconsciously looking out for suicide-bombers or al-Qaeda assassins in accordance with the Western negative image of Iran, I felt safe and I did not think there was any risk. "Al-Qaeda are not active in Iran," Farhad said. The truth was, if al-Qaeda had now moved their headquarters to Tehran, as reports claimed, they would not be active in their own backyard – they had not been active in the vicinity of the Taliban when they were in Afghanistan – and so despite the misgivings in the British Foreign and Commonwealth Office's assessment, there was probably no risk that they would be active against Westerners in Tehran.

Then, after the jostling, we were suddenly through and into a courtyard and I saw two minarets bisected by a clock over a barrel-vaulted arch, under a cloudless blue sky. This was *Imam* Khomeini mosque, formerly Shah mosque, Farhad said. It had been built in the early 19th century and finished in 1830 under Fath Ali Shah, the Qajar ruler. It was inside the bazaar but was a working mosque. The courtyard was clean – completely free from litter – and I remarked on this. Farhad told me, "In Iran the refuse collectors come every day. Everyone's rubbish is collected every day. My rubbish is collected every day. There is no litter in the streets anywhere in Iran." I was to find this comment for the most part true. "In every courtyard of every mosque there has to be a place for ablutions," Farhad said. This courtyard joined the tinsmiths' alley to the east and the goldsmiths' and silversmiths' alley to the west.

Farhad took me to the entrance of the mosque. "We take our shoes off here," he told me. I took my shoes off and he took them to an attendant. I followed him in my socks into the mosque where some two dozen Iranian men, some in Western shirts, some in traditional dress, sat or stood and prayed towards a window or knelt and bowed their heads to the floor in prayer. (Of course, there were no women.) A man lay by a column on his back with a heavily bandaged leg, and another seemed to be unconscious, possibly dead, on his side with his eyes closed. They were ignored. Several of those praying looked up at me as if to say "What is the Westerner doing here?" but I was left to myself.

"Look," Farhad explained, "We go over to the shelves at the side here and take one of these ground-clay blocks. It is made of special clay mixed with the clay of Mecca, but it is from the earth. We put it in front of us and when we bow our heads to the ground we rest our foreheads on this clay. Then we put the clay block back when we have finished with it. You see on the shelves here there are holy books. The *Koran* is always here, and one or two books sacred to Shias. Let's sit down."

I sat down, ignoring the others as they now ignored me, and crossed my legs and meditated. I was tired, having hardly slept the previous night, but I went deep even though I was vulnerable while my eyes were closed. The Light came up before my inner eye, and I wordlessly held the people of Iran up to the Light, sensing that they were about to suffer at the hands of the West. Afterwards we went into a side room, which was plainly and simply furnished, and Farhad explained the architecture while an Iranian tried to pray near us, standing up and kneeling down with his head to the floor.

We went into the side room on the other side, and then returned to the entrance and put our shoes on and came out into the courtyard and bazaar, and walked back up the crowded alley-way to our car. "The mosque," Farhad explained, "is always by the bazaar in Iranian towns and cities."

*

I had asked to see the Parliament and Presidential buildings. I was told we could not see the new Parliament or the President's building as they were cordoned off. We did, however, pass the Supreme Leader's complex, where armed guards manned the gates. I could see a white two-storey rectangular house set back behind the high surrounding wall, and Farhad said that the President's complex was behind it. Ahmadinejad could therefore appear quickly for meetings with the Supreme Leader. We drove down tree-lined roads and passed the Old Parliament until 2003, which had now been given to the Council of Experts who nominate the Supreme Leader. The expert jurists were housed in a modern ferro-concrete building. It had a carving on it of Zal killing the dragon, a mythical figure like our St George who Farhad said came from the *Shahnameh*, the Epic of the Kings. Then we drove up Navvab Street towards the snowy mountains to the north and into Eisenhower Street, which was associated with the Tehran conference of 1943, Farhad said.

As we drove back to Mehrabad airport to catch our flight on to Shiraz, Farhad explained that Tehran suffered from pollution and was split into traffic zones. "To reduce congestion and pollution, odd numbers on car registration plates can go into a zone on odd days and even numbers on even days. We've had this system for more than fifteen years."

Farhad asked me how I spelt my surname – and also what my father's first name had been, a question I deflected and which he repeated twice (a strange question for a Westerner, suggesting an impending computer search that had something to do with the secret police).

I said that in Arabic my surname was pronounced "*hajr*", meaning "stone".

He said "Yes, four sounds cannot be pronounced in Arabic: p, g, szh and ch. Arabs say 'Farsee' instead of 'Parsee'. But all four sounds exist and are pronounced in Parsee. So I can say your surname, Hagger."

I asked if Parsee was his first language?

"Of course. I can't speak much Arabic. Arabic is the language of religious form and ceremony – the *Koran* is in Arabic and certain prayers are in Arabic – but otherwise we speak Parsee among ourselves. The Parsees are the Persians who went to India in the 7th and 8th centuries and again in the 10th century, mainly for religious reasons. They were Zoroastrians and felt persecuted by the Islamic religion. But Parsee is the language spoken by us Persians who stayed behind." He said again, "We Persians are more cultured than the Arabs." Then, when I commented on the number of cars at the airport, without seeing the contradiction, "It is because of the *Haj* (pilgrimage to Mecca). Men are returning from Mecca and are being met by their families."

I had made the best use of my few hours in Tehran. I had stepped off the plane before dawn with very little sleep but I had kept going until my 15.30 flight to Shiraz. I had wanted to see the Crown Jewels Museum but it did not open until 2 p.m.pm, and then only a few days of the week. And I had wanted to visit the Golestan

Palace of the 19th-century Qajars and see the Marble Throne in a mirrored open-fronted audience hall built in 1801 for Fath Ali Shah, the monarch who had about 200 wives and at least 170 (and perhaps 189) children. This Marble Throne was named the Peacock Throne after his wife, who was nicknamed Lady Peacock. It replaced an earlier Peacock Throne created in 1736 for Nader Shah Afshar, who invaded India to seize it from the Moghul ruler Mohammad Shah along with the Koh-e Nor diamond, which the British took and locked in the Tower of London.

But though Qajar luxury was to influence Reza Shah, who was crowned on the Peacock Throne in 1925, and his son, Mohammad Reza Shah (the last Shah), I had prioritised and done what mattered to me. I had obtained an overview in Tehran of the early Iranian (Achaemenian and pre- and post-Islamic) cultural heritage and of the effect of the Khomeini Revolution – of the old and the new.

3

AMONG PILGRIMS AND SUFIS

IN SHIRAZ

The journey to Shiraz was comfortable enough. We said goodbye to our driver, and Farhad then looked after me, wheeling my suitcase away out of sight to check it in while I sat restfully, then bringing milkless tea (with lollipop-like sticky-sugar sticks to dip), which we sipped before boarding, and sitting attentively next to me on the Russian plane. "You see," he said, "there's a sign in Russian near the front. During Ayatollah Khomeini's rule, Russia was very supportive and offered a plane deal." The English translation of an announcement in Parsee began "Dear passengers…"

For much of the short flight lasting an hour and twenty minutes, my second flight since last going to bed, I resisted the temptation to snooze and could see out of the cabin window far below a chain of tiny sand-coloured mountains in what appeared to be a desert waste under a clear blue sky.

Farhad did not let me out of his sight as he steered me to collect my suitcase from the carousel. As we waited he introduced me to our new driver, a balding, retired banker called Ali, who would be with us for the rest of the tour. "He has driven our car from Tehran, he set off while we were seeing Tehran, an eleven-hour drive," Farhad said.

I wondered why we had not hired a car and driver in Shiraz. Was there something special about the car that had required it to be driven for eleven hours from Tehran – was it bugged? Or perhaps it was natural to work out where the car and driver needed to be at the end of our tour, in Tehran, and start from there? And why did I have one national guide rather than a guide in each place?

To this last question, Farhad later told me, "It is good to have one guide throughout for otherwise you can be told the same thing over and over again." And he had a point.

In Iran, which has a long tradition of dualism (a later Zoroastrian and Manichaean corruption of the One) in which opposites co-exist, it is wise to accept circumstances at face value and not ask too many questions.

Shiraz is set in hills. The winters are short and spring long, and at one time it was regarded as a green place full of gardens, most of which have long since disappeared. There, poets hailed its roses and nightingales, perfumes and rose-water, its immortal cypress trees and at one time its wine and love. (Wine, as in Omar Khayyam, is a symbol for Sufi intoxication then the soul is drunk with the ecstatic vision of God.) It had been founded by the Achaemenians, grown under the Sasanians, risen to provincial capital under the Arabs in 693, prospered under the Saffarids and Buyids of the 9th-11th centuries, and was undamaged by the invasions of Genghis Khan and Timur Lenk (Tamburlaine the Great). It became Persia's literary centre on account of Sadi in the 13th century and Hafez in the 14th century.

We drove along a street with low buildings and stalls on either side, past orange trees and palm trees, a statue of Khomeini and hints of gardens, straight to the tomb of Hafez. Farhad said, "Every Iranian home must have two things: a *Koran* and the poems of Hafez. Hafez means 'The man who knows the *Koran* by heart' and Hafez did know it by heart." For hundreds of years Persians recited Hafez's poems when they held a cup of wine in their hand.

It was dark when we arrived at the tomb. A crowd of hawkers stood round the entrance gate. I could see the floodlit open eight-columned pavilion with a small dome over the tomb up a few steps at the end of a wide tree-lined path, and orange trees with floodlit oranges on them. Farhad said, "They are Seville oranges, too bitter to eat."

The marble tombstone of the 14th-century poet lay beneath the dome. It had been put there in 1773 by Karim Khan, the first ruler of the Zand dynasty who made Shiraz his capital in 1750 and built the citadel. It was engraved with two of Hafez's *ghazals* (or lyric poems of between six and fifteen couplets), which had Sufi associations. Pilgrims came to meet in the garden, walk by the two pools and under the orange trees and place a finger on the marble tomb in homage, as I now did. It was an Iranian custom to lay an open book of Hafez's poems on his tomb and let the wind blow the pages. There was a belief that the first line to be read would happen, that the future is contained in his words. Sometimes sung poems of Hafez's could be heard as background music.

Beyond the tomb, by a walled garden, there was a summer-house, and through the windows I could see a striking man with a long beard and a tall hat sitting in meditation. He wore a black outer robe over a white pleated frock that showed in his lap.

"Oh," Farhad said, "a Sufi *dervish*. Not all *dervish*es howl and whirl and dance. Those from some sects contemplate rather than dance, and live in poverty and austerity."

I could see the *dervish* was lost in the One. To my horror Farhad went into the summer-house, opening the door and closing it behind him, and through the window I watched as he stooped and spoke to him, disturbing him in his mystic vision. He backed away sheepishly and returned to me.

"He told me he cannot come now, but he will be in the courtyard later," Farhad said. "Let's go into the teahouse."

The teahouse was in the walled garden beyond traditional Persian seats like wooden-frame beds covered with carpets, with rolled pillows at each side. It was large and had over 20 tables well spaced out, round most of which sat groups of Iranians. On most tables stood a bubbling *ghalyan* (*narghile* or *hookah*).

We sat down at a table. A waiter in a long robe tied with a white sash and wearing a small round white-mitre hat – "1920s Persian dress," Farhad said – came and served us tea and asked if we wanted a *ghalyan*. I said, "No."

This was where those who came to meet round Hafez's tomb could converse more deeply, puffing smoke drawn through bubbling water. Farhad told me how people made jam from the flowers of the Seville oranges, and he said, "Hafez has a line, 'The flowering of oranges makes you drunk.'" After a while I began clearing my throat and my eyes began watering from the smoke of the *ghalyans*, and we drank up our tea and left.

Shiraz. Waiter who brings the *ghalyans* (pipes).

The Sufi *dervish* was wandering about in the dark beyond the floodlit tomb. Farhad said he was going to speak to him to ask if I could photograph him.

I said I would rather speak to him. "Say, 'Sorry if I disturbed you in the One,'" I said.

"In the One," Farhad said. And he went over to the *dervish* and spoke to him. I could see the *dervish* shaking his head and speaking in a fierce way.

Farhad returned. "He said, 'It doesn't matter, that's all right,' but he won't be photographed."

I knew that *dervish*es were members of a Muslim religious fraternity (*tariqah*), that some *dervish*es were mendicants, that in the 12th century *dervish*es learned the *silsilah*, the spiritual descent of their fraternity to which they were bound through their initiator, and that *dervish*es' most important practice was the "*dhikr*", "remembering" of God in ecstatic trance – going to the One. I knew that the tall hat was a camel's-hair hat which represented the headstone of a grave and that the black robe symbolised the grave – it was appropriate that this *dervish* was hanging round near Hafez's marble tomb (although he was also probably paying respect to one who had memorised the whole *Koran* by heart).

I knew that the name "Sufi" came from the woollen garment worn by Sufis – "*suf*" meant "wool" – and that this Sufi was wearing the Sufi equivalent of a monk's habit that characterised his fraternity's dress. I knew that this black robe, representing his mortal body, was cast off in ecstasy so that the *dervish* appeared in his white undergarment, his radiant, spiritual body symbolised in the white shroud of resurrection and at one with the Light, in the One. I had hoped to ask him about his experience of the One, but he had been too fierce in his austere rejection of Western appearance and photography to entertain my question.

As we came away Farhad said, "Look, cypresses." The trees that bordered the wide path leading to the floodlit tomb were cypresses. "The cypress symbolises immortality and longevity, and is found at the tombs of all Sufis in Iran."

Outside the gate a man with a canary on his wrist was holding out a stack of cards. "The canary will pick one card with its bill," Farhad said. "It's your fortune. Each card contains a line of Hafez."

Sortilege: divination by lots! Farhad slipped the man a couple of notes with Ayatollah Khomeini on them, and the canary picked a picture of Hafez (presumably) with two followers under a tree addressing a half-naked mendicant and listening animals and birds. On the back was writing in Parsee.

"Now pick an interpretation."

I picked a flimsy green paper covered with Parsee. A boy was importuning me with beseeching eyes, selling something I did not want, and I asked Farhad to give him 5,000 *rials* (half a dollar) on my behalf.

We got into our car and I asked what the card and interpretation said.

Farhad's first attempt at translation was faltering as he was trying to read small writing in the dark while the car was moving and jogging. He read out, "You have suffered a lot, some are jealous of you. If you pray you are already healed. You are a perfectionist and are never satisfied." He seemed reluctant to continue.

A few days later I asked him over dinner if he would translate the card and interpretation accurately. I wrote down his translation. He said after studying the Parsee, "First I should say that the word 'beloved' has two meanings in Hafez and in all Sufi poets. It means God as well as one's beloved. Bearing this in mind, on the back of the card is a line of Hafez's poems: 'I was so interested in your lips and in kissing you that Hafez forgot the nightly lessons and the words of prayer at dawn.' The interpretation says: 'You're thinking about something. You're not satisfied with what you're doing now in your career. There are many difficulties in the path you are taking, but you should try and defeat these challenges and diffi- culties. Don't be afraid of the difficulties, unhappiness and grief that you might face on this path. And think about the end and the result of what you are doing. And there's a very happy, good result to what you are doing which will lead to your future.' That's your fortune. 'You have actually made a lot of effort in your life. You had difficulties with the people around you. They were good friends of yours and in your career don't forget God. You have a very good life now, you have been very well treated now. For this bounteous gift of God, thank Him so that you will always be healthy and you will achieve whatever you like, God willing. Your actual beloved will come back and you will start your friendship.'"

It seemed a very different translation from the one he had attempted in the car. I pondered a call back to the Beloved, to God, the One. The canary had drawn my lot, and I could read into it whatever I liked and the words would retain their essential ambiguity and would neither confirm nor deny any interpretation.

*

We went on to Sadi's tomb, which was like a small well-lit columned temple with a blue dome against a tiled marble wall beside orange trees, near water. The underneath of the dome was tiled with two superimposed suns in the centre – one spiritual, one physical – shining out with rays that became petals, and the wall had two rose motifs. The marble tomb of the 13th-century poet was under the dome. It had been completed in 1952, and replaced a tomb of the 1860s. "Sadi travelled and then wrote *Rose Garden*

(*Golestan*) in prose and *Orchard or Fruit Garden (Bustan)* in verse," Farhad said. "He wrote, 'The sons of men are limbs of one another.' It's on the UN building in New York. Sadi was the best lyric Persian poet. Hafez stayed at home and learned the *Koran*, and was the most important didactic Persian poet."

Shiraz. Sadi's tomb with Nicholas Hagger and rose garden/Paradisal motif.

Like all pilgrims I lingered by the tomb, touching it with my forefinger, and asked Farhad to translate the text on the wall behind me.

He translated: "Your other hand is wrapped round the neck of your beloved, what else do you expect from the world?" There was another poem: "I have committed a lot of sins. I am happy because the world is delighted on account of Him (ie God), I love everything in the world because the whole world has been created by him." Farhad added, "In other words, he loves all creatures because they are created by God."

Farhad drew me away. "Sadi lived in a convent on this spot and composed in an area called Roknabad," he said. "He composed near a spring. There is a spring here, the waters come out of the mountains. People make rose-water from the spring here. They heat a rose, the smoke goes through a pipe, they cool it and it becomes liquid again, cooled steam. It's distillation of the rose, the essence of the rose, making odiferous water by distilling the flower. Come, let us see the spring water."

A short colonnade led into an underground octagonal tiled "pavilion" that looked down onto a sunken central pool of limpid water, in which swam brown trout. The pool seemed to be fed by a spring along a channel. There was a small counter near the viewing area that served as a teahouse. It was in one of the eight bays, and seats round the other walls were for drinking tea. I sat and looked down at the clear water and brown trout a storey below me and thought of us humans swimming in clear air. And thinking of the water, roses, rose-water and orange trees which quench thirst and satisfy the senses of smell and taste (or did once when Seville oranges did not seem so bitter) and how Islamic gardens reflect Paradise, I thought it would be easy to pass into the *dervish*'s ecstatic union outside in the early summer if one could have the garden all to oneself, as now. The garden of Sadi could induce a sense of the One very easily.

*

We returned to the car and drove to the centre of Shiraz and stopped near the tall, sand-coloured walls of the citadel (*arg*) built by Karim Khan, the first Zand ruler, around 1767. Over its entrance there was a tiled panel based on an episode in the *Shahnameh,* of Rostam fighting the white Div or demon – further evidence that traditional Persian art reflects traditional legendary-historical epic material as a common culture. I thought of Matthew Arnold's poem, 'Sohrab and Rustam', which drew on this same traditional matter.

"It's late," Farhad said, "and you've had a very long day, but I want to take you to something that is not on the itinerary. I would like you to see this. I want to take you to a shrine. Since 2002 non-Muslims have not been allowed to enter even the courtyard, but if you follow me you will be all right."

We saw the outside of the shrine across Ahmadi Square, a golden-floodlit, bulbous, onion-like dome above a tiled arch, alongside a golden-roofed minaret. This was the mausoleum of Shah Cheragh ("King of Light"), the name by which Sayyid Amir Ahmad, the brother of the eighth *Imam* (*Imam* Reza) who is buried in Mashad, came to be known. ("Sayyid" indicates a descendant of the Prophet.) Sayyid Amir Ahmad came to Shiraz in 808 and died here in 835 – hence this shrine. A mausoleum was built over his grave in the 1340s and rebuilt periodically since then. Most of what can be seen today is 19th-century (an earthquake having destroyed the dome and damaged the inside) and is now a place of Shiite pilgrimage to commemorate the eighth *Imam*'s brother. In this spirit the dome was built in 1959 and the minaret around 1970.

The shrine was crowded. As usual we took off our shoes at the entrance, and I was soon among jostling Iranian pilgrims. The entrance doors were of silver. Some Iranians kissed the silver door frame. What I saw beyond it was truly astounding (even if 19th-century): an ornate silver mausoleum, or cenotaph, with grille bars, set in a massive domed hall covered with minute mirror-tiles, bits of mirror, each individually cut and pressed into place, giving an exquisite shining, indeed dazzling, effect.

I took in the silvery green above the shrine, but it was the shrine I focused on. There was a scrum of some fifty Iranian pilgrims trying to get near it, pushing through kissing the silverwork in an swoon, eyes in trance and perhaps ecstasy, clutching the silver criss-cross bars and peering through them for the tomb, young and old alike. Touching the silverwork round the shrine with lips or fingers brought instant rapture, and I understood what it must be like to go to Mecca (or Mashad) and visit the tombs of the *Imam*s there. Mecca and Mashad would witness this swooning fervour only on a larger scale for this was merely the brother of one of the *Imam*s, and his other brother, Sayyid Mir Mohammad, had his own shrine nearby. Every inch of this domed hall reflected the electric lights and so shone with light. No wonder Sayyid Amir Ahmad was known as "the King of Light". Here, the symbolism was of a shrine within the Light.

We left the scrimmage among the pilgrims and looked up at the dome, which resembled the whorls, small petals and sepals of a stylised chrysanthemum, and went to a side room where pilgrims stood and sat on the floor in prayer, or bowed their heads to the earth, and looked at a redder mirror-work on the ceiling. I was so consumed with all I saw that I did not once think, 'I am the only Westerner here and should not be in this building, I am in danger.' Initially I had been aware of some glances, but I was soon ignored as each Muslim bared his soul to the One, in contact with the brother of the Holy *Imam* who would serve as an intermediary between all praying Muslims and their yearned-for Paradise.

Farhad said, "Let's sit down." We sat on carpet, crossing our legs in our socks, and Farhad closed his eyes and prayed and I meditated for the second time that day, like the *dervish* regarded my body as an outer garment to be laid aside to reveal the radiant spirit body. I went deep and as the Light shone within I focused on the nuclear crisis and asked the Hidden *Imam* to solve it. While I had my eyes closed, resting on the Light, I felt serene and the idea came to me that I could be a messenger for peace. It was only when I stood up that I realised how vulnerable I had been. In Iraq suicide-bombers were exploding their bombs in mosques, and with my eyes closed I would not have seen an attacker approach; nor would Farhad, who had had his eyes shut for a long while.

We padded out of the mausoleum, picking our way between praying Iranians and bypassing the *mêlée* round the shrine trying to touch the silverwork and the groups trying to kiss the silver frame of the doors. The fervour I had witnessed must have been similar to what Britain experienced in the 17th century, when the Civil Wars were fought over religious denominations, Cromwell's army sang psalms and Fox, Penn and Bunyan were imprisoned for preaching their views. Perhaps a better analogy would be Italian Roman Catholic crowds kissing sacred relics and statues on holy days.

Outside Farhad said, "I am so glad it was open and you were able to see it. You got close to what it means to be a Shia in there, seeing all those pilgrims visiting that shrine. Please always remember that in every Arab city or town four things are always close together: the Friday mosque, the bazaar, a *caravanserai* (literally 'caravan palace' or 'palace for caravans') and public baths. Caravans of 200 camels, which have been travelling in the desert for up to 15 days without their leaders being able to bath, needed facilities and a mosque. So as they approached a town they could see the minaret of the mosque in the distance and they made for it. The *caravanserai* was like a hotel for the caravan people and their camels. They could go to the baths and perform their ablutions and go to the mosque. They could stock up for the next phase of their journey from the warehouses in the bazaar."

*

We drove to the Homa Hotel, a modern building with sloping sides by a quiet, wide road opposite the trees of Azadi Park. I was in room 525, and Farhad was in the room opposite me, room 526. My room was large with a double bed and looked out on a sweep of mountains.

My first act was to make a thorough and exhaustive search for my reporter's book. I went through my suitcase and hand luggage item-by-item twice, but there was still no sign of it. I then made an international telephone call to my wife to tell her that I was safe. She had been my travelling companion to so many places over the years, but she knew this was not a country without risk and that I had left her behind for safety reasons. It was a Sunday before 6 pm in England, and I told her that I was very reassured by how things had gone but lamented the loss of my "notebook". "It's definitely not in my luggage," I said. I asked her to look for it on the floor where I had packed my suitcase to see if it had fallen out. I knew it had not – I could recall the carpet as it was when I wheeled my suitcase away – but it was my way of indirectly communicating what had happened.

I washed, shaved and changed, and locked my suitcase, but not my hand luggage (a small leather case with several zipped compartments that had travelled in the aircraft cabin and contained books and papers for the flight). I went down to dinner.

I had arranged to meet Farhad in the first-floor dining-room but there was no sign of him. I found a window-seat overlooking softly floodlit orange trees and he found me while I was studying the menu. He ordered shrimps and I ordered, on his recommendation, a cooked Persian stew to avoid any cold salad that might upset me. Our driver did not join us.

Over dinner we reviewed what we had done during the day and I clarified my understanding regarding some of the things we had seen.

He told me, "I could have had an academic career, but this work is addictive, I like moving about and so for ten years I have done this." He certainly had expertise – degrees in English Literature and Old Persian, knowledge of Islamic architecture, on which he had spoken at a conference, and of *caravanserai*s, on which he was doing research for a book – and he had a very good way of telling me something while I was in one place, leading me forward to the next place and telling me something new that built on what he had just said. He would have been a very good teacher. He said, "This is the most compact tour I have done in ten years. Normally this would take two weeks – three weeks in the summer heat when everything is more slow."

He told me he lived with his parents in Tehran, and he was careful not to contradict the official line. He had a very high regard for the Supreme Leader and he had been interested in the previous President's – Khatami's – "dialogue of civilizations" and wondered if a more diplomatic approach on the part of the current President would ease "the international crisis" (as he called the nuclear crisis): "There are some things that are better not said. You can think them but not say them." I took this to refer to the President's remark about wiping Israel off the map. I asked him if he realised that Israel might bomb Iran. He said, repeating the official line, "No, Iran is too strong, they wouldn't dare."

I had had little sleep for nearly two days and I went straight to my room after dinner. I opened my hand luggage to remove – and write in – my desk diary, which served as a journal, and there, in the book compartment of my hand luggage, lying loosely on top, was my reporter's book. I could not believe what I was seeing. In my thorough searches in that same compartment there had been no trace of it, but miraculously it had returned – or been returned – on top of that section while I was at dinner, and after I had referred to my loss in my international telephone call. Its reappearance was truly mysterious.

Had I overlooked the reporter's book all along despite my searches and blindly not seen it lying on the top all the time? No. Had it been brought down on the car that had driven from Tehran? I had no means of knowing. Where was Farhad before he joined me at dinner? Where had the driver been while Farhad and I were at dinner?

I decided it would be wise not to speculate as to how the reporter's book had been returned. I had no evidence for any allegation. This was one of those situations in which, in the words of Keats' 1817 letter, one should be "capable of being in uncertainties, mysteries, doubts, without any irritable reaching after fact and reason". It was better that the events concerning my reporter's book should remain a mystery. The important thing was, I had my notebook back and would no longer have to make notes on folded sheets of paper. I could approach the rest of my tour with the coherent, systematic note-taking I had originally planned.

After writing my diary, or journal, I lay in the bath. I had good reason to feel satisfied that things had gone well, better than I expected. In Shiraz I had joined pilgrims in two Paradisal gardens that reflected two Sufi poets, and I had observed the Sufi *dervish*. I had also joined pilgrims to the shrine of the eighth *Imam*'s brother, which had been closed to Westerners since 2002. I had been among pilgrims in Shiraz, and though the hotel room was hot with no means of turning the radiator down, all the subconscious apprehension I had felt in the previous weeks about being kidnapped, paraded on television and beheaded, had been replaced by relief, and I slept soundly.

4

BACK WITH THE ACHAEMENIANS,

OUR SOURCE

We had to be off early the next morning as we were taking in the Achaemenian ruins in and around Persepolis and Pasargadae and then driving on to the desert town of Yazd, a long day.

I woke to a view of a long range of the Zagros mountains with part of Shiraz in their foothills. I was down to breakfast early, and helped myself to wheatflakes and milk, yoghurt, fried egg and split sausage, flat bread, butter, honey and carrot jam, orange juice and coffee. I had almost finished when Farhad joined me and I told him I had now found my "notebook" – in my hand luggage. He took the news in his stride.

I returned to my room, locked my luggage, handed it over to the hotel porter and took the lift downstairs. There was a framed pledge by the lift on the ground floor: *Imam* Ali, the first *Imam*, promising from the 7th century AD that all travellers to Iran would be protected. While Farhad settled the hotel bill I sauntered outside and stood in warm sunshine with a view of a palm tree under a cloudless blue sky and breathed in air so pure I felt almost intoxicated. Our driver, Ali, was standing by our Peugeot with his door open, and I savoured the "ever-green city" and its mild climate. Farhad joined me and said, "This weather is like late March."

On the way out to Persepolis we passed alongside the *Koran* gateway. It was an arch with a room above it, which had been added by Karim Khan, the first Zand ruler, in which a copy of the *Koran* was kept for it was a tradition that all travellers in and out of Shiraz should pass under the *Koran*. An earlier building, reputedly 9th century was taken down in 1936 but had to be rebuilt five years later due to public demand.

We went through a narrow pass with spectacular views of the Zagros mountains on a glorious spring morning. The previous day I had worn a mac-proofed fleece for warmth, and had then changed into a body-warmer when it was less cold. Now I was in a sweater as the temperature rose. We passed the railway built by the Allies in the First World War (in which Iran was neutral), linking the Gulf to North Iran. Shiraz had not been connected.

We passed some nomads, the women in colourful red and black *chadors* over green undergarments. Farhad said, "They are Qashqai, they're Kurdish Shia, they speak Turkish. They winter in the foothills of the Zagros mountains south of Shiraz and move up to mountains in the north when it's spring."

As we drove I refreshed my memory of the Achaemenian dynasty (see Appendix). It began with Achaemenes (ruled c. 700-675 BC), chief of the "tribes" of Persians (as opposed to Aryan Medes, Bactrians and other Iranian-speaking peoples) who came from the south-west of modern Iran (the eastern part of the Elamite Empire), which they called *Parsa* (in Old Persian, Greek *Persis*). The dynasty descended through Achaemenes' son Teispes to Cyrus I, and through his son Cambyses I to Cyrus II. From his son Cambyses II it passed under circumstances that are not wholly clear, to another branch of the family, Darius I. It descended through his son Xerxes, his son Artaxerxes I and his son Darius II to Artaxerxes II and then Artaxerxes III and his son Arses. It then passed to another branch of the family, to Darius III, who ruled until Alexander's conquest in 330 BC. In all, therefore, it spanned getting on for 400 years.

"Oh, look," Farhad said suddenly. "The river Kor, with a Sasanian bridge."

I saw a dilapidated humped-back bridge over two arches. It spanned a bluish river wide enough for two small boats to pass.

"Kor is short for Korash," Farhad said, "and Korash means Cyrus. So it's the River Cyrus."

"And Pasargadae is not far from here," I said, "so it was named the River Cyrus after the King of Kings?"

"That's right. Persepolis was built near the confluence of the Kor and the Pulvar. This river must have been named after Cyrus during his lifetime. Darab in the south-west was named after Darius."

Again I was confronted with the living legacy of the 2,500-year old tradition of kingship that is still spoken of in Iran.

We approached the nearest small town to Persepolis, Mardasht. Farhad said: "Cyrus had three capitals: Pasargadae (near here), Ecbatana (modern Hamadan) and Sardis. Darius had three capitals: Susa (his winter capital), Ecbatana and Babylon. He built Persepolis as a ceremonial city. It was called by the Greeks – Herodotus and later Alexander – the 'city of the Persians' (*Persepolis*).

"Knowledge of the Achaemenian time was lost in the late Parthian or early Sasanian time. The Iranians who came later didn't know about the Achaemenians and related their ruins to the time of Jamshid, the mythical first king of the Persians whose exploits are in Ferdowsi's 11th-century verse epic *Shahnameh* ('book of kings'). They called Persepolis 'Takt-e Jamshid'. Before that it was called 'Parsa', 'the place of the Persians'. So this place was named Parsa, then Takt-e Jamshid, then Persepolis (in Herodotus)."

*

We were now approaching an avenue that led towards distant mountains. "Here the last Shah planted 2,500 trees in 1971 to mark 2,500 years of kingship." We left the car and walked between the trees to steps up to a platform beneath low mountains.

At the foot of the steps we encountered a nomad woman wearing a colourful reddish dress with a plain reddish-black scarf and shawl. She was with a moustached man in a Western jacket, trousers and open-necked shirt, and he had his hands in his pockets. Farhad talked to her and said to me, "She is a Qashqai." I asked if I could take her photograph and she smiled and said I could.

We climbed the 111 shallow steps of the terrace stairway. "They were shallow so that the king could look majestic with his sceptre and also to help the older members of the royal family," Farhad said. We stood at the extreme left of a platform, a terrace leaning against the Mount of Mercy at the back and surrounded on three sides by a retaining wall from 4 to 12 metres high. I stood, breathing in the pure air, before the Gate of All Nations. It was guarded on either side by bull-like colossi with wings, and I looked across at the ruins of colossal buildings, the blocks of stone that formed them hewn from the mountain. The stone was grey but in the sunlight it looked yellow. Before me were distant columns and trilithons of doorways, the remains of Darius I's alternative to Cyrus's Pasargadae. Below the platform the plain spread out beyond the trees to distant mountains.

Persepolis. Platform.

Persepolis. Gate of All Nations.

"Persia ruled 30 countries under Xerxes I," Farhad said, "And the ambassadors came here to the Gate of All Nations, which was built by Xerxes I, at the New Year to bring offerings. Persepolis was probably used for ceremonial purposes, for rituals connected with the New Year ('*No-Ruz*', literally 'New Day'), the vernal equinox."

I knew from my own research that Darius I and his successors worshipped "Auramazda" (Ahura Mazda) "and the other gods who exist" and (elsewhere) "Ahura Mazda, the greatest god". They had the rudiments of monotheism within a cultural heritage that had been polytheistic (Mithras, Anahita and Indra being other Iranian gods). I thought of the Egyptian rituals to the sun-god Ra. In Egypt the rituals made the Nile flood. I wondered, did the king in conjunction with Ahura Mazda, make the New Year happen, or did the ritual merely acknowledge the arrival of the New Year?

"Of course, ambassadors came to pay tribute to Darius I, Xerxes' father, before this Gate was built. Both Darius and Xerxes were seated on the throne in the hall over there, which we shall soon see. In Xerxes' time, these ledges were where the ambassadors sat to wait for the procession into the throne room. These huge blocks of stones were hauled up by pulleys."

I looked at the mythical and legendary winged-bull colossi, which were like the Assyrian winged bulls. They had a headdress adorned with sun-rosettes. The human head of the colossi portrayed wisdom, the body of the bull abundance and fertility, and the eagle's wings (as in Assyria) power and speed. They were to west and east, and on the inside of the gateway, high up, there was a cuneiform inscription by Xerxes I in Old Persian, Akkadian/Babylonian and Elamite, listing his family tree and referring to the gate as "the Gate of All Nations" or "Entrance-Hall of all Countries".

The inscription says: "A great God (is Ahura Mazda), who created this earth, who created that heaven, who created man, who created happiness for man, who made Xerxes king, the one King of many (kings), the one Commander of many (commanders). I (am) Xerxes the great King, the King of kings, the King of countries having many (kinds of) human beings, the King in this great earth far and wide, the son of Darius the King an Achaemenian. Xerxes the King says: By the favour of Ahura Mazda this Entrance-Hall of all countries I built. Much else (that is) beautiful was built in this Persepolis, which I built and my father built. Whatever has been built (and) seems beautiful (or, whatever beautiful thing built is seen) all that by the favour Ahura Mazda we built. Xerxes the King says: May Ahura Mazda preserve me and my kingdom, and what has been built by me, and what has been built by my father – that indeed may Ahura Mazda preserve."

The Gate was based on a gate at Pasargadae built by Cyrus II. There were three columns over 16 metres high, on the capital of one of which could be seen the Ionic scrolls ending in rosettes similar to the ones I had seen in the Tehran Archaeological

Museum, dating from the time of Xerxes I (around 476 BC). Graffiti had been scratched into the stone. I read "1897" and the insignia of the British Forces' "Central Indian Force, 1912".

Farhad and I had Persepolis to ourselves except for a couple of Iranian women who had come and spoken to Farhad. They were students of ancient Iranian languages, and they were studying the inscriptions for their university course. Farhad gave them some information and advice. While they chatted, I took in the location, the plain below the platform which stretched beyond the pines planted by the late Shah to distant mountains tipped with snow. At the back in the mountain were the tombs – entrances cut high up into rock – of the only two kings buried in Persepolis: Artaxerxes II and Darius III. (The earlier kings from Darius I onwards were at Naqsh-e Rostam, and these two tombs copied the cross-shaped style of those four.)

I thought of the might of Cyrus II, Darius I and Xerxes I. I thought of how this site was burned by Alexander's troops in 330 BC. I had read that Persepolis burned because all the ceilings were made of timber. The Roman historian Quintus Curtius Rufus reports that "mounds of gold and silver, huge quantities of clothing, and furniture which was not functional but ostentatiously ornate" were seized, and that "the quantity of money captured here was huge almost beyond belief ". Though Alexander destroyed Persepolis in surely the greatest act of vandalism – *barbarism* – ever, people still lived around its ruins for centuries afterwards, and I thought of words Marlowe (who had not visited Persia) put into the mouth of Tamburlaine the Great (not realising that Persepolis in Tamburlaine's day was a platform):

"Is it not passing brave to be a king,
And ride in triumph through Persepolis?"

We wandered behind the Gate and saw ruins and fallen capitals of columns with griffins on them. The fabulous griffin had the head of an eagle and was half-lion. The capitals were usually adorned with the heads of bulls. Farhad said, "The University of Chicago excavated this part of the site. They found financial records showing that the workmen were paid and were not slaves, and that women worked here and had maternity benefits. The records were preserved by the fire Alexander caused. The fire turned the clay records to brick and preserved them."

We made our way towards the Apadana palace of Darius I and Xerxes I, where the ambassadors brought their offerings. Under a roof to shield them from the sun two flights of steps that met in the middle led to the Apadana's raised platform, which the delegates used. On either side of the steps there were numerous reliefs. On the outside of the steps, on either side under the slopes were identical motifs of a lion biting a unicorn under sun-rosettes, which perhaps symbolised the summer biting winter at the vernal

Persepolis. Carvings, lion biting unicorn.

equinox, the warm weather defeating cold weather.

"Between them," Farhad said, "are immortal soldiers. They are called that because when one died there was always another to take his place. These soldiers were Darius's guard. See, they are standing holding their lances upright with two hands and they're resting the base of the handle on their three-ridged shoes."

On the base of the Apadana platform, in three rows easily visible from both flights of steps, there were 23 scenes, separated by cypress trees, of the delegates from 23 nations who, led by a Persian or a Median official, had come to make their offerings to Darius. Each delegation was shown as a short procession, often with a horse.

Farhad pointed out details. The Armenian horse's mane was tied with ribbons, and the Armenians carried a golden jug, presumably for wine or perhaps for sacred water. He pointed to a bound lioness's rage, while children were held away from her. Cappadocians were pushing forward rams that did not want to move. The Chorasmians wore pointed caps. The Indians carried spices. The Libyans had a chariot with detailed wheels. The

Persepolis. Armenians with golden jug and leading a horse whose mane is tied with ribbons.

Scythians bore cloth and led a horse. They had pointed hats. The Syrians led rams. The Ionians, wearing curved, pointed hats, carried fabrics, bundles of wood and jars. The Libyans bore loads and folded fabrics. The Roxyis carried valuable cups. The Ethiopians were on the outside as one of the least important nations. The Medes were the most important as Astyages was Cyrus's maternal grandfather. The Babylonians were next in importance. The quality of the carving was amazing.

Among the carvings on the outer wall of the eastern and northern staircases of the Apadana was an inscription by Xerxes I in Old Persian, Elamite and Babylonian. The first two sentences are identical to the inscription quoted above. The third and fourth sentences are slightly different: "Xerxes the great King says: What has been done by me here, and what has been done by me farther off, all that I did by the favour of Ahura Mazda. Me may Ahura Mazda, with the gods, preserve, and my kingdom, and what has been done by me." It is the same sentiment: everything Xerxes did was due to Ahura Mazda.

We entered the Apadana palace. I saw the holes for the gateposts. "Apadana" means "castle". It took 13 years to build and had a counterpart at Susa. It had a central hall and three porticoes or "*eivans*" (*iwans*), leaving the centre of the hall as a square. There used to be 36 limestone columns, each 20 metres high, which supported the no-longer-existing ceiling. Only three have survived. Their bases were circular, the capitals were carved with bulls. On a column is a carving of the king, Darius I, walking under an umbrella to shield him from the sun. This is carried by an attendant, and another attendant beside him is carrying a fly-whisk and towel.

The throne was before the gate on the far side. We found the exact spot, and worked out where the ambassadors would have stopped. I thought of Darius I sitting here, lord of the known world in the 6th century, receiving his tribute, and I thought of the inscription on a tablet found with gold and silver tablets discovered in a chest beneath a five-metre thick wall in the Apadana: "Darius, the Great King, the King of kings, the King of vast lands, the son of Hystaspes, an Achaemenian. When Ahura Mazda saw his land in chaos, he bestowed this land on me. He made me king, and I am the king by the will of Ahura Mazda. I subdued this land. If you wish to know how many there were, the lands that belonged to me, look at the figures carrying my throne. Then you will know that the Persian spear has flown far and you will know that the Persians have fought beyond their territory." "If you wish to know how many there were…." Perhaps Darius was aware that there might be more conquests between the carving of the inscription and the date of his death, and cannily linked the tally to a carving by his tomb not yet done.

We moved on to the private residence of Darius when he came to Persepolis, the Tacharan, generally called Darius's "Winter Palace" but which the Rev. Ralph Norman Sharp translates as "Summer Palace", an idea that goes better with the advent of

Persepolis, Apadana. Nicholas Hagger standing exactly where Xerxes I sat on his throne to receive ambassadors. .

summer at the vernal equinox and the New Year. It is on a platform 2.5 metres above the base of the Apadana, 30 metres by 40 metres, and is a stone ruin of more than a dozen trilithon door-frames.

A bas-relief in the entrance to the main hall shows a long-bearded royal hero, presumably Darius, grappling with a fabulous winged unicorn. With his left hands he grasps the unicorn's horn, with his right hand he plunges a dagger into his body. The same room acted as his office and living-room. Farhad said, "In Persia, there was no furniture or bed. A bed could be carpets, mattresses, material put down and taken up so one room could be bedroom, living-room and office at different times of the day." On the western stairway is an inscription by Artaxerxes III detailing the

Persepolis. Darius I's palace and living-room

Achaemenian lineage and pointing out that he had added a stone staircase to Darius's palace.

There is an inscription by Darius I in a block of stone 26 feet long, in Old Persian (the language of those at Pasargadae) on the southern wall of the palace and in Akkadian/Babylonian (the language of Babylon) and Elamite (the language of Susa) on the eastern side of the same block of stone. Akkadian/Babylonian was the international language of the time. The inscription says: "The Great Ahura Mazda, the greatest of the gods – he created Darius the King; he bestowed on him the kingdom. By the favour of Ahura Mazda Darius (is) the King. Darius the King says: This country, Persia, which Ahura Mazda bestowed on me, which (is) beautiful, having good horses, having good men, by the favour of Ahura Mazda, and of me, Darius the King, has no fear of another (country). Darius the King says: may Ahura Mazda bear me aid with the gods of the (Royal) household, and may Ahura Mazda preserve this country from foe, from famine, from falsehood (or the Lie, *drauga*)! Upon this country may there come neither foe, nor famine nor falsehood! This I, as a boon, request of Ahura Mazda, with the gods of the (Royal) household; this to me, as a boon, may Ahura Mazda, with the gods of the (Royal) household, give!"

The inscription continues: "I (am) Darius, the great King, the King of kings, the King of countries which (are) many, the son of Hystaspes, an Achaemenian. Darius the King says: By the favour of Ahura Mazda these (are) the countries which I acquired with this Persian people, which had fear of me (and) bore me tribute: Elam, Media, Babylonia, Arabia, Assyria, Egypt, Armenia, Cappadocia, Sardis, the Ionians of the mainland and of the sea and the countries beyond the sea, Sagartia, Parthia, Drangiana, Bactria, Sogdiana, Chorasmia, Sattagydia, Arachosia, India, Gandara, the Scythians, Maka. Darius the King says: If thus thou shalt think, 'May I not have fear of another,' preserve this Persian people! If the Persian people shall be preserved, henceforward to the longest time, happiness unbroken – this will descend from Ahura upon this (royal) house." Darius mentions 22 of the 23 nations he ruled (assuming that the mainland Ionians are not counted separately

Persepolis. *Faravahar* above inscription on wall of Darius I's palace.

from the Ionian islands). The 23rd country is Persia, which was too obvious to list.

Above the inscription is the *Faravahar*, the Achaemenian crest which is sometimes regarded as a winged soul. A bearded human figure in a hat facing to the right holds the ring of life. From the waist down he becomes an eagle with two wings and tail feathers and an eagle's legs and talons, all of which are joined by a central ring.

Farhad said, "I have studied Ahura Mazda very carefully and read all the books. No image was ever made of Ahura Mazda. The ring in the picture is a symbol of life. The *Faravahar* may be the spirit of the king, Darius I. The books say that that winged image did not exist before Artaxerxes I, that all the *Faravahar*s in Persepolis were later than Darius I and Xerxes I."

And, standing before the palace of Darius I, thinking of research I had done, I thought of Egypt, where the Pharaoh was the winged Horus in life and Ra, the sun-god, in death in as much as he became Ra on his death. "In the same way," I said, "might not Darius I have become Ahura Mazda on his death, become one with Him? In which case, the *Faravahar* shows the spirit of the king as Ahura Mazda with the king's face, and with wings to denote the spiritual body being shown. This idea would have been around in the time of Cyrus even if it was not shown in art until later, and so it was the origin of the Angels' wings which the Jews brought back from their captivity in Babylon when released by Cyrus. During his life the Egyptian Pharaoh had brought down the power of Ra – in the case of Akhenaton, the power of the Aton – and transmitted it to his people and caused the Nile to flood. In the same way, during his life Darius I brought down the power of Ahura Mazda and transmitted it to his people and caused the vernal equinox to happen."

I said, "Both the Pharaoh and the Persian King of kings were priest-kings who were at the centre of rituals that made the seasons change. It was the same with the Chinese Emperor at the Temple of Heaven in Beijing, rituals involving his transmission of the power of *T'ien* (Heaven) enabled the Chinese harvest to be good.

The Egyptian Pharaoh, the Chinese Emperor and the Persian King all embodied the god in rituals and *were* the god and gave their face to the god. Hence the constant references in Persia to Ahura Mazda."

Farhad had listened in silence. He said, "That is very interesting. It is an entirely new way of understanding the connection between the Persian king and Ahura Mazda." But it wasn't a new way of understanding history, it was merely a restating of the old way that had been known in Egypt and China and was also known in Persia. All new insights take place on the borders between disciplines and civilizations, and mine had come by comparing the religious rituals of different civilizations.

Now, excited and mentally on heat, I said, "And what's more, I want to return to the carvings on the staircase to the Apadana for they were here between 515 and 485 BC, the 30 years during which the palace was built. Ionian workmen were here and took back news of the carvings to Greece. Indeed, the Persians brought news with them when they invaded Greece between 492 and 479 BC. How did Greek art arise so spectacularly? Because they got it from Persepolis, here, via the Ionians. How did they develop the Ionic column? Because they got it from Persepolis, here, via the Ionians. Persia was behind Greece. Persia was producing superlative carvings eighty years before Pheidias. Pheidias, the sculptor of the classical carvings on the Acropolis, developed what was happening in Persia. Greece is the source, via Rome, of our European civilization and therefore also of the North-American civilization, the two civilizations which together make Western civilization. Persia is behind Greece. So Persia is actually the source via Greece and Rome of Western civilization."

Farhad listened very quietly as I talked near Darius I's palace, and he said, "No one has said that before. If it is true, it is very good for Iran. But this is an entirely new way of understanding history."

Later I looked in books and found confirmation for the Persian inspiration of Greek art and philosophy in Nadereh Nafisi's *Persepolis* which holds that the *Faravahar* came from the winged Horus, symbol of divine and solar power. Early Zoroastrianism focused on the sun and its light as opposed to darkness. As in Egypt, royal power came from the sun and was symbolised by the eagle, which was akin to the hawk of Horus. "Farrh", an Old Persian word, was echoed in other languages and suggests royal fortune, health, prosperity and fertility, perhaps as a guardian spirit of kings sent by Ahura Mazda. The battle between Ahura Mazda and Ahriman, or Angra Mainyu, the evil spirit expressed as *Druj* or *Druga*, "the Lie", which is central to Zoroastrianism and Persian dualism, is to possess the Farrh, a divine blessing which helps revive the dead – and therefore stands for immortality. It is possible that Darius thought that by revering Farrh he would be worshipping his creator, Ahura Mazda.

I found confirmation for the *Faravahar*'s not being Ahura Mazda in Dr Ardeshir Khorshidian's *A New Look at Persepolis:* "A good example of... unfamiliarity with the ancient Iranian culture can be found in the way the '*Faravahar*' (the Achaemenian symbol or emblem) was treated by... foreign scholars. This symbol that depicts an elderly man clad in regal Achaemenian attire holding one hand up high as if in prayer to the almighty, was held most highly by the ancient Persians. The Achaemenians carved this symbol on the highest mountains and rock faces they were able to reach in Iran and lands that they conquered. This emblem has been wrongly attributed to Ahura Mazda, while the Achaemenians never attributed any shapes, or carved any statues to be a representation of the Almighty. The *Faravahar*, therefore, is a mere symbol or emblem that holds within her profound meaning and is not a pictorial depiction of the monotheistic Achaemenians' Almighty

God Ahura Mazda.... Why... would Ahura Mazda hold a hand aloft in Prayer? Since he was the highest held deity, who would he be praying to?"

Later still, I found corroboration that Ionian workmen had helped build Persepolis and had taken ideas back with them in Josef Wiesehöfer's *Ancient Persia* which I found in Tehran on my last night: "The Ionian artists and builders taking part in constructing Persepolis must have talked about the splendour of the residence when they returned west and some scholars indeed tend to believe that the ideas carved in stone in Persepolis were adopted in parts of the Acropolis building programme in Athens (the Parthenon frieze)." Also: "Under the Achaemenids, Greek philosophy flourished in Ionia, Greek mercenaries fought for Persian interests, and Greek statesmen served as counsellors to the great kings." And in Khorshidian: "The writer (Jim Hicks in *The Persians*) attempts to show that the art of the Achaemenians was borrowed and copied from foreigners and that Persepolis was built at the hands of Greek workers and artisans. However, nothing is further from the truth." The movement was in fact in the other direction.

I returned to J. B. Bury, *History of Greece*, which I had studied for 'A' level Ancient History as a schoolboy and there was is no mention of Persia as being the context for, and influence on, Greek art and philosophy although there is a very full treatment of the Persian wars.

*

We went on to the Xerxes I's palace, to which he turned his attention after being defeated by the Greeks at the battles of Salamis (480 BC) and Plataea (479 BC). Lacking the firmness and resolve of Darius I, being more unpredictable (now severe, now kind), he resolved to build a palace even more glorious than that of his father Darius. The Gate of All Nations came first, then Xerxes built this palace he called Hadish in an inscription: "I made this Hadish by the will of Ahura Mazda." An inscription on the entrance of the palace reads: "King Xerxes, the King of kings, son of the Achaemenian King Darius."

Xerxes I also built a palace called Three Gateways, which was finished by his son Artaxerxes I. Stairs leading to the Three Gateways are adorned with carvings of Persian soldiers equipped with lances and shields, and on the southern portal Artaxerxes I wears a robe with folds – the Elamite garment of honour Darius wore in the headless statue in the Tehran Archaeological Museum.

Inscriptions engraved on the northern and southern entrances resemble those found on the southern gate of Darius I's palace and say: "A great God (is) Ahura Mazda, who created this earth, who created that heaven, who created man, who created happiness for man, who made Artaxerxes king, the one King of many (kings), the one Commander of many (commanders). I (am) Artaxerxes the great King, the King of kings, the King of countries having many (kinds of) human beings, the King in this great earth far and wide, the son of Xerxes the King, the grandson of Darius, an Achaemenian. Artaxerxes the great King says: By the favour of Ahura Mazda this palace Xerxes the King, my father, previously (began to build). After that I built (it). Me may Ahura Mazda, with the gods, preserve, and my kingdom, and what has been done by me." On the western staircase is the *Faravahar* and beside it a winged lion with a human head – a sphinx, which was a feature of Xerxes' reign.

Avoiding the harem, we returned to the staircase the ambassadors used, with the reliefs of 23 nations, and looked briefly at Xerxes I's palace of A Hundred Columns which lies to the northeast, towards the mountains. When it was discovered in 1878 it was under three metres of soil and cedar ash. This was Xerxes I's audience hall, his attempt to go one better than his father Darius I's Apadana.

Here was a wonderful carving at the north-western gate of the king sitting on the throne with the master of ceremonies before him, and an attendant with a fly-whisk standing behind him, holding a towel. Below him are his Persian and Median guards near a bull's head which has lost its horns. On the south-eastern gate the king is on his throne and below him are emissaries bearing gifts. On both eastern and western gates the king stabs a fabulous unicorn. Among the ruined column bases are fallen capitals in the shape of a crown.

We went down past the Treasury, a rectangle of identical column bases over 120 metres long and nearly 62 metres wide. I thought of the Athenian Treasury, which was established at the sacred island of Delos, the ancient centre of Ionian worship, soon after the beginning of the Athenian Empire c. 478 BC. The idea for the Athenian Empire's Treasury had come from Persepolis, where Darius had begun the Treasury building before his death in 486 BC. The idea had been brought to the Greeks from Persia during the Persian invasions between 492 and 479 (the battle of Plataea). It was of Alexander's troops plundering this Treasury building in 330 BC that Rufus wrote, "The quantity of money captured there was huge almost beyond belief."

Outside the museum there was a double-bull capital and inside in a glass case was a pulley which had lifted the stones. There was a corroded trumpet which presumably played royal fanfares.

We walked back to the car soon after 11 am. Farhad pointed out the decaying remains of a tent city built by the last Shah in 1971 to host the lavish event for 60 monarchs or heads of state at the 2,500th anniversary of Persian monarchy. Many of the visitors were accommodated in tented apartments with marble bathrooms, and food was transported by air from Maxim's of Paris. The huge amounts of money squandered on the event at a time when roads needed improving appalled the Iranians, few of whom were invited, and the ostentatious opulence arguably began the movement for Revolution which was to end the long tradition of Iranian monarchy before the close of the decade.

*

We drove on and stopped briefly at Naqsh-e Rajab, where there are Sasanian bas-reliefs. Ardashir I receives a circle of kingship from Ahura Mazda during his investiture (which is like a coronation). His son Shapur stands behind him holding a *barsam* (a stick used in rituals, with his finger crooked in respect). There is a Middle Persian inscription. In another relief, Shapur I the Great, Ardashir I's son, is shown on horseback being given the circle of kingship by Ahura Mazda during his investiture. There is an inscription in Greek, Middle Persian and Parthian. Assuming that the reliefs commemorate two investitures, then they can be dated to AD c. 225 and AD c. 242 respectively.

We drove on to Naqsh-e Rostam, parked and walked on sloping sandy soil where small rats scurried to and from holes. Above us were the entrances to four Achaemenian tombs high up a rock-face in low mountains to be out of reach of tomb raiders. The tombs had reliefs above them after the manner of the Elamites, who were the first to use this style. The Achaemenians appear to have learned from Egypt that shaft graves can be penetrated, and they excavated their tombs in perpendicular rock with cross-shaped entrances a considerable height above ground level. They could only be reached by a steep ascent in a basket fastened to ropes on pulleys, braving the sheer drop below. As knowledge of the Achaemenian time was lost in the late Parthian or early Sasanian periods, the

Achaemenians do not appear in the 11th-century *Shahnameh*, Ferdowsi's verse-epic "book of kings", which starts with the legendary Jamshid and soon passes to the Sasanians. The later Persians did not know that these were Achaemenian tombs and, looking at Sasanian reliefs at ground level below, thought they were carvings that showed the legendary hero Rostam of the *Shahnemeh* – hence the name, "pictures of Rostam" (Matthew Arnold's Rustam). Persepolis was to do with Jamshid, they

Naqsh-e Rostam. Darius I's tomb with inscriptions on either side of the door.

thought, and this place with Rostam.

Of the four tombs, there is general agreement that the third tomb from the left is Darius I's and this is borne out by inscriptions beside it; and that the first from the left is Darius II's. The other two tombs belong to Xerxes I and Artaxerxes I. Opinion is divided as to which is which, but there is some consensus that the extreme right-hand one is Xerxes I's.

Farhad said that the bodies of the kings were first exposed on the mountainside above for their bones to be picked clean by vultures and other birds, as the Zoroastrian *Videvdat* dictates, and their bones were then brought down and interred in these rock-

Naqsh-e Rostam. A view of Xerxes I's tomb showing its height.

faced tombs.

The reliefs above the tomb doorways show the king standing at the Zoroastrian fire-altars under the *Faravahar*. Farhad pointed out that the king on the extreme right-hand relief, thought to be Xerxes I, is shown with 30 representatives from 30 nations carrying his throne. More throne-bearers are under Darius I's throne. One wonders if they number 23 because of the 23 delegates on the Apadana staircase, but even through binoculars it is hard to be sure of the exact number shown. Above his tomb doorway Ahura Mazda is shown between him and his son Xerxes, who tends the fire.

There are two inscriptions in Old Persian of Darius I, one behind the carved figure of Darius above his tomb, the other to the left of his tomb doorway. Together they confirm that this is the tomb mentioned by the Greek historian Ctesias, who wrote that it was in a cliff-face and could only be reached by ropes.

The inscriptions communicate lineages and events to succeeding generations, and in the case of the first inscription the countries Darius I ruled: "A great God (is) Ahura Mazda, who created this earth, who created that heaven, who created man, who created happiness for man, who made Darius king, the one King of many (kings), the one Commander of many (commanders). I am Darius the great king, the King of kings, the King of countries having all (kinds) of human beings, the King in this great earth far and wide, the son of Hystaspes, an Achaemenian, a Persian, the son of a Persian, an Aryan, having Aryan lineage. Darius the King says:

By the favour of Ahura Mazda these (are) the countries which I seized far away from Persia. I ruled over them; they bore me tributes. What was said to them by me, that they did. My law, that held them. Media, Elam, Parthia, Aria, Bactria, Sogdiana, Chorasmia, Drangiana, Arachosia, Sattagydia, Gandara, India, the *haoma*-drinking Scythians, the pointed-helmeted Scythians, Babylonia, Assyria, Arabia, Egypt, Armenia, Cappadocia, Sardis, Ionia, the Scythians beyond the sea, Skudra, the shield-bearing Ionians, the Libyans, the Ethiopians, the men of Maka, the Carians."

If the Ionians and the Scythians are treated as two nations and Persia is included, then the tally is 27. If all the Ionians and Scythians are treated separately, it is 30. Either way it exceeds 23, the number of delegations on the Apadana staircase. Between the building of the Apadana staircase and his death Darius conquered at least four more nations.

The inscription continues, echoing the tablet: "Darius the King says: Ahura Mazda, when he saw this earth disturbed, after that bestowed it on me; made me king. I am the King. By the favour of Ahura Mazda I put it down in its place. What I said to them, that they did, as my desire was. If thou shalt think that how many were those countries which Darius the King held, look at the sculptured figures, which bear the throne. Then thou shalt know; then to thee it will become clear (that) the spear of the Persian man (has) gone forth far; then to thee it will become clear (that) the Persian man very far from Persia engaged in battle. Darius the king says: "This which has been done, all that I did by the favour of Ahura Mazda. Ahura Mazda bore me aid until I did what has been done. Me may Ahura Mazda preserve from harm, and my (royal) house, and this country. This I request of Ahura Mazda. This may Ahura Mazda give to me. O man! The command of Ahura Mazda, let this to thee not seem repugnant! Do not leave the right path! Do not revolt!"

The other inscription says: "A great God (is) Ahura Mazda, who created this excellence which is seen, who created happiness for man, who cause wisdom and activity to descend on Darius the King. Darius the King says: By the favour of Ahura Mazda I am that sort (of man) that I am the friend of right. I am not the friend of wrong. (It is) not my desire that the weak (man) should have wrong done (to him) by the strong, nor (is) that my desire that the strong should have wrong done (to him) by the weak. What (is) right, that (is) my desire. I am not the friend of the deceitful man (or, of *Druj* or *Druja*, the Lie, *drujanam*). I am not quick-tempered. Those things which happen in my anger are firmly held (in control) by (my) thought. I am firmly ruling (my) impulses. The man who co-operates, him according to the co-operation, so I reward him. He who does harm, him according to the harm so I punish. (It is) not my desire to do harm, nor (is) that my desire if he should do harm, he should not be punished. What a man says against a man, that does not convince me until he satisfies the well-ordered statute. What a man does or when he performs according to his powers, I am satisfied (with that), and my pleasure is extreme, and I am well satisfied. And of that sort (is) my intelligence and command. When what has been done by me thou shalt see, or when thou shalt hear (it), both in the palace and in the camp, this (is) my activity over and above (my) thought and intelligence."

The inscription continues: "This (is) indeed my activity, that my body has strength. As a warrior, I am a good a warrior. Once it be seen with intelligence in the place (of battle) what I see (to be) rebellious – what I do not see (to be rebellious), both with intelligence and with command, then I am more forward (than others) to think with intelligence, when I see a rebel, as when I do not see one. Skilled I am both with hands and with feet. As a horseman, a good horseman I am; as a bowman, a good bowman I am, both on foot and on horseback. As a spearman, I am a good spearman, both on foot and on horseback. And the skilfulnesses which Ahura Mazda has caused to descend on me, and I have had the strength to use them, by the favour of Ahura Mazda what has been done by me I have done with these skilfulnesses which Ahura Mazda has caused to descend on me. Oh menial, vigorously make clear what sort (of man) I am; what sort my skilfulnesses (are); what sort my superiority (is). Let it not to thee seem false which has been heard by thy ears. Hear that which is conveyed to thee! Oh menial, let not to thee be made false that which has been done by me. See that which has been written! Let not the laws (be broken) by thee. Let not (anyone) be untrained. Oh menial, may the King not inflict punishment."

Standing apart from the cliff-face is a cube-shaped tower known as the Zoroastrian Kabah. It takes its name from the cube-shaped

Naqsh-e Rostam. Kabah with (probably) Darius II's tomb.

Islamic Kabah at Mecca. Both buildings are constructed of grey-and-white stone – the Zoroastrian Kabah is the only Achaemenian building to be constructed of grey-and-white stone, and to have niches all over its outside. The purpose of the Zoroastrian Kabah is unknown. It stands in front of Darius I's tomb and has an empty, windowless room, like the Mecca Kabah, and some believe that a *magus* guarded the sacred fire there, but it has no smoke vents. Some believe that it housed the *Avesta,* the Zoroastrian holy scripture. Some believe it was the Sasanian treasury or archives room, or even that it was an observatory for viewing the stars. Some even believe it was a place where battle flags were stored.

There are two inscriptions on the wall inside, one in Middle Persian, one in Sasanid Pahlavi, Parthian Pahlavi and Greek, carved by the High Priest Kartir. He recorded Shapur I's victories over the Emperor Gordian of Rome and the defeat of a Roman army of 60,000 under Philip the Arab and the capture of Antioch – also the capture of the Emperor Valerian. He also recorded his own building of fire temples throughout the Empire. In the Sasanian time Zoroastrianism was the State religion and the Zoroastrian High Priest was very powerful and could tell the king what he should do. In the earlier Achaemenian time, as we have seen, the king may have been as close to Ahura Mazda as, or even closer than, the Zoroastrian priests.

The Mecca Kabah was reputedly built by Abraham and Ishmael. Pilgrims there kiss and touch the Black Stone which was reputedly given to Adam as he left Paradise. The shrine was destroyed and rebuilt several times. I remarked that Mohammad originally prayed towards Jerusalem but after his migration to Medina and his difficulties there with Jews he prayed in the direction of the Mecca Kabah, which, like the Christian tabernacle, was an "empty" dwelling-place of God – where Allah, like Yahweh, could be found. I said that on this analogy, it is likely that the Zoroastrian Kabah was an "empty" dwelling-place where Ahura Mazda could be found. Darius I and his three Achaemenian successors therefore rested near Ahura Mazda.

Below the cliff-face tombs are seven Sasanian reliefs, the "pictures of Rostam". Ardashir I is shown AD c. 240. Shapur I, his son, holds the Roman Emperor Valerian captive while Philip the Arab kneels before him, suing for peace. Bahram II (who reigned from AD 276 to 293) is superimposed on a panel of a 9th-century-BC Elamite king. Narseh or Narses (who reigned from AD 293 to 302) receives the circle of kingship from Anahita, goddess of war and fertility – one of the few representations of Anahita in art. The figure that seems to be Hormizd II (who reigned from AD 302 to 309) is shown with his enemy upside down. In the carvings Medes are shown with round hats, Persians with cylindrical hats.

*

We drove on to the Cyrus II's capital at Pasargadae through deserted countryside. The driver played traditional Sasanian taped music in which an instrument called a *santur* was played with small sticks. We passed the railway that is being built from Isfahan to the Gulf via Shiraz – I counted four tunnels that had been driven through rock – and we eventually approached the village of Pasargadae and encountered Cyrus II's tomb, a yellowy "gable-roofed house" under scaffolding on a high-stepped pyramid, built in the Urartian (north Turkish) style by Greek stonecutters. There was a low line of distant mountains behind it under blue sky and all round a flat sand-coloured plain. "We'll come back to this later," Farhad said.

It was here, where he defeated the Median army led by his maternal grandfather Astyages, overlord of the Persians, in 550 BC, a battle which led to the beginning of the Achaemenian Empire, that Cyrus II decided to build his capital from 546 BC. He conquered Lydia, Ionia and Babylonia by 539 BC – the year on which the last Shah based the 2,500th anniversary of Iranian kingship celebrated in 1971 – and then much of Central Asia. He ruled the first world state, a universal empire which extended from the Aegean to the Indus River, from Pasargadae, which may have been named after the main Persian tribe. Xenophon described him as tolerant and merciful. According to Herodotus, Xerxes I, on the other hand, lacked tolerance towards other religions and suppressed rebellions in Egypt and Babylonia, and was relentless towards Greece. Wiesehöfer shows that Cyrus was less kindly than Xenophon allowed and Xerxes more kindly than Herodotus allowed.

We drove across the flat sand-coloured plain, which we had to ourselves, to the Entrance Palace, which served as a gatehouse. A large corner-pillar carries an inscription in three languages, Old Persian, Elamite and Babylonian. Farhad translated it aloud: "I (am) Cyrus, the Achaemenian." The word "king" was missing at the end. Here on a block of stone under a corrugated-iron roof to shield it from the elements was a winged "genie", Farhad called him, wearing an Egyptian crown and an Elamite robe, and adopting an Assyrian four-winged stance, the oldest well-preserved Achaemenian monument reconciling Egypt, Elam and Babylonia in one universalist image. As Egypt became part of the Persian Empire under Cambyses II in 525 BC, this relief may date to his reign and symbolise Cambyses' expansion of the Persian Empire. Perhaps the statue showed Cambyses with an Egyptian Pharaoh's power to channel Horus/Ra to his people, but depicted here in Persian terms: a winged Ahura Mazda who channelled Ahura Mazda to Egypt, Elam and Babylonia.

There were mosquitoes about, and I had been told that anti-malarial precautions would normally be necessary in the south but would not be necessary in January. The mosquitoes were very aggressive, dive-bombing me as if they had not seen a tourist for several weeks, delighting in the unseasonally warm weather, and I was relieved to move on to the Reception Palace, which stood on a foundation of two layers of limestone blocks. There were base-markings or bottom fragments of 12 columns, and a line of rounded segments of fallen columns. I looked for evidence that the capitals were Ionic but there seemed to be no capitals. On the inside of the waist-high stone doorways are carvings of the bottom half of a bull's legs and of a man in a fish-like costume, or a fishman, which according to Farhad was a figure in Phoenician mythology who symbolised fertility, while the bull was a symbol of abundance. On a corner block was a trilingual inscription in Old Persian, Elamite and Babylonian: "I, Cyrus the King, built this."

Farhad said, "The first mention of a Persian garden is about this palace, in Herodotus and Plutarch. There was water to irrigate trees which would have linked this Reception Palace to the private Residential Palace so Cyrus could walk back home in shade."

We passed water channels – blocks of stone above conduits in straight lines – on our way to Cyrus's private Residential Palace. It covers 3,192 square metres, Farhad said, and has five rows of six columns and self-contained gardens. Farhad took me to another waist-high stone doorway under a roof to shade it from sun. The inside of the doorway showed a man in an Elamite robe, and on the hem were Old Persian words which Farhad read out for me: "I am Cyrus the King, (an) Achaemenian." Farhad said, "In Persian architecture whatever is on the left is always reflected on the right," and he read another inscription on the inside of the opposite doorway: "I am Cyrus, son of Cambyses (ie Cambyses I), the Achaemenian King." Farhad said, "I think Cyrus and his father Cambyses were shown."

I lingered in Cyrus's living-room, gazing across the plain towards the distant low snow-white mountains. Then we returned to the car and drove back to Cyrus's tomb, and I got out. It was by itself on the flat plain, and it was as if nothing had changed since

Pasargadae. Cyrus II's Residential Palace, inscription on hem of robe above Cyrus II's feet.

Pasargadae. Cyrus II's Residential Palace and living-room, with Nicholas Hagger.

Alexander's day – except that it was now under scaffolding (put up in October 2001 and still there five years later). The entrance was on the west side (where the sun set), and Zoroastrians looked for light in the direction of the sun. It was discovered in the late 1950s, when it was under a mound of earth. There was a problem with a fig-tree growing on top of the mound, and solving the problem of the fig-tree led to the discovery of this tomb.

Pasargadae. Tomb of Cyrus II, mountains in distance.

Pasargadae. Tomb of Cyrus II, Nicholas Hagger standing where Alexander stood.

I walked round it while Farhad, walking with me, reminded me that Alexander the Great, arriving here in the spring of 324 BC, had found it desecrated with Cyrus's bones scattered and no trace of his gold sarcophagus or kingly clothes. Alexander had been disgusted' and, sensing a precursor, a kindred spirit who had also ruled a universal empire from the Aegean to the Indus, ordered that the tomb should be repaired. It was not possible to climb up the steep steps and look inside the doorway of the "roofed house", and to my regret Farhad said there was no trace of the famous inscription I had read as a schoolboy. According to both Arrian and Strabo, Cyrus placed an inscription over the tomb saying, "O man, I am Cyrus, son of Cambyses, who founded the empire of Persia and ruled over Asia. Do not grudge me my monument."

Cyrus had been influenced by north Turkey when he conquered Sardis – hence the north-Turkish style of the tomb. There is reputedly a rosette on the roof gable, perhaps symbolising fertility or the wingless sun disk of Ahura Mazda, but I was unable to locate it. The Persians, not knowing that Pasargadae was Cyrus's capital, called this the "Tomb of Solomon", and they called a terraced wall in rocky hills nearby the "Throne of Solomon's Mother" and a distant single-storey building that resembled the Zoroastrian Kabah "Solomon's Prison". According to inscriptions of the 3rd century AD, Solomon was considered to be the same person as Jamshid, who was responsible for all ancient monuments, including those at Persepolis and Pasargadae. As we have seen, throughout Persia, knowledge of the Achaemenian time became forgotten very rapidly, until it was unearthed, understood and retrieved.

I stood where Herodotus, Alexander, Strabo and Plutarch had stood at various times between the 5th century BC and the 1st/2nd centuries AD, and thought of the Shah of Persia in 1971 saying, as told by Farhad, "O Cyrus, sleep calm and peaceful for *I* am here" – betraying an arrogance that would lead to the Revolution at the end of the decade and terminate the long tradition of 2,500 years of kingship, the very thing he wanted to celebrate. He did not know when he stood before the tomb of the first king of Iran in 1971 that he would be the last king of Iran before the end of the decade.

*

We drove back to the village and stopped at the simple Pasargadae restaurant for lunch. The toilets – like all those outside our hotels – had two enamel footprints on either side of a hole in the floor and smelt vile. I "washed" my hands in anti-bacterial gel I carried in my bag. We ordered three kinds of kebab, soup, yoghurt and bottled water. The driver, Ali sat at our table. We were the only visitors and were served by Pasargadaean descendants from the time of Cyrus.

My head was full of wonderful stones and carvings, the monuments of the Achaemenian dynasty from Cyrus II to Xerxes I and beyond and their superb art which was the missing link between Assyria/Egypt and Greece. I had much to mull over. I had had a revelation on which I needed to reflect. The Achaemenians were the classical Greeks' source, and therefore our source too. Yet the Greek civilization had begun with the Minoans, so exactly what had happened during the Persian influence?

Now, musing in the simple Pasargadae restaurant as a student of the rise and fall of civilizations, I confirmed my pre-existing view of the Greek and Arab civilizations. I realised I had already accommodated the Persian impact on Greek culture. The Aegean-Greek civilization had begun with the Minoans and had developed a strong religion. The temple of Hera at Olympia had been firmly dated by pottery to c. 600-590 BC, *before* Cyrus. It was not the structure of the Greek civilization that was affected by Persia, but the quality of its art. The Aegean-Greek civilization had experienced a breakdown of certainties as a result of the Persian invasions of 492-479 BC. In stages 38 and 39 of its progress a civilization that has just broken down suffers a weakened religion and its visual arts become secular and restless, as did Greek art in the time of Pheidias, whose huge statues wore calm and serene classical expressions from c. 456 to 430 BC. There is philosophical rationalism and scepticism due to the weakening of the civilization's religious outlook, and this reflected itself in the rationalism of the Ionian philosophers and Sophists. Greek religion weakened in the time of Parmenides, who was born c. 515 BC and would have been thirty c. 485 BC, and is known for holding "all is one" (or "all is One"). The Iranian civilization, for its part, had been in its stage of political unification (stage 15) under Cyrus and had undergone expansion at this time, an expansion that had been checked by the defence of the Greeks.

The Iranian civilization had run its course by the early 16th century and had passed into the Arab civilization and fully adopted Islam. Following the decline of the Ottoman Empire and the loss of Arab sovereignty to Western (British and French) colonial occupation, there was a yearning for, and a revival of, fundamentalist Islamic values (in stage 45 of the Arab civilization) as the Middle East groped towards a federation of Arab and Islamic states. Its high point was the Khomeini Revolution. The fervour I had experienced in the Shiraz shrine was an aspect of this revival, and I knew it was a phase and would eventually be replaced by a new phase.

My stunning perception had not changed the structure of my pattern of history, it had just brought detail to a couple of stages in the Greek civilization. Those stages included Pheidias and Parmenides, who were at the source of Western art (sculpture and philosophy), and so my perception had carried forward my understanding of the source of Western art and philosophy.

5

IN DESERT YAZD, AMONG ZOROASTRIANS

The journey to Yazd was along a relatively deserted road through rugged mountains. We climbed and there was snow on either side of the road for a while, then scree again. From time to time we overtook a lorry, but there was little traffic. We passed a *caravanserai*. As we journeyed we talked. Farhad conversed with Ali in Parsee and after a laugh he turned round and shared their conversation.

"We are discussing the Turks in Iran," he said. "They are like your Irish, they are strange, and there are many jokes about them. Ali was telling me, 'A Turk was told, "Your son has died." He was distressed and jumped off the roof of his fourth-floor apartment. As he passed the third floor he thought, 'But I have no son,' and as he passed the second floor, 'And I am not married.' And as he passed the first floor, 'I haven't been called Papa.'" He laughed. "Another Turk was told so-and-so has got HIV. He replied, 'He had a GLX last year.'"

The Iranians feel superior to the Turks – and to the Arabs. Farhad had said again, "The Arabs have had little civilization until the 20th century, whereas the Persians have had 2,500 years of kingship." In fact, the Mesopotamian civilization in what is now Iraq was every bit as old as the Iranian civilization, and despite their disdain for the Arab, they shared a reverence for Islam with them.

"Do you Shias dislike the Sunnis?" I asked.

"Oh no, Sunnis are fine, we are all Muslims. We have no problems with Sunnis in Iran. Saddam Hussein was bad because he invaded Iran, not because he was a Sunni." He made it sound as if it were like Catholics and Protestants: in mainland UK we were barely aware of the difference, but in Northern Ireland there had virtually been a civil war between them. So it was with the Iranians, he led me to believe: Sunnis and Shias were no problem within Iran but were in virtual civil war in Iraq.

In fact it was more complex than that. The Human Rights Report of 1997 had said that Sunnis were persecuted in Iran, and the 2001 Human Rights Report had said that Shias were persecuted in Saudi Arabia. The Sunni-Shia divide included persecutions that recalled the persecutions of the European Catholics and Protestants in the 16th and 17th centuries.

I said I had not seen any soldiers during our travels, that soldiers had a low profile in Iran. "In fact," Farhad said, "the army are in barracks *outside* the cities. They're not in the cities because we need the space. Three years ago a barracks in Tehran was changed into a park for citizens. That is how it should be, the citizens should come first."

We talked about cars. "This is a Peugeot Persia, it's mainly Iranian but its gearbox and engine are French. It's the only car made in Iran. We have a lot of SsangYong cars. You know, they are Korean."

"North Korean?" I asked, thinking of reports that North Koreans were helping Iran develop nuclear weapons.

"Oh no, South Korean. We have no relations with North Korea."

'Does he believe that?' I wondered. 'Does he know?' "Iran and North Korea were linked by Bush in the Axis of Evil," I said.

He scoffed: "When we heard that we laughed. Bush is so stupid. We can't be linked with North Korea. He's never travelled. He doesn't know about other countries. He didn't have a passport until 1991. He'd been to two countries before he became Head of State

I believe, China and France." In fact, he had been to China, Mexico (three times) and Israel (twice), and had briefly visited Rome. According to his staff he had also visited Bermuda, Canada, Egypt, England, Scotland, France and Gambia.

We had travelled through mountains and plains, and now reached the fringe of the Abarkuh Desert. "Abarkuh is the most faraway place you can reach," Farhad said. "It's like your Timbuctoo." Timbuktu is in West Africa. "It means 'in the middle of nowhere'. I had a letter from a friend recently. He wrote 'I'm studying at university in

Abarkuh. 4,500-5,000-year-old cypress tree. Below, girth of tree's trunk.

Abarkuh', meaning a long way from everywhere. Look at the traditional 19th-century houses. They have pomegranate orchards. And
look, Sasanian chicken-farms. You see, a lot of small arches, like
the arch at Ctesiphon."

We had reached the town of Abarkuh and we turned down a
lane. "I want to show you something that is not on the itinerary,"
Farhad said. "A very old cypress tree in the middle of the desert."
We drove down a lane with mud huts and mud-and-straw walls and
stopped in a wide parking area with a view of a distant mosque.

"There it is," Farhad said, pointing to a cypress more than 60
feet tall and with an enormous girth. It stood near a runnel of clear
running water, ringed by a shoulder-high hedge that allowed it
considerable space. "That tree is 4,500 years old, may be 5,000
years old. It's fourteen and a half metres in diameter."

Four thousand five hundred to five thousand years old. Five
thousand years was as old as recorded history, as old as the first
writing. It had been a sapling when the Great Pyramid and
Stonehenge were being built. It had been alive before the
beginning of the Iranian civilization, from the time of the Elamites
before the Indo-European migrations. It was older than the Tree of
Life of the *Kabbalah*. It was much older than Abraham and Moses.
It was a mature tree by the time Cyrus conquered Media. It was
older than the events in the *Bible*, it was an ancient tree on the day
of the crucifixion. It had withstood all the events that had befallen
Iran since then, from the Arab conquest to the rise of Khomeini. To
it, a Shah's fall and an Ayatollah's reign of terror were of little
more significance than wind disturbing its leaves.

I wandered off and looked at its trunk. It was gnarled and riven.
There was a kind of hollow room in the centre waist-high to me,
that a child could sit in. From its massive base four, perhaps half a
dozen, trees seemed to grow up, like half a dozen poplar trees close
together. People had tied bits of white paper to its leaves as wishes

to divine power, which it seemed natural to associate with this awesome tree. Because of its antiquity this really could have been the Tree of the Knowledge of Good and Evil in Paradise, more so than the small offshoot of the original tree in Iraq's al-Gourna (or al-Qurna), which I had visited at the confluence of the Tigris and Euphrates while working in Baghdad.

Ali had the boot open and was making tea. A little swarthy gnome of a man in a green shirt worn outside blue trousers, a pinkish work-jacket, plimsolls and a green hat had appeared. Farhad offered him a carton of tea. Farhad said to me in some triumph, "This is the guardian of the tree."

"Can you ask him how old the tree is?" I asked.

Farhad translated while the gnome gratefully clutched his tea. "Four thousand five hundred years, perhaps five thousand years. Experts have examined it and they have said that about its age. Many scientific tests have proved its age. It was damaged in a fire about twelve years ago. The Municipality of Abarkuh appointed me to guard the tree eleven years ago. I work here from 7.30 to 5. I have been 32 years with the Municipality but only 11 years as guardian of the tree. I am a descendant of the prophet with lineage to prove it." Farhad added reverentially, "He is wearing a green hat, that means he is a descendant of the Prophet."

Abarkuh. The guardian of the tree.

I asked if his father worked for the Municipality as well.

"Yes, he did. This man lives in one of the mud-houses a short walk away. Some of the houses have domes so that part of the room below is cool as the sun moves round in the hot months."

We had been watched by a woman in a black *chador* sitting on a wooden seat, and Farhad took my carton of tea, which I had not touched, and ran over and gave it to her. She accepted it with much nodding and smiling and sipped it. Farhad returned and realised what he had done. "Oh," he said, "where is your tea?" I said it was all right, I couldn't hold it as I wanted to write in my notebook.

"Where does the fresh water come from?" I asked.

Farhad interpreted. "They dug into the ground and made a well. They installed an electric pump, and the pump pumps water along channels. They are called *qanats*. Persians started digging *qanats*, underground water channels, 2,000 years ago to irrigate crops and supply drinking-water. The well has to be 100 metres deep. A tunnel wide enough to crawl up was dug with a slight downward slope from near the top of the well. Well water was pumped up to the tunnel and the gradient then brought it gushing out into the open water channels. The water irrigates the ground round the tree and the garden here, and it is so pure the women come and fill jugs of water to take away and they wash their clothes in the running water. It is good to have this water when the hot weather comes. It is very cool.

"Now," Farhad said, "we must go," and he pressed banknotes with Ayatollah Khomeini's head on them into the hands of the guardian of the tree and of the lady who had watched and drunk my tea, and we drove on.

*

We now skirted the Abarkuh Desert. Dusk was approaching and the sand met the sky just as from the coast the sea meets the sky. Farhad said, "Look, a mosque. Its minaret was like a lighthouse, it guided caravans of camels."

Soon afterwards we passed a 17th-century *caravanserai*. We stopped and I got out to look and wandered away from the car.

There were scorpions here, Farhad had said, and I trod carefully. I had nearly trodden on a scorpion in bare feet in Baghdad. It was on the marble floor of our kitchen. The servant had lit a small fire round it so it was enclosed in a wall of small flames, and it had brought its sting over its body and stung itself to death.

I looked at the *caravanserai* in the dusk and thought of Edward Fitzgerald's translation of Omar Khayyam (4th edition):

"Think, in this batter'd Caravanserai
Whose Portals are alternate Night and Day,
  How Sultan after Sultan with his pomp
Abode his destin'd Hour and went his way."

In the car as night fell and we sped past flat desert Farhad turned from the front seat and said, "A caravan comprised about 200 camels conveying goods or pilgrims. There were 20 to 30 people with it: a leader, a security man, a navigator, a scribe, a *mullah* and 25 others too look after the camels. When they put in at a *caravanserai*, the camels were tethered in corridors, unless it was full, in which case they were in the courtyard or even outside in special stables. The men slept in raised alcoves open at the front so they could guard their tethered camels. They passed the evening talking with other caravan people and told stories. *The Arabian Nights* began as a *caravanserai* tale."

I asked if the local desert people believed in the Evil Eye.

"Yes, they guard against it with dried beans and incense."

We talked about the international crisis, and I said to Farhad, "An idea came to me during the meditation in the shrine at Shiraz last night. The Iranian leadership are supposed to reply to an American offer to negotiate, but they haven't replied. There's been no message. If they want to reply but don't want to lose face by using a diplomatic channel, then I can be their messenger. I can take back a message and put it in a newspaper article. The trouble is, we return to Tehran on Friday evening, and there may be nobody in the government who can see me on a Friday evening. It's like asking to meet a spokesman on a Sunday evening in the West."

He said, "I don't know anyone to ask."

I said, "Couldn't you ask a friend who might have an idea as to how to get to the top, to the President or Supreme Leader?"

He said, "Yes I could, I will ring him."

We passed through Deh Shir, a small village in the dark desert under bright desert stars with no light pollution – I could see Orion's belt very clearly – and we went through a mountain pass. It was 3 degrees Centigrade outside. And then we were approaching Yazd.

*

Yazd was named after the last Sasanian king Yazd I, Farhad said. Or perhaps from the Middle Persian word *yazd*, which means "worshipper". (Its ancient name was Isisatis.) "It was a Sasanian town and remained a Zoroastrian centre after it was conquered by the Arabs in 642. It is between deserts to north and south – Dasht-e Kavir and Dasht-e Lut, and on one of the ancient Silk Routes to Afghanistan and Pakistan Marco Polo passed through in 1272. It was on a caravan route to Central Asia and India, exporting its silks, fabrics and carpets. It was spared during the invasions of the Mongol Genghis Khan and the Turkic/Uzbek Timur (Tamburlaine). It now has a community of 5,000 Zoroastrians out of a population of 300,000. From the 7th and 8th centuries onwards, feeling persecuted, Zoroastrians have migrated to India as Parsees, just as the Pilgrim Fathers migrated to America, and because of the caravan links with India, many would have left Yazd for there."

Around 7.30 we arrived at the 19th century Hotel Garden Moshir, a colourful traditional hotel built round a long garden – a luxury in the desert, where gardens tried to replicate Paradise – with a long central water channel (*qanat*) to irrigate plants and avenues of trees. I was shown to a first-floor room off a lobby overlooking this garden, room 307, an Islamic-style room with traditional patterns on grilles and tiles and a barrel-vaulted brick ceiling and semi-brick walls that I eyed for mosquitoes (and immediately plugged in anti-mosquito liquid). Farhad was in the room opposite on the other side of the lobby.

I washed and shaved and was down at 8 in the long Islamic dining-area, a former camel-stable, Farhad said, which had two green, red and blue macaws perched on a small tree at the end. As the chef was Caspian, I chose a Caspian dish of *fesenjan*: meat balls, pomegranate sauce and crushed walnut. Soup and yoghurt were served unasked-for while we waited and took in wall-paintings of scenes from the *Shahnameh* in bays all along the side walls. I was sitting in front of a picture of Rostam, the father who kills his son Sohrab in battle (Matthew Arnold's Rustam). Farhad said of the wall-paintings, "In Arab countries the old tradition was lost. In Egypt, the Coptic became Arab. In Syria, the Byzantine became Arab. But Persia was different. Persian survived and the *Shahnameh* preserved pre-Arab Persian legends and history, the old sources." The driver came in late and shared our flat-bread. I had a diet coke and Farhad a non-alcoholic beer (which was permitted under Iran's strict prohibition rules).

Over dinner I wanted to see how freely we – or rather, they –

could talk. The conversation was about revolutions. Farhad believed the Iranian revolution finished during the Iran-Iraq war, which ended in 1988, and he said that the present President was inflexible.

Ali, the driver, said he was anxious during the Revolution, while working in a bank.

Farhad said, "Because of the Iran-Iraq war, everything was controlled by the State, including banks, shortly after the Revolution. Khomeini made everyone pure. There was no corruption. In 1989 Khomeini died, and after Rafsanjani was elected President corruption returned, people made money for themselves out of government."

Ali saw men arrested and was uneasy.

An Iranian who knew Farhad came in on the conversation and said, "I have not been able to understand why so many good people were shot."

I said that revolutionary leaders exist to eliminate a particular class and have to be inflexible to achieve their aim, and that the only way to achieve a sudden and abrupt change in society is to be universally ruthless and not make exceptions for individuals. I asked them all, "Do you feel you can speak freely now?"

They said they could, and then Ali said, "Our President was barracked during a speech at the University of Tehran a few days ago. Students started burning a picture of him. He said, 'It does not matter, you're free to express your opinions. This is a democracy. You can burn my picture, but you can't burn me!'" Farhad and Ali laughed.

After supper I rang my wife to confirm that I had arrived in Yazd and to reassure her that I was safe. I wrote my journal and went to bed.

*

The next morning I breakfasted on the other side of the dining-area, looking across at the picture of Sohrab and Rostam. It was the usual help-yourself breakfast, and the choice of jams included cedrate jam. I did not take any but commented on it to Farhad when he joined me, and asked what it was.

"Cedrate is a fruit, like an orange. It is a variety of the citron or lemon." He rushed to the self-service table and returned with cedrate jam, opened it and said, "Try it." This was another example of Iranians' eagerness to please.

I returned went up to my room to put out my suitcase and hand-luggage for the hotel porter. I returned to Reception to settle for my telephone call the previous night. Now the dining-area was filled with schoolgirls all wearing black headscarves (*maghwaes*), sitting at the long central table and along the sides. Every seat was taken. The young porter looked stressed, and he half-ran back with me to collect my luggage. He went in and took Farhad's luggage. From the lobby I saw Farhad heading off into the gardens, I thought to greet one of the gardeners I could see crouching on the far side, prodding the earth – he went round shaking hands with a lot of people everywhere we went – but in fact, he later said, he was looking for me. We did not then know it but the hurried porter left behind Farhad's briefcase in his room, and the driver did not notice.

We set off and passed a large "mourning house" in a square, a 19th-century *façade* with an arch for open-air ceremonies and parades, including the mourning on 10 *Moharram*. We drove to a spacious confectionery shop, a well-known sweetmeat-and-biscuit shop, Haj Khalife Ali Rabar, where we were the only customers and bought a box of Iranian sweetmeats. Not two but three *Ayatollah*s looked down from a picture on a wall: Ayatollah Khomeini and Supreme Leader Ali Khamenei, of course, but also a smiling ex-President Khatami, who had come from Yazd and had therefore crept into the Head-of-State portrait. Yazd was the only place where I saw him in a portrait, and there was not one portrait of Ahmadinejad in any room I entered in Iran, which in itself perhaps conveyed where the balance of power lay. The sweemeats were put in the boot of our car and were brought out and offered round whenever we stopped for tea.

Robert Byron visited Yazd in 1934 and recorded his impressions in *The Road to Oxiana:* "Yezd (ie Yazd) is unlike other Persians towns. No belt of gardens, no cool blue domes, defend it from the forbidding wastes outside. Town and desert are of one colour, one substance; the first grows out of the second."

We drove straight to the sand-coloured Old City and the 15th-century Friday mosque, which has a magnificent front, a blue diamond-patterned dome and two minarets. We went in. It was completely deserted. We stood before a blue-tiled *iwan* or hall that opened onto the courtyard, and Farhad pointed out the Kufic calligraphy and explained six other styles of calligraphy, of which five were in the mosque. The decorative tiles were in the Timurid style, Timur (Tamburlaine) having ruled here. Farhad pointed out

Yazd. Old City square, with Tomb of the 12 Imams on left.

stalactite designs.

We stood under the dome and Farhad said, "I want you to understand the architecture of a mosque. The *mihrab*, the niche there, is the most sacred area, and so the most decorated, with tiles and calligraphy. It points to Mecca, God is in the centre. Then look up and see how the square floor becomes a dome. The square represents the earth, the dome the sky. Each corner of the walls has a diagonal squinch. Then above the squinches there are eight sides, there's an octagonal holding-structure, and the dome rests on top. This is true of all mosques." We passed a playing area covered in carpets. In the courtyard a staircase led down to a *qanat* for ablutions.

We walked to a 14th-century theological school or *madraseh*, Khanegha, where 14th-century Sufi *dervish*es gathered. We went into the main room, which was small but vertically high and with a dome on top. It was in a state of disrepair; in fact, it looked as if it had not been touched since the 14th century. Out in the courtyard there was a window with local finds relating to hunting in c.1500 BC and a *sitar*, a three-stringed instrument. Steps down led to an ablutions area which could be viewed through a circular grate. This was known as Alexander's Prison – in the same way that Achaemenian buildings at Persepolis were attributed to Jamshid and tombs at Naqsh-e Rostam were attributed to Rostam. It actually had nothing to do with Alexander, though

Yazd. Alexander's prison (below circle in ground) with *badgir* or wind tower (top right).

his army conquered Yazd – according to Safavid history, he built a castle (known as Kasah) in Yazd – but local tradition claims he was imprisoned in the room under the courtyard grate. It is just possible that he did have a prison here in the Sasanian Old City.

From the courtyard we looked at *badgirs* or wind towers, tall four-sided towers with up to a dozen slits or vents each side which rise above many rooftops in Yazd. This ancient cooling system used natural air-conditioning by catching any breeze or wind and diverting it into the rooms of the house below or through water. Besides the body of the tower there were vents to shut out the hot air and flaps to circulate and cool the wind over a pool of cool water. The warm air rises up a different shaft. Byron writes of 1934 in *The Road to Oxiana*: "The towers of Yezd (ie Yazd) are square, and catch the wind from all four quarters by means of hollow grooves, which impel it down into chambers beneath. Two such chambers at either end of a house set up a draft through the length of it."

Yazd. Shia *Husaynieh*.

The caretaker wore a red *fez*-like woven hat and a Western suit. We followed him across the modern *Husaynieh*, an open courtyard surrounded by arched bays used in the *Moharram* festivities. It was where religious plays (*tazias*) were put on. Here the *Ashura* ceremonies take place on 10 *Moharram*.

We went into an 11th-century, pre-Crusade, sand-coloured, domed Seljuq mausoleum of Azadoleh, Governor of Yazd (who was not buried there). It was built in 1038 and dedicated to the 12 Shia *Imam*s, whose names appear on a frieze inside. Hence it is called the Tomb of the 12 *Imam*s, Boghae Davazdah *Imam*. Again, the square floor became, via squinches, an octagonal holding-

Yazd. Inside Tomb of the 12 Imams with pre-Crusade frieze.

Yazd. Caretaker.

structure for the dome, and the calligraphic frieze naming each of the 12 *Imam*s was above 11th-century stuccowork and plasterwork, each letter of which ended beautifully in a flower. The reverential care with which the holy names was written took me deep into the Muslim mind before the Crusades and into why the Muslims resisted the Crusaders occupying Arab land.

The caretaker left us to walk back across the tree-bordered square enclosed by mud-walls and mud-domes to his mud-walled house (to which natural gas was supplied in large head-high pipes, as Farhad pointed out). We returned to our car. Three old men of the Old City sat on a ledge where a mud-wall jutted out, gazing into space. Our caretaker changed his mind and veered towards them and sat with them. They all ignored us as we drove off, their minds in their own world, not ours. Farhad said, "There are two kinds of bricks in Yazd: sun-baked bricks in the 19th-century traditional houses, and fire-baked bricks in the more modern houses. Sun-baked bricks are laid out in the sun for two days and are rebaked in an oven when they have dried in the sun."

We drove to a street with arches over it and to a 19th-century house made of sun-baked bricks beneath a mud-on-straw *façade* that was now the Kohankashaneh Hotel. There were two knockers on the wooden double-doors, a long one for men and a ringed one for women. They made different sounds so that those inside would know if it were a man or woman calling. We were greeted by the owner, a grey man who said *"Salaam"* and put his right palm across his heart, which I reciprocated. At the end of a passage was a sitting-area with seats like carpeted wooden double-beds, overlooking a courtyard: a central rectangular fish-pond with trees on either side and a tented awning, folds rising to an apex.

Farhad said, "The family live in the basement from June to September when it gets very hot, sometimes 45 degrees. Down in the basement it is cool. You can judge how cool by looking at the well. There's a well lower than the water-table down a long flight of steps beyond the fish-pond."

Farhad took me to look. He opened a door. "Go down and see," he suggested.

There were enormous mosquitoes on the sloping tunnel ceiling that led down to a quite wide ablution area. "I can see from here, thank you," I said, eyeing the mosquitoes and backing out.

We sat on the bed-seats, the only visitors, and drank tea served in glasses and ate some of our Iranian sweetmeats. I went to the gents and noticed two huge mosquitoes on a wall near my head, which I watched very carefully. This desert living was full of hardship – sweltering heat, remoteness, lack of modern conveniences – and high among them to those, like myself, who had been advised that anti-malarial tablets were not necessary, were mosquitoes. I recalled going on safari in a Land Rover in Tanzania, and, as we edged between lions, our policeman lying at the back, sweating and delirious from malaria and a temperature of 106, a tsetse fly settled on the top of the door near my head, which I watched, ready to leap out and take my chance among the lions rather than be bitten by it. I had no plans to return to the UK with malaria, sweats and delirium.

*

We left the hotel and walked down more mud-walled streets with arches over them and crossed a small garden square where four boys of about 12 were noisily playing marbles, pushing each other between throws and flicks, and then we drove to the main Zoroastrian fire temple (one of 18 fire temples in Yazd), the Atash

Yazd. Zoroastrian fire temple.

Kadeh, a low arched building up wide steps with a modern *Faravahar* on its low roof, which was built in the 1930s. It holds the sacred eternal flame, which was visible through a large floor-to-ceiling window, a screen to prevent the sacred fire from being contaminated by human breath. The guardian of the fire had to wear a cloth over his mouth to prevent his breath from contaminating the flames. Through the window, flames leapt from wood (supposed to be apricot or almond) heaped in a cauldron. The fire was said to have been burning since AD470, to have been transferred to Ardakan in 1174, to Yazd in 1474 and to its present site in 1940.

Yazd. Caretaker.

The crowd of Iranian school-girls in black *maghwaes* I had encountered breakfasting in our hotel were now crowding round the glass and causing a hubbub. A swarthy, elderly, grey-moustached, fierce Zoroastrian with a disdainful look and a pointed knitted hat and spectacles, in a brown leather coat over faded blue trousers, was trying to sell them packs of postcards of Yazd. He was the caretaker. He told Farhad that the priest was "not here".

Farhad said, "This man keeps the fire together with another man. They work a shift, rota system so someone is here 24 hours a day."

I told Farhad I had some questions to ask him, and I firmly engaged him in conversation (having learned from the Shiraz *dervish* that tact and sensitivity did not work in Iran), to his evident irritation as I was preventing him from offering his postcards of

Yazd to the girls. He had the Shiraz *dervish*'s determination not to be questioned.

"Does he worship Ahura Mazda as they did in Darius I's day?" I asked while black-headscarfed girls milled about, chattering loudly, and an Iranian man I had bad vibes about blatantly listened, thrusting his face between mine and the Zoroastrian's while I guarded my wallet.

"Yes," Farhad interpreted, "he says the religion hasn't changed."

"When was Zoroaster born?" I asked. "He says 6000 BC," Farhad interpreted, "eight thousand years ago. But," he added, "I have studied the *Avesta* and I will explain in a minute, the real date is likely to be the 7th century BC."

"Does he believe in *Druja (*or *Druj* or *Druga)*, the Lie, and in Ahriman?" I asked.

"Yes, he does," Farhad said.

"So he believes in the light and darkness, in Ahriman/*Druja* as the Lie, deception. How does he regard the light and the sun? Are they symbols of Ahura Mazda?" I asked.

"Yes," Farhad interpreted. "They are symbols of Ahura Mazda."

"Does he pray with his eyes open or closed?"

"Eyes open," Farhad interpreted, "looking at the light and the sun."

"Does he ever close his eyes and see Ahura Mazda as Inner Light?"

"No, we don't experience Ahura Mazda inside as Inner Light," Farhad translated. "However, Ahura Mazda is everywhere."

That was the best I could do. The man who was listening had almost interposed his body between the Zoroastrian and me, the girls had moved out of the vicinity of the sacred fire and were heading down the steps and the Zoroastrian was darting off to sell them postcards of Yazd. The least I could do was to buy a pack. It cost 20,000 *rials*, just over $2 or £1 for 20 sturdy postcards within a folder, just over 10 cents or 5p per card. But with a good salary being $450 or £250 a month – I did not like to ask Farhad exactly how much he earned as it would force up the end-of-tour tip – everything would have to be cheap to be affordable. And I knew from what Farhad had told me of the newspaper headlines, there was disquiet because inflation was running at 30 per cent.

Now Farhad said, "I have studied the *Avesta* as I said. Zoroaster's dialect is north-eastern, from Tajikistan. He was born in western Iran, Azerbaijan, which was then within the Persian culture. He migrated to the north-west to the north-east. The *Avesta* is written in a different dialect from Old Persian. Most scholars believed it's between 900 and 500 BC, but c. 630 BC is the most likely to be right. 6000 BC could not be true. The *Avesta* is five books. It is different from the *Koran*, it was written from the 7th century BC to the 6th century AD, much of it written by Sasanian priests. Only a small part of the first book was in Zoroaster's words. Yasht 1. In the whole of the *Avesta* there are paradoxical ideas because it was written by many hands. Sacrifices, for example. Zoroaster is against sacrifices, but later on sacrifices bring abundance. The instructions for burial change in the same way. Zoroaster did not specify laying bodies out for vultures, but later on it was required. The first *Magi* were Medians. The Medians had five tribes, one of which was called *Magus* – it's in Assyrian annals of the 7th and 6th centuries BC. One of the five tribes was a tribe of trained clergy. Zoroaster was one of them. Some *Magi* were against the king."

*

We went on to the Towers of Silence, *dakhmehs* (literally "places for leaving dead bodies"), circular stone walls on adjoining hills outside Yazd where until the 1960s the bodies of dead Zoroastrians were laid out on stones for vultures and wild birds to pick clean. It was logical to do this. Fire was sacred and eternal and must not come into contact with dead bodies, death being an evil introduced into the universe by Ahriman, the power of darkness. The same applied to earth, which must not be contaminated by dead flesh. The dead could not be cremated or buried, so laying the bodies on stones and allowing birds to pick skeletons clean was what happened until the 1960s, when people began finding bits of dead flesh in their gardens, dropped by overflying birds. After 1978 all dead bodies were buried in stone coffins in graves lined with cement in the cemetery below the Towers.

Before then, a few hours after a death a dead body was brought to a wooden building on the outskirts of Yazd. The body was washed and a ceremony was held. The dead body was then carried up to one of the Towers of Silence and put in a sitting position. "For the first night," Farhad said, "the priest recited Yasht 3 on fire, water, stars, the sky, the sun. And book 4, the Sasanian *Vendidad (or Videvdat)* rites for burial." The priest would watch to see which eye the vulture pecked out first – if the right eye, the soul would be with Ahura Mazda, god of light; if the left eye, with Ahriman, principle of darkness. Until the 18th century there was only one Tower of Silence, but it could not cope with the increased demand of a rising population and an increasing number of deaths. So another Tower of Silence was opened. The bones were thrown into a central pit within the circular Tower.

In the Achaemenian time, the dead (including Darius I and the other kings in the Naqsh-e Rostam tombs), were laid on rock and their bones later gathered and put in rock tombs. The dead were buried in rock-faces to avoid grave-robbers and so the bodies would not contaminate the earth. Later on, circular stone walls were built and the dead were put on a stone platform. A small

Yazd. Picture of Zoroaster near Faravahar on wall in mortuary reception.

centralised pit contained sand, charcoal and phosphorus acted as a drain so as not to contaminate the earth.

We went to the wooden building which acted as mortuary reception. It stood at the foot of the hills whose peaks held the two Towers of Silence and looked like a small village hall in the English countryside. The body was laid on a table and washed and dressed in a sacred shirt before being tied with a girdle to a metal bier. On the wall

Yazd. Towers of Silence on hilltops.

was a picture of Zoroaster, the sun's rays streaming all round his head by the *Faravahar*, standing between two cauldrons of sacred fire, holding a bough, presumably of apricot or almond wood, to fuel the sacred flames. There was a white ceremonial hat lying on a window-sill, which I tried on.

We walked across the mortuary's enclosed compound. With a

key Farhad had acquired at the entrance we let ourselves out through a back gate and headed up a steep smooth path towards the right-hand, 19th-century (new) Tower of Silence. We passed old sand-coloured, domed, arched stone walls: a disused Zoroastrian

Yazd. Inside a Tower of Silence, pit in centre, priest's room behind small wall at back.

kitchen, well and water cistern for feeding those attending ceremonies. We passed a sand-coloured building with an arch in the centre, under which bodies were laid during a ceremony that preceded the journey up to the Tower of Silence.

Then we started the steep climb. No one else was about. The last bit was a scramble over uneven rock, but I was fit for my years and made it to

Yazd. Priest's room, entrance.

the top quite comfortably. The circular wall was head-high and made of stones. The outer part of the ring within the wall, which was open to the elements, had blocks of stone laid into the ground. The inner part was of sandstone. The square pit in the centre was two or three feet deep with small boulders at the bottom. There was a small mud-faced wall at one end of the circular wall, and behind it was a mud lean-to built against the circular wall with a low arch and a door. This was a tiny "house" with just room for a priest to shelter in during his vigil under the stars during the first night a body was laid here.

We left the circular wall and stood outside it. Yazd stretched away beneath us from left to right, with mountains in the distance under a blue sky with some white clouds. There were isolated domed mud-buildings in the desert before the town began. Farhad pointed out our hotel far in the distance, and that there had been a massive amount of new building since the 1970s.

During our descent from the lofty Tower of Silence Farhad talked about the British in 19th-century Persia. "Persia had been a staging post for India," he said. "Kerman was the gateway to India, and there were British bases in Persia, for example at Tehran, Shiraz and Kerman."

Back in the compound via the back gate, we encountered a stooping man by a donkey laden with a couple of bulging bags slung over its back. He had a reddish wound-round head-covering and a white sash in a cross over his shoulders and under his arms, tied at his back. His trousers bulged above his footwear as if fastened by cycle-clips.

I asked Farhad to find out if he was a Zoroastrian.

"Yes, he is," Farhad translated.

"How long has he lived in Yazd?"

"Thirty years."

"What does he do?"

"He says he's caretaker of the cemetery over there."

"Does he remember the Towers of Silence in use?"

The Zoroastrian spoke at some length. "Yes, the bodies were washed in that wooden building and then carried from there. There were two priests. They stayed up in the Tower just for a few minutes. They visited it every two weeks and when the bones had been picked clean by the vultures they put the bones in a rock hole at the top of the hill."

"Are there still vultures?"

"Yes, but farther away in the mountains, now. We don't see them so much now," Farhad interpreted.

"Where is Ahura Mazda?" I asked. "Is he localised in the sun or everywhere?"

"Everywhere," Farhad interpreted. "Ahura Mazda is like Allah, everywhere."

"How does he pray, with eyes open or closed?"

"Eyes open," Farhad translated. "He prays to the light with his eyes open. The light and the sun are symbols of Ahura Mazda, he looks on these symbols and prays to Ahura Mazda."

"And fire?"

"Fire is a symbol of purity and Ahura Mazda," Farhad translated. "We respect fire, we don't worship fire."

"Does he see Ahura Mazda behind closed eyes?"

"No, he always prays with his eyes open. Ahura Mazda cannot be seen."

"Is he aware of Ahriman and *Druja*, the Lie?"

The Zoroastrian spoke at length and very animatedly. "He prays, 'O Ahura Mazda, please protect us from *Druja* and injustice, and protect our family.' He is very cultured," Farhad added, "though he is a simple man. He quoted poetry, including Ferdowsi. He said the young don't care about religion, they see religion as being in the past. In fact, Darius I referred to *Druja* in an inscription. Darius says, 'I am not a friend to the man who is a lie-follower.'"

"And his donkey?"

"He rides it to the cemetery and back home. It is his transport. In the cemetery the headstones are all made of concrete, he says."

I smiled at the little Zoroastrian and he smiled back at me and nodded, and as Farhad slipped him a couple of notes with the Muslim Khomeini's head on them I felt like Wordsworth asking the leech-gatherer in 'Resolution and Independence', "How is it that you live, and what is it you do?" The self-sufficient leech-gatherer scratched a living by catching leeches in ponds on moors and selling them to doctors for a pittance and seemed part of the craggy mountainous scenery in which he worked. And similarly this hardy, self-sufficient man, who was equally resolute and independent, scratched a living by riding his donkey into the cemetery every day, proudly guarding the concrete headstones, making sure Zoroastrians were buried without the darkness of human flesh contaminating the earth and praying to the light with his eyes open. He too lived close to the elements and, with his knowledge of past journeys up to the Towers of Silence, he also seemed a part of the craggy mountainous scenery in which he lived, courting light and eschewing darkness.

We returned to the car. The driver made tea and served sweet-meats from the boot and we sat in the car, looking round us, and Farhad resumed the conversation we had been having during our descent. "The British have a bad reputation in Iran," he said. "They have a century of colonization behind them, things they did in the 19th century here. The Americans are newer, they have less of a bad record. In many ways Iranians prefer the Americans."

I said, "But Bush called Iran part of the Axis of Evil."

"We laughed when Bush said that," Farhad repeated from earlier that morning. "We are not like North Korea. We laughed because he is so stupid. Iran isn't like that, it doesn't want these people."

"Al-Qaeda?" I asked. "Al-Qaeda is supposed to be based in Iran."

"Here? Al-Qaeda is not active in Iran. I believe not, that's my view."

I reminded Farhad that I had wanted to go to Susa, and that I had been told it was not safe round Ahwaz as it was strongly Arab and al-Qaeda were there. I said that there had been reports that al-Qaeda had moved to Iran, and they wouldn't be active in their own backyard, would they? "It's where they were *not* active that you would expect them to be based."

Farhad frowned. "I believe not, that's my view," he said.

And so it came down to his belief in Iran's light as opposed to darkness. If they had wanted to achieve some publicity from the lone Westerner touring Iran, al-Qaeda could have followed me up to the Tower of Silence, killed me and left my body for the vultures. But no one had been following us. We had been completely alone in desert Iran – by the 4,500 year old cypress tree, by the 17th-century *caravanserai*, in the 11th-century Tomb of the Twelve *Imam*s and climbing to the Tower of Silence. The only people who could have been following me on behalf of the Iranian State, which was allegedly harbouring al-Qaeda following its defeat at Tora Bora in Afghanistan, or the Terror Alliance were Farhad himself and our driver – who denied that terrorism was present in Iran or that Iran was part of an Axis of Evil.

6

ISFAHAN'S SAFAVID BEAUTY

We began the drive to Isfahan skirting desert – the Dar Anjir Desert to our right and beyond it the Great Central Desert, Kavir-e Lut. As we went through the barren terrain Farhad talked about *caravanserai*s: "In the 17th century security increased and there was more demand for caravans to carry silk from China to Venice, for export to Europe. King Abbas gave orders that 999 *caravanserai*s should be built. He was asked, 'Why nine hundred and ninety-nine, why not a thousand?' He replied, 'Because nine hundred and ninety-nine sounds more than a thousand.' We are going to have lunch in one of his 999 *caravanserai*s. In Meybod."

Meybod was a sand-coloured desert town. We parked near low sun-baked brick walls and low domed houses, and opened the car boot. Now Farhad discovered he had left his briefcase in Yazd. "It's got my money in it," he said. We walked down a slope to the *caravanserai*, a one-storey brick building with arched unloading bays on the outside wall. We entered the square brick courtyard

Meynob. *Caravanserai* courtyard, loading/unloading island.

which was surrounded by more arched unloading bays. There was a head-high brick "island" in the middle with five planks of wood sticking out as ascending steps, where camels could be unloaded. We hung around while Farhad telephoned the hotel in Yazd and they rang him back to confirm that they had his briefcase. "It's all right," he said, "it's being sent by taxi, here."

Within one wall of the square there was an enclosed arched corridor which was the restaurant. Wooden tables were laid with tablecloths and china drinking vessels where the camels used to stand. On either side there were raised waist-high carpeted bays where the caravan people unloaded their camels and slept by their goods and valuables. Less valuable merchandise would have been outside.

"Look," Farhad said, "that pipe was for tethering the camel for the night. The camel spent the night where we are, or if this was full they were put out in the courtyard or in stables outside the *caravanserai*. These bays are where the caravan people told each other stories in the evenings, including tales from the *Arabian Nights* – tales from India and Arabia as well as Persia – such as 'Ali Baba' and 'Sindbad the Sailor'. See, each one has a hearth and there are holes in the ceiling above where we are sitting for the smoke to escape. The ceiling bricks have been scoured, they were smoke-blackened before they were cleaned. The caravan routes were vernacular conditions used for hundreds of years and can't be traced back to an origin." I thought again of Omar Khayyam's *caravanserai* which was "battered" during his lifetime in the late 11th or early 12th century. Presumably there had been caravans and *caravanserai*s in the Sasanian time, certainly in the early Arab period.

We ordered mushroom soup, kebab and desert yoghurt. Farhad said, "The yoghurt is strained to get rid of the juice, it is a speciality of desert towns." It tasted slightly sour and tingled on the

Meynob. Restaurant where camels were once tethered.

tongue, leaving a tang.

Music wafted across to us. Farhad said, "It's Sufi music, about birds and the souls of people compared." I thought of the traditional Persian common culture that was still available whereas secularization had withered the roots of our traditional common culture in the West. Another song was about picking flowers in the garden. "Our culture is multi-layered," Farhad said. "You can't separate the mystical from the physical. To a Persian listener there is a mystical meaning even though it's about picking flowers. It's like Hafez's poems, ambiguous."

Farhad mused and said, "All *caravanserais* are different. Some are rectangular and have four *iwans* – openings to a courtyard – like a mosque. Some are round. They're more rare. Some are covered *caravanserais*. In some you can sleep overlooking the courtyard, which is where the camels were tethered."

At the end of lunch Farhad's briefcase arrived by taxi. We drove to a local pottery, where there were garish designs, and waited while the driver bought some pottery for a friend. Then we set off past pistachio trees and a plantation of barley, and journeyed through an arid plain, an empty desert with no vegetation: the Siyah Kuh Desert.

*

We stopped at a checkpoint manned by revolutionary guards. Farhad said, "Our road has joined the road from Afghanistan, and trucks are being thoroughly searched." A guard in military uniform gave me a penetratingly suspicious look but let us through after speaking with the driver and Farhad, both of whom raised their voices, indicating I was a tourist and had not come from Afghanistan.

We passed occasional isolated ruined *caravanserai*s and at Nain, "a crossroads, the centre of the desert" (Farhad said), we stopped for petrol. I got out near a workman who was chipping away at the kerb with an axe. An Iranian swept by with two women in *chador*s trying to keep up.

"Two wives?" I asked Farhad.

"No, probably wife and her sister," he said. "Sometimes in the past you would see a man with two wives, but not now, not so frequently."

We passed the snowy Sarj mountains and approached Isfahan. The temperature fell to 2 degrees, and as it grew dark I steered the conversation to the leadership. I asked, "Why did the students burn Ahmadinejad's picture?"

Farhad said, "Because of his stupid policies. They want more contact with the West. They don't want to be isolationist. This isn't Stalin's time. We live in a global world now, with the internet. We don't want isolation. We want more Westerners coming. He's right about some things, about America, for example."

I asked, "Does the Supreme Leader want isolation?"

"I don't know if he's isolationist or being told to be."

I said, "Perhaps the Supreme Leader wants to purify laws?"

"The Supreme Leader is not that severe. He should be reformist like Khatami and have a dialogue with the West, not conservative and confrontational. There are some things that can't be said. The Iranian people don't want conservatism."

I said I had been welcomed everywhere by Iranians, who seemed to have a good attitude to the West. I said, "Your President Ahmadinejad is now in Latin America putting together an anti-American oil alliance of Ecuador, Venezuela and Nicaragua, and this visit may be interpreted as being confrontational. Why is Ahmadinejad anti-West, not like them?"

"He hasn't travelled enough," Farhad said.

*

Isfahan, the third biggest city in Iran after Tehran and Mashad, stands on the eastern edge of the Zagros mountains with desert on the other side. (In terms of Iranian pronunciation, it should perhaps be transcribed "Esfahan", but in that case "*Imam*" must be "*Emam*", which is not so immediately understood, and I have preferred to stick with "Isfahan".) It began as a small town, Gey, in a suburb (Yahadiyeh) of which the Jewish wife of the Sasanian Yazdegerd I settled a colony of Jews in the 4th century AD. It became a provincial capital after it was captured by the Arabs in 642. The Seljuq Turks, Oguz Turkmen from the Jand region of Central Asia, made it their capital from c.1050 to their fall c.1200. (The Tomb of the 12 *Imam*s in Yazd, 1038, had been right at the beginning of Toghril Beg's Seljuq rule for Toghril I proclaimed himself Sultan in Nishapur in 1038.)

The Turkic Safavids had headed a militant Sufi order founded by Sheikh Safi of Ardabil in north-west Iran. His descendant Ismail I conquered Tabriz and the rest of Iran, and in 1501 proclaimed himself Shah (the pre-Islamic title used by Iranian rulers), united the whole of Iran into an independent state and made Shiism the State religion. Then in 1578 the Safavid Shah Abbas I, the Great, made Isfahan his capital and rebuilt it into one of the largest and most beautiful cities of the 17th century. In the 17th century Armenians moved here to shelter from the Ottomans, and there are 13 Armenian churches. They are Gregorian Orthodox and venerate St Gregory's image. Their language is Indo-European and does not belong to any of the known branches of Indo-European languages. Isfahan was besieged by the Ghilzai Afghans, fell in 1722, and was in decline until its industrial growth in the 20th century. The 4th-century-AD Jewish settlement had flourished and had now become the second-largest Jewish community in Iran after Tehran: 4,000 Jews with three active synagogues.

"Isfahan has been made the cultural capital of Islamic countries," Farhad said. "It is a cultural town, it is like Edinburgh. There are festivals, religious people and artists. It has the best stucco and miniaturists. Shah Abbas I brought the best artists to Iran. It also has best textiles and fabrics, it is like Manchester, there are a lot of factories."

It began to snow about 5pm. We arrived in heavy snow that turned to slush as it settled and saw no sign of the Isfahan nuclear site, which is supposed to be in a suburb of Isfahan. We drove down tree-lined streets and booked in at the Abbasi Hotel, a regal building – indeed, it had been the last Shah's favourite hotel – with beautiful Persian decorations and paintings. Three of the four sides of the Hotel were in a two-storey 17th-century *caravanserai* that enclosed a large courtyard hung with lanterns that lit shrubs, trees and fountains through the falling snow.

*

I made a brief visit to my room, 324, and went straight out with Farhad into the whirling snow. He hailed a taxi, and we drove to a carpet shop for my wife had given me precise measurements and asked me to find a couple of short runners which, because of their atypical length, would be hard to find at carpet auctions in the UK. Where better to look than in Isfahan, the town most associated with Persian carpets?

Farhad had rung ahead with the measurements to save time, so we were expected. The carpet shop opened just for me. It was really a warehouse. There were Persian carpets on the walls and draped over furniture at the sides. The owner spoke English and was about forty. He showed us to chairs where we were served tea in glasses and we watched as a dozen runners of approximately my measurements were laid out on the Persian carpet on the floor. By a process of elimination I whittled them down to two and asked the price. I had a shock: over $8,000 around £4,500. As usual my eye had picked out the best-quality, and therefore most costly, carpets. Good taste is a very expensive boon.

I explained that in the UK I had picked up equivalent Persian carpets at auction for £100 each even though they had been valued at twenty times as much, and I said I would ring my wife about them and let him know tomorrow. I also said that if I were having them I would have to pay by card and that there was a problem as the US administration had called on banks, including my own, to refuse to honour all transactions to which Iran was party.

The fellow knew how to get round sanctions. "Don't worry, you can pay a small deposit in cash and send the rest to another account in Dubai. Or else you pay the whole amount to a foreign account, which I will nominate."

Farhad said in an undertone to me, "I will make a call to another carpet shop. We'll go there later."

We left the shop and put up our macproof hoods and walked through driving snow and slush to nearby *Imam* Square: long, dimly-lit rectangular gardens surrounded by Shah Abbas I's 17th-century buildings – two mosques with snow on their domes and a small royal palace with an open balcony from which Shah Abbas I and other Safavid monarchs watched polo in the square below. "We shall see all these buildings tomorrow morning," Farhad said. We walked the length of the square to peep into the bazaar through an open 17th-century door: a long arched tunnel with lights and stall-like shops that held wares. The bazaar seemed to be closing.

We returned to the square and went up a steep narrow staircase to a small teahouse's terrace that looked down on a dark *Imam* Square. We stood in the open air and Farhad said, "Look, the polo goals." And in the dark I saw two quite fat, waist-high bollards on the curve of a road used by taxis, farther apart from each other than football goalposts. "Polo is a Persian game," Farhad said. "It was played in Persia from the Sasanian time. Persians took it to India" – I assumed it went with the Zoroastrians who fled there from the 7th and 8th centuries onwards and settled as Parsees – "and from there it went to Britain."

We retraced our steps down to the square and took a taxi to another carpet shop. There were no seat-belts in the back of the taxi, and Farhad said, "Seat-belts in the back are optional in Iran." (I pointed out that Princess Diana would now be alive if she had fastened her seat-belt at the start of her last drive.) Again Farhad had rung ahead with the measurements, and again the shop opened specially for me. This one was even larger, with two rooms. Tea arrived in glasses as we thawed out in front of a powerful heater, and then we went through to the second room and I described the kind of pattern I was looking for.

The owner of the shop, a very forthright, definite man of about forty whose name was Mohammad, said, "The other shop had very expensive carpets. I can tell you, this carpet I am holding is the usual, conventional size. If you depart from that with a longer, narrower runner, it can be up to three times as expensive because of the rare size, even though the square metrage is the same. But now I know what you want, I am sure I can do it much cheaper. I have a warehouse with fifteen hundred carpets. I will check your measurements against each carpet – truly, I will search through fifteen hundred carpets tonight, and I will have those of the right size here for you tomorrow morning. I will not waste any more of your time now."

We walked back through the falling snow with our hoods up. We came down Chaharbagh Bala Avenue, "the Boulevard where everyone walks," Farhad said, "the Champs Elysées or Oxford Street of Isfahan".

We crossed the square by our hotel and dived down some steps where Farhad found a bookseller of Persian books still open. He bought three books, and then further along found a lit window of books. "Look, the *Shahnameh*, the Persian epic," he said. I went in and bought the book with some of my *rials*, and another two books at the same time.

We then climbed steps and crossed back towards the hotel. We encountered a large 18th-century building in a side street. "That's a very famous *madraseh*," Farhad said, "the Chahar Bagh. It has 300 students. Visitors are not allowed as they may interfere with the studies."

We returned to our hotel. My room was several doors away from Farhad down the carpeted corridor, in a lobby area where sat three uniformed staff. They were not doing anything so I put my head round the door and pointed out that I had no plug for my wash-basin. All three came in and tried the loose bath plug, which did not fit, and then left, unable to solve the problem. I shaved in running water as there was no plug.

I dined with Farhad in the luxurious dining-room on the ground floor. We both ate soup, yoghurt and fried shrimps. The driver did not join us, and Farhad brought in one of the books he had bought and with some formality presented it to me. "It's a book of Persian poems, one of the best I know," he said. The title was *A Study of Islamic Texts in English Translation (II)* by Dr Hossein Elahi Ghomshei. "It's in Persian and English." He inscribed it for me, "To my dear friend Nicholas Hagger..." Then he read a couple of poems, Sadi's 'Oneness of Mankind' and 'The Alchemy of Love'. He read beautifully with great feeling, and I realised that the traditional Persian sensitivity was still strong among all Persians, who knew their poems as a kind of common culture: the Zoroastrian guardian of the cemetery and this expert in Old Persian languages both knew the Persian poetic heritage as well as the historical and legendary stories in the *Shahnameh*, which I also had on the table.

I returned to the international crisis. I asked "Is your President helping by having gone to Latin America – Ecuador, Venezuela and Nicaragua – and putting together an agreement with all three countries to stop the flow of oil if Iran is attacked? America might regard this as confrontational. Diplomacy seeks to defuse. If a small boy in a school playground goes and hits a big boy and is then hit back, he only has himself to blame. I don't want to see innocent people hurt. You know Israel is set to bomb Iran?"

He mused on what I had said, reluctant to express an opinion.

Then a plane went over very noisily, and I said, "I hope that isn't Israel."

He said, "Israel wouldn't dare attack Iran. We're very strong."

I said, "Iran has gone up."

He said, "Yes."

And then I knew that the hawkish outlook of the leadership – reflected in this dove's sensitive and gentle voice – had pervaded

Iran's intelligentsia, who parroted it, and that Iran was too inflexible to make peace. I felt that war was now a certainty and felt sad that Iranians' eagerness to please and beautiful tradition would be crippled by an assault from the air. We had finished our meal and we stood up and went out into the lobby, and I felt a sense of impending doom gather above the reception desk and hang like a cloud of smoke above all the Iranians within view.

I went to my room and rang my wife and, aware that the US ban on banks trading with Iran was an issue in an international telephone call, told her indirectly how much I had been asked for two carpets. She said, "That's far too much. I got my last one for…." I said, "I know how much." We agreed not to go ahead with the first carpet vendor.

*

Next morning I walked down the nearest stairs to the breakfast area, which looked down on to the lobby. I sat with a view of the snow-covered grounds, the flat-roofed 17th-century *caravanserai* and distant domes. Snow had stopped falling, there was a cloudless blue sky with early sun and a glare from the white covering of snow in the garden.

Farhad came down as I finished breakfast, and I reported our decision on the first carpet shop. "The US does not want my bank to trade with Iran," I said.

He went very quiet. Then he said, "So many tourists have cancelled, I have no clients for at least two months after you, and it's the same with the other national guides."

I said, "Sanctions must have contributed to the cancellations." And, looking round me and sensing I was the only Westerner breakfasting at this hotel and touring in Isfahan, again I felt a sense of impending doom, that I was the last tourist to go round before the bombing began and that no other outcome was possible for peace had ceased to be an option due to the Iranians' mental outlook, which was one of studied denial.

We drove to near *Imam* Square, which looked magnificent, its flat-roofed walls with two-storeyed arches golden in the early morning sunshine. The snow had melted on the pavement but still whitened every flower-bed, adding to the heady effect of the gleaming square. We walked to the Shah mosque, or Abbasi Friday mosque, Majid-e *Imam*, which Shah Abbas I began in 1611/12 and which, despite his urgings as his years advanced, was still unfinished when he died in 1629. He had been 52 when work started and

Isfahan. Abassi Friday (or Shah) mosque from Imam Square.

he insisted that the work should be speeded up as he grew older. This led to the use of prefabricated patterned tiles rather than of the more time-consuming individual mosaic tiles.

We were the only visitors and gazed at the wonderful blue, white and yellow tiled entrance with stalactites in honeycomb and the open doors, two slabs of plane-tree covered with silver.

We went through a domed vestibule that entered the north *iwan* (or hall that opens to a courtyard) at 45 degrees, to take us from the end of *Imam* Square to being aligned towards Mecca. We came out in a courtyard that was screened off so we could not see the ablutions pool. Off this courtyard there were four *iwans*. We

Isfahan. South *iwan*, entrance with suns and stalactite architecture.

Isfahan. Main sanctuary, *mihrab* and central paving-stone.

Main sanctuary dome: golden rose.

walked to the south *iwan*. It had two minarets before the dome. I looked up and saw two suns under the dome: an inner sun suggesting the spiritual sun, the One; and an outer one suggesting the physical sun. We went into the main sanctuary and stood under a wonderful yellow, blue and green dome in which a central blue orb exploded out in a golden rose and rippled in concentric circles through the most intricate patterns in green and then in blue. Beneath the orb there was a central spot in the sanctuary floor. I stood on the central black paving-stone.

Farhad said, "Clap," and when I clapped my hands there was an echo. I could even hear a rustle. A *mullah* standing on this central spot could be heard throughout the mosque. Under the windows there was a text from the *Koran* in calligraphy. It recognised "the importance of praying", Farhad said, "and how the seven skies are". I asked, "Doesn't it say seven heavens rather than seven skies?" He said, "No, it says seven skies." The *mihrab* pointed towards Mecca.

From the main sanctuary I could see the two turquoise minarets. Farhad said, "They have calligraphy on them. One says Mohammad, the other says Ali. (Ali was the first Shiite *Imam*.) The tile designs made these two names over and over again. Some of the tiles are covered with gold and have lines of Persian poetry on them. The tiles on the wall have a floral design and suggest a garden. This sanctuary was recreating Paradise."

We came out through a side hall with two large bowls, one for drinking from and one to echo, Farhad said. We emerged into the deserted courtyard of one of the two *madrasehs*.

"Look," Farhad said, "this column is a sundial, it works on a slope above that step by your foot. The shadow of the sundial meets the stone at noon, prayer time, all the year round – slope, step and shadow converge at noon. When the shadow meets the stone, it's time for prayer. Nothing else mattered. The sundial only points to the time at noon, not to any other time."

Farhad continued, "Praying is one function of a mosque. It is also for business chat, news, study (in its *madrasehs*), debating." I thought again of the fervour I had seen in the Shiraz shrine. Although Islam was younger than Christianity, the Arab civilization was older than European civilization and both were older than the North American civilization. I thought that Islam was in a fervent phase that archaistically looked back to an earlier

Isfahan. The mosque's dome which has a message of peace round it.

fervent period, and that the West had yet to experience an equivalent archaistic recreation of its 16th- and 17th-century fervour.

We stood and looked at the beautiful dome from the outside. Farhad said, "Round its base there is calligraphy. It says, 'Peace be unto the Prophet and his household.'" And I saw how peaceful Islam was in its original idea, and how warlike al-Qaeda and Muslim confrontationalists had departed from the basic, peaceful message which was inscribed on the outside of the dome for all to see in *Imam* Square as all entered and left the bazaar or market.

"Which came first," I asked, looking at the elaborate pattern on the dome, "tiles or carpets?"

"It is not known," Farhad said. "From carpets to tiles? From tiles to carpets? Both are lost in antiquity. And look on that minaret and on those tiles. Angular Kufic or masonry Kufic, curved Persian becoming angular and saying 'Ali'. Ali was the first *Imam*, the father of Husayn, the third *Imam*."

I wandered back out, stunned at the sheer beauty of what I had seen and how it objectivized the inner harmony of the soul. Farhad said, "This is one of the top five mosques, along with Cairo, Damascus, Samarra and Cordoba." Here, for me, was the supreme perfection of Islamic civilization, which expressed the religion's

Isfahan. Entrance to Abassi Friday mosque showing deliberate imperfection - compare columns on either side of the open doors.

harmony and peace in exquisite and intricate patterns with a spiritual sun and a physical sun below it in the south *iwan*. Everyone should come here and know that the dome proclaims a message of peace as opposed to war.

Farhad stood outside the entrance with me and said intensely, "Look, there is a deliberate mistake in the columns on either side of the silver doors. One column is straight and the other has a motif in it. They deliberately made the mosque imperfect – to say that only God is perfect. And look," he said, "this mosque has its arms out – the two sides of the square – towards the bazaar, embracing

Isfahan. Sheikh Lotfollah mosque.

the people there and beckoning them in."

There was a bookstall nearby which had a couple of books I needed. I bought them and they were put in a bag. With typical Persian warmth Farhad insisted on carrying them for me.

*

We crossed the square, stepping on snow in places, to the Sheikh Lotfollah mosque or Ladies' mosque, the mosque used by Shah Abbas I for his private devotions but dedicated to his father-in-law, a famous theologian who supervised his mosque and theological school. It was built between 1602 and 1619. Its dome was pale gold with white and blue almond shapes which got smaller as they approached the dome's centre. There was no minaret.

We went up steep steps, whose steepness denoted respect, looked at the superb blue mosaic work – the best of the Safavid period – and plunged along an angled corridor which aligned us to Mecca. We came out in a wonderful sanctuary or prayer hall. The dome was like a gold net stretched between surrounding lattice windows. There was a central rose.

"Look," said Farhad, "in the centre of the rose is a peacock and beneath the peacock is light from one of the lattice windows. It's the peacock's tail. It's been designed so the peacock always has a tail of light. The tail moves with the sun, and where it is depends on where the sun is. The peacock's tail was a Safavid symbol and suggests the Peacock Throne." The concept of a peacock's tail like a hand on a clock took my breath away. I recalled Robert Byron's reaction: "I have never encountered splendour of this kind before."

We went to the *mihrab*, which faced Mecca. It was decorated with flowers. "There is no signature of the artist as miniaturist," Farhad said, "as he is worshipping God in this work. The inscription by the artist says, 'This is the work of a poor, humble, miserable man in need of God's grace. Master Mohammad Reza Ibn Husayn Isfahani, 1028AH.' 17th century." Then he commented on the mosaic styles nearby. "There's the mosaic faience style which is assembled like a jigsaw, and there's the seven-colour style, each colour requires a different temperature. The other Shah mosque had a seven-colour style. This one is faience from head height. Below that it's a garden. You see, leaves and trees, the same motif as the lattice windows and the door of the mosque. Each lattice window was one block of stone cut into tracery." There were no courtyard or *iwan*s and as we left I looked again at the peacock's tail on the dome ceiling, which had moved during our time in the mosque.

*

We went on to the royal palace, Ali Qapu palace, from which large

Isfahan. Royal Palace and viewing veranda, Imam Square

portraits of Khomeini and Khamenei stared disapprovingly down. It is a square Timurid building with a veranda in front of it (added by Shah Abbas I, then under scaffolding) and an arch behind built c. 1600, from which the Shah and his court viewed parades and celebrations. The staircase rises steeply, and it may or may not have been intended as a Safavid residence. We came across a fireplace. "That fireplace is shaped like the hat of a Safavid king," said Farhad.

We ascended level by level, dwelling on stucco, floor tiles, murals and mosaics, until we reached the throne room and we then went out onto the veranda, which had a beautiful wooden ceiling of roses and the view, through 18 columns, of the square Shah Abbas and the Safavid kings had when they watched polo below.

We looked across the rooftops and dome the other side of the square at the buildings of distant Isfahan. "That tower on the skyline was for a fire, to signal to caravans coming in from the desert," said Farhad. "Over there is the Jewish quarter. That is the Friday mosque, Jameh mosque." I saw a sandy, domed Seljuq building – "it is 11th-century, rebuilt in 1121 with its Nizam al-Mulk dome c.1087 (the grand vizier of the Seljuq Turks Nizam being a colleague of Omar Khayyam's), and added to in the 15th century," Farhad said – and I am now dismayed that although the mosque was on my itinerary we somehow did not visit it: judging from pictures, the *iwan*s and tilework are spectacular. "Here the king watched the life of the city," Farhad said, "his people going to the bazaar and to the mosque." They, in turn, would be able to look up and see him.

We left the royal palace. We passed a group of secondary-school children, who were not in uniform. I remarked on this. "Secondary pupils don't wear uniform in Iran," Farhad said, "primary do."

*

We stopped at a shop on the edge of the bazaar. There were minia-tures in the window. "Come in," said Farhad, and I found myself greeting a slight, moustached Iranian who was painting a miniature.

He spoke and Farhad interpreted: "He uses a peacock feather, the hair of a cat and a porcupine quill as a handle. That is the best brush for miniatures. He paints on camel bone – the lower part of the leg of a camel. It is left for three months in lime water, then two months in petrol to get the fat and gristle out. Then it's cut into segments. The older the camel, the bigger the camel bone. The maximum length is 7 cms. A cow bone can crack. Using ivory is forbidden. He's done, look, Omar Khayyam here, Schehezerade there. He uses lapis-lazuli powder, gum and turquoise stone. He uses walnut, pomegranate for red, saffron for yellow. Natural dyes don't fade. Chemical colours fade in light."

Farhad added, "He is the best known miniature artist in Iran. Look, he has done the design for these postage stamps, a lot of stamps. His father was a miniaturist and his brother is as famous as he is. Look at the paintings on these boxes. This one took two months. This one three months. It's a scene from the royal palace, Shah Abbas watching polo. Look at the detail of the costumes. Look at the Persian on the dome, you can read it with a magnifying glass. Would you like to buy?"

The miniaturist was charming and he gave me one of his porcupine quill brushes to give to my wife. He also gave me a quick sketch he had done of Omar Khayyam while Farhad interpreted. "I have him in my mind's eye, that is how I see him." He showed me miniatures of Hafez and Sadi, adding, "They did not look like that. It's how I see them." But it was another instance of Persians having a common culture of traditional material, all recognised and believed. The boxes were all well over $100 each, and he offered me framed pictures costing hundreds of dollars. The problem was to find a box that was not covered with a detailed scene that would mean nothing to an English recipient, for a mere $30 or $40 (the minimum price for his quality, hand-painted work). I made three purchases of small boxes with designs to show willing. It was only later that I realised that without being consulted I had sacrificed the Friday mosque to be sold boxes.

I insisted we left, and we went back to the second carpet shop. The carpet-seller, Mohammad, was in a Western shirt and trousers. He greeted me like an old friend, thrust glasses of tea in our hands, sat us down and said in English, "I have sorted through fifteen hundred carpets for the sizes and styles you want, and I've brought three to show you." And he and his assistants spread them on the floor and told me their measurements.

They were exactly what I was after. One was very good and I thought my wife would also be pleased with another. I asked how much, and was relieved that it was less than a quarter of what the previous carpet-seller had demanded. I bargained him down, watched in silence by three or four elderly, seated assistants. When we finally reached agreement there was spontaneous applause. I was able to pay him out of spare dollars.

He said he would put a leather hem on the underneath edges of the carpets free of charge, and send them to me in Tehran before my flight out. "Iran is not like Arab countries, Dubai only cares about gold. If this were Dubai, do the deal, then out. We Iranians are cultured and want to give quality, so I will do the hem for nothing. This boy will do it. Tip him 10 dollars."

However, Farhad said, "I think five is enough." So I tipped the boy five dollars. He seemed well pleased with it, and Mohammad seemed unaware of how "Dubai-like" his request for me to give the boy gold had been.

Mohammad said, "Come through," and he led me to a large wooden desk with carpets hanging on the surrounding walls.

I commented on a beautifully golden carved box on the desk, next to a globe.

"It came from the Shah's palace," he said. "I bought it at auction. It was on the Shah's desk."

He gave me three small pieces of carpet as a gift. He said, "This one is Baluchi, 30 years old, and these two are Baktiar."

Knowing that if all went according to plan I would soon be driving past one of Iran's nuclear sites, I took the opportunity to get him on to politics. I said, "I remember a cry, '*La, la,* Baktiar,' 'No, no, Baktiar,' the Prime Minister between the Shah and Khomeini."

He laughed and said, " '*Margbar* Baktiar,' 'Down with Baktiar.' That was the chant at the demonstrations."

"And now," I asked? "It's not 'Down with the present leadership'?"

Mohammad said, "I am for nuclear. Nine nuclear countries have it: the US, Russia, the United Kingdom, France and China; India, Pakistan, Israel and Brazil. Even Brazil has it and now a tenth country, North Korea. Why if Brazil can have it can't we have it?"

In fact the first five countries are considered to be "nuclear weapons states", an internationally recognised status confirmed by the Nuclear Non-Proliferation Treaty or NPT, while India, Pakistan, Israel and North Korea have conducted tests but are not formally recognised by international bodies as they have not signed the NPT. Brazil's military regime conducted a nuclear weapon research program in 1978, which was ended by an elected government in 1985. Brazil signed the NPT in 1998, denying that Brazil had developed nuclear weapons.

I said, "With nuclear power comes responsibility, to use it wisely, and your leader has said he wants to wipe Israel off the map. If he's going to have nuclear weapons, he must speak more responsibly than that."

Mohammad said, "I'm for Ahmadinejad. In his heart he is gentle but in his words angry. His heart is right but he must appear angry to Bush. Last night Bush was saying that Iran must leave Iraq – or Iran will be bombed. He wants our oil and gas."

I said, "But isolation will be bad for your business, you want Westerners to come here and buy from you."

"Of course I do," Mohammad said. "My last customer was a week ago, and I don't have any more in my diary but I don't say 'My business is suffering', I say 'I support Ahmadinejad, as nuclear is our right'. You are like Straw," Mohammad continued. (Jack Straw had made several visits to Tehran when British Foreign Secretary.) "Straw here, no problems. Beckett here, problems. Straw sorted everything out. Why did he stop coming here?"

I said, "He was moved from his position following a visit to England by Condoleezza Rice. She visited his constituency and was shocked by how many Muslims there were and reckoned he'd gone soft on Muslims. I think she told Bush, and Bush asked Blair to sack him."

"Ahmadinejad has to talk tough," Mohammad said, "but in his heart he will not attack Israel. But I am for nuclear."

I thanked him for the carpets and we left. Outside Farhad said, "I was very surprised at the way he spoke. So many businessmen want business and don't think like that. Yes, I am very surprised."

We drove to Shahrzad restaurant in Abbas Abad Avenue where plane-trees meet overhead. We passed blue taxis. ("Taxis are blue in Isfahan," Farhad said, "green in Shiraz and traditionally orange in Tehran, now yellow – jasmine.") Over lunch of kebabs again (in the interest of speed), soup and yoghurt, with the driver present, we again discussed the nuclear crisis.

I said I too was surprised that a merchant like Mohammad should be in favour of Iran's defiance and conservatism. I said that even reformists believe Iran was too strong to be attacked.

Farhad said, "I think our government will change its mind."

"What, back down?" I asked.

"Yes. It will change its mind."

I inwardly shook my head. The conservatives were defiant, the reformists thought the nuclear policies were "stupid" for being unnecessarily confrontational and isolationist (a view Farhad had

7

IN *HUSAYNIEH* AND NUCLEAR NATANZ

On the way out to Natanz we called at Hotel Ali Qapu as Farhad had left the bag of books he had insisted on carrying, in the minia-turist's shop, and had arranged over his mobile for them to be sent by taxi to the hotel nearest to our restaurant. We drove past the *madraseh*, which I could now see was under scaffolding, and I saw pictures of a long-haired young man who did not look unlike Ché Guevara on the back window of two taxis in front of us.

"Who's that?" I asked.

"That's Abbas," Farhad said, "the brother of Husayn, the third *Imam* and younger son of Ali, the first *Imam*: Abbas Abu'l Fazl. Husayn was the true successor of the Prophet according to Shiite belief, and so there is interest in his brother Abbas, who devoted his life to children and people who were thirsty. I told you the story of Husayn, what happened when Yazid became the Ummayad *caliph* in 680 AD. The people of Kufa, Iraq, invited Husayn to their town and said, 'We'll support you to be leader.' Yazid threatened people, saying 'If you follow Husayn I'll kill you all' and he used bribes. Yazid took troops to the desert of Kerbala where Husayn and 72 followers were alone. Yazid told people, 'You must not go to Kerbala.' His Ummayad pursuers poisoned the water-holes Husayn's 72 followers used, and Abbas went off to find drinking-water. He found some, filled a container and carried it in his left hand back to Husayn's 72 supporters. The Ummayads caught him and cut off his left hand. He carried the water in his right hand. They cut off his right hand, and then he carried it between his teeth until they shot him dead with arrows. On the 10th day of *Moharram* Husayn fell on the battlefield. His head was cut off. He was martyred and his blood watered the Tree of Life. I was brought

Natanz. Above, gate of Sufi *dervish* monastery (left); Seljuq funerary complex of Abd al-Samad and Mongol mosque (centre); and Buyid pavilion turned into another Mongol mosque (right). Below, Al-Samad's tomb with Nicholas Hagger.

up as an orthodox, not a devout, Shiite, and as a child I learned about bravery and freedom from the stories about Husayn's life and its not just Shiites who give for *Moharram*. My upstairs neighbour is a Jew and my downstairs neighbour is an Armenian. Both give offerings to *Imam* Husayn on the 10th of *Moharram*."

We drove past the low, thousand-peaked, snowy Karkas mountains – " '*Karkas*' means 'vulture'," Farhad said – along clear roads with frozen snow piled at the sides. There was still snow on the branches of the roadside trees. We headed for snowy mountains

Natanz. Pyramid dome above tomb, inside.

Natanz. Pyramid dome, outside.

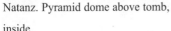

and soon we were surrounded by white peaks. We approached Natanz along a tree-lined road amid flurries of snow. Flags hung from lampposts, alternate blue and green. Farhad said, "Flags for *Moharram* are generally green and red. Perhaps these were left over from the Eid, the festival of the Breaking of the Fast at the end of Ramadan." We were now in a peaceful town in the foothills of the Karkas mountains.

We parked before a portal or gate of 1317 with glazed turquoise and cobalt adornment. It is all that remains of a Sufi *dervish* monastery, a *khanahqeh* to accommodate visiting Sufis. Beside it was the decorated funerary complex of the 11th-century Sufi mystic, Abd al-Samad al-Isfahani, which includes the Friday mosque. It stands under a blue octagonal "tent", a pyramid dome and a minaret, next to a domed building. We went through a door

Natanz. One of four *iwans* in former Buyid pavilion turned into Mongol mosque, an Afghan praying, snow on the central courtyard.

from the street and turned left through a silver door off a passage into the tomb and, ignoring the tombstone behind a wooden screen at first, focused on an 11th-century Seljuq cruciform building that had been updated and turned into a mosque by Mongols in 1307.

141

Natanz. View of minaret from courtyard

Brick calligraphy under the octagonal dome said in angular calligraphy (Farhad translated), "In the name of God, the most merciful,
the most beneficent, Mohammad is the Prophet of God and Ali is
God's successor."

Farhad said, "Look at the 14th-century Mongol-style raised

tesserae on the wall here, combined with the brickwork and crosses." Between four crosses was a tile of a white dove on an octagonal gold star with a decorated blue background. Farhad continued, "The lattice under the dome is more geometric, less floral than in Isfahan. Look at the flowers on the tiles, floral Kufic." The dome was in stalactite style and resembled the centre of a chrysanthemum, radiating outward with angular, not curved, lines, or like a sun with rays spreading outwards, disguising its pyramidal external shape. Farhad said, "The *mihrab* has been destroyed."

The 1307 box tomb was surrounded by colourful yellow, green and blue tiles from the 19th century. (As in the case of Hafez and Sadi, tombs of Sufis were built long after the Sufis' death.) Abd al-Samad had come from Isfahan to Natanz in the 11th century, before the Crusades, and had become a Sufi teacher. Translating 14th-century calligraphy, Farhad read out: " 'This is the tomb of a great man, light of the nation and the world, Abd al-Samad.'" Here with this pre-Crusade Sufi could be found the true peace Islam upholds, peace as palpable as the tiled dove.

We left the tomb and in the passage went to a building at the back of the complex, an octagonal Buyid pavilion turned into a four-*iwan* mosque that had been built between 1304 and 1309. There were two storeys of arches between each *iwan* round a courtyard heaped with snow and steps to an ablutions area level with the water-table below, which was replenished from the mountains.

In the *iwan*s opposite us a little old man in a woollen hat was praying in the snow. He was kneeling on a carpet. He stood and then knelt and bowed his head to the earth.

"He is Afghan," said Farhad. "I can tell."

We turned and entered the *iwan* opposite. Farhad said, "The *mihrab* was stolen from that wall. It's now in the Victoria and

Albert museum. The calligraphy here is 14th-century. The calligraphy there says 'Ali'." The dome ceiling was as bare as the outside of the dome the other side looked, Seljuq-style.

*

We left the mosque. I moved away to view the complex as a whole. Behind was a lane that ended in a door, and suddenly Farhad was calling me from inside the door. "Come in, this is a mourning house, a *Husaynieh*, a place where the mourning ceremony is held for Husayn." And I thought of the annual mourning ceremonies for Tammuz and Adonis in the Mesopotamian and Syrian civilizations, and grasped that the Arabs had taken over these ancient ceremonies that pre-dated 2000 BC and grafted on their mourning for Husayn on 10 *Moharram*.

Natanz. Civil servant (right), teacher (left).

Through the door I encountered what looked like a *caravanserai* under a large tent that was sporadically decorated with pairs of red lions. Two storeys of arched bays above a waist-high wall surrounded a dusty-sandy courtyard, in the centre of which there was a raised platform. On this stood five tent-poles. They supported the tent which rose to a height and whose edges were fastened to the top of the arches. There was a stage at the near end, and at the far end an open fire blazed on a grate on the dust, near which stood, sat or wandered up to a dozen men and children, keeping warm on a day when frozen snow was piled up outside. On strange ribbed wooden chests with oval ends behind me, parked on the stage, hung pictures of Husayn and Abbas.

"Here are the committee of those organising *Moharram*," Farhad said.

These were the men of Natanz who would be affected if the nearby nuclear site were bombed.

"On the 9th and 10th days of *Moharram* they put on mystery plays which retell the story of the martyrdom of Husayn. The 9th day is known as *Tasua* ('the day preceding the martyrdom') and the 10th day is known as *Ashura* ('the day of the martyrdom'). On the 9th day they put on a *taziyeh*, a popular religious passion play, on the eve of Husayn's death and they carry his coffin, there, a *nakhia*, with ends like giant palm leaves. It is draped in a black cloth and carried by 72 young men – the 72 followers." He pointed at the chests. "They have his picture, or Abbas's, on them. On the 10th day the mystery play is *Ashura*. The young men beat their hands on their breasts or on their backs, and the public who come to watch weep. There are processions which begin here, and in costume will be Husayn, *Caliph* Yazid, Abbas, Shem (the soldier who attacked Husayn); and the two who survived the massacre: Zeynals (Husayn's sister) and Ali (his son)."

The local dignitaries had come to meet me, all wearing Western jackets and trousers and shirts without ties. The arrival of a Westerner was clearly a big event in their lives and did not happen very often. I smiled at them and tried to radiate goodwill, and convey how impressed I was by what I saw. A little old man who wore a green woollen hat, a beard and spectacles – a civil servant, Farhad said – was the elder's spokesman, ably abetted by a grinning tall man who, Farhad told me, was a teacher.

Farhad translated what the civil servant was saying: "If you are staying in Natanz, you are welcome to have dinner with us."

It was as though I had passed them in the desert, and they had invited me to share their desert meal. I thanked them and smilingly declined, saying we had to be on the road soon.

But they insisted on making me welcome. "They say you can take any photos you want."

And I obliged, taking the two of them on the *Moharram* platform, and clicking a third elder who seemed reluctant to acknowledge Westerners and was clearly a figure to be reckoned with and humoured.

The two men, along with others who had come over, proudly showed me half a dozen ribbed coffins that were standing on the stage or in one of the bays ready for *Ashura*, and I felt the warmth of their contact and their spontaneously generous invitation, their humanity, and was almost moved to tears at the thought of the air attack on the nearby nuclear site with tactical nuclear weapons that was being prepared and might be only weeks away, and which might contaminate them all with a radioactive cloud. What would next year's *Ashura* be like as a whole community who mourned for Husayn shed tears while suffering from radiation sickness, Natanz then being as well-known as Hiroshima?

I dragged myself away from these good people of Natanz and took my terrible feeling that they were all awaiting an awful fate back out with me, a reluctant Tiresias who had glimpsed an imminent horror hanging over their future of which they, smiling, beaming, seemed unaware. I went back to the lane, at the end of which rose the tented eight-sided dome like a sharpened pencil and the minaret above it, and we returned to our car and set off for Kashan.

*

We had not gone far when we stopped. Farhad leaned across the driver and spoke to a very old man in a green woollen hat who was walking on a central reservation that included an open flower-bed under snow. He was carrying a shopping-bag.

28 FURTHER VIEWS OF IRAN

26

27

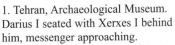

28

1. Tehran, Archaeological Museum. Darius I seated with Xerxes I behind him, messenger approaching.
2/3. Persepolis. Carvings of delegates from 23 nations including chariots, realistic horses and rams.
4. Yazd. Sacred fire behind glass.
5. Shiraz. Hafez's tomb and oranges.
6. Yazd. Zoroastrian cemetery caretaker with his donkey.
7. Natanz, *Husaynieh*, open courtyard under large tent, open fire for warmth.
8. Natanz, *Husaynieh*. The third elder.
9. Natanz, *Husaynieh*. Picture of Husayn on a *nakhia* (coffin with ends like palm leaves).
10. Isfahan. Dome with central peacock and peacock's tail of light.
11. Natanz, uranium enrichment site.Mountain behind site (taken after passing complex).
12. Hamadan. The site of Ecbatana, under snow.
13. Tehran, Jamaran. Khomeini's living-room behind glass, connected by walkway to *Husaynieh*.
14. Jamkaran, near Qom. A lady in a *chador* posts a message to the Hidden Imam through the bars above the well.
15. Jamkaran, near Qom. Nicholas Hagger by the well, site of the Hidden Imam's imminent Second Coming with Jesus.
16. Jamkaran, near Qom. Close-up of the cover above the well.
17. Qom. Khomeini and Khamenei with the name Allah as Light between them.
18. Qom. Khomeini's house.

19. Tehran. The upstairs sitting-room where the Shah is thought to have received Kermit Roosevelt of the CIA at midnight in 1953, sitting on the French settee in the centre.
20. Tehran, Jamaran. The street that leads to Khomeini's house.
21. Tehran, Jamaran.The slope with runnel beyond checkpoint.
22. Tehran, Jamaran. Entrance to Khomeini's house at top of slope.
23. Tehran, Jamaran. The other end of the walkway, the door into the *Husaynieh*.
24. Tehran, Jamaran. Inside the *Husaynieh*. Khomeini entered the door on the raised platform from the walkway and walked to his chair and microphone.
25. Tehran, Jamaran. Khomeini's living-room with his white-covered settee, slippers, ten books and furled umbrella – his sole possessions.
26. Near Arak. Martyrs from the Iran/Iraq war of 1980-88, on the side of a house.
27. Hamadan. *Ganjnameh*, rock carvings of Darius I and Xerxes I.
28 Natanz, uranium enrichment site. Machine-guns on two mounds trained on cars.

Farhad spoke to him in Parsee, and as the old man was bent double by my rear window I had a close view of his face. Tears came into his creased eyes as he nodded and then looked up to heaven and expressed his gratitude to the Almighty. Farhad got out and opened the boot and handed over a plastic container. The man thanked him profusely and again looked to Heaven. We drove on.

"What was that about?" I asked.

Farhad said, "The driver and I agreed in the restaurant that we would take whatever food we could not eat with us, in a plastic box, and give it to a poor person we found who needed food. I said to him, 'Hello, Haj' – that's a mark of respect, treating him as if he had just returned from Mecca – 'old man, we've had lunch and had some food left over. Would you like it?' He blessed us. He said, 'This is Allah's doing. Thanks to you and thanks to Allah. Whatever your wishes, I hope you reach them.' He behaved as if he was poor, he was moved to tears. The *Koran* says, 'Clutch the poor to your breast and help them.'"

I said, "What a lovely thing to do. It's like what we British used to do in the Georgian and Victorian times. Then tramps could come to your door and be given food. Wordsworth wrote about wanderers who did that. Nowadays in Britain everyone is provided for by the Welfare State, everyone is entitled to some benefit, and he would be entitled to a pension of around £300 a month which would mean that if he was hungry he could buy his own food."

News of such a large hand-out impressed Farhad, who told the driver, and I could tell from the driver's reaction that it was above the average wage in Iran. Later I pondered this Muslim act of charity towards a man they had perceived as poor, and I was haunted by it.

Farhad said, "We are leaving Natanz on the old road. I prefer these old roads." I was pleased, for I knew the old road to Kashan went straight past the Natanz nuclear site whereas the motorway skirted it a considerable distance away. I knew that the nuclear site was 17 miles north-west of Natanz. Our car's speedometer clocked kilometres as we progressed. I did a rough calculation: $17 \times 8 \div 5$ (1 km being five-eighths of a mile). I worked out we had just over 27 kms to go and watched the clocking band on the speedometer over the driver's shoulder.

We drove through snow-covered mountains and then a plain with mountains on either side. I took photos of the scenery. Then we reached the one-kilometre-to-go mark and came over the brow of a slight hill and I could see the site beside the road on the left. It was in a snow-free plain with snowy Alp-like mountains, clouds beneath their peaks, beyond it. The snow-free plain continued to the right of the road. I clicked on my camera.

Farhad said, "We're approaching the nuclear site now and you can't take pictures. Restricted zone."

"Can I take one picture?" I asked.

"Well, quickly take one picture."

"Where?"

"There."

I had just taken a picture without a flash and clicked again as we approached. This time there was an enormous flash throughout the car.

"It's very dangerous," Farhad said, turning anxiously. "They are watching cars and have machine-guns. Look, there are machine-guns trained on us on the right now. Sometimes someone has taken a photo and they pursue the car. They can pursue us and take us to court even in Tehran. Put the camera away."

As I hid my camera under my shoulder-bag the nuclear site was on top of us. I tried to take everything in. I could see the machine-guns 50 to 100 yards away on the hump of a hill on the right, and then we were passing a green earthwork wall round the enclosed – fenced – nuclear site 30 yards to our left. We went under the long barrel of a green anti-aircraft gun, and then another.

The site was huge, it seemed to be a couple kilometres long, and we must have passed under at least 10 anti-aircraft guns trained above us at the sky. Behind these were concrete roads, mounds and sheds and I could see a barrier to stop cars, guards and a lorry moving. I could see tiny people moving in different parts of the site when the grassed earthwork that linked the guns dropped, permitting a glimpse. There were in fact about two dozen anti-aircraft guns on a security perimeter of 4.7 miles, which meant that the square site had sides of just under 1.2 miles or just under 2 kilometres. Then we were past the site.

It was incredibly near the road. There was an obvious practical reason for this: it was convenient for haulage, lorries could just turn in with what they were carrying. On the other hand, it was very hard to keep it secret, with the road so near. Of course, if Iran was only developing nuclear energy here and was not developing a nuclear weapon, as the leadership claimed, then there was no need to hide it away. In which case, why the machine-guns and pursuing cars? Why the heavy security? I had found the site on the internet back in England. Aerial photographs showed that the above-ground signature did not match the earlier foundation work. There were photographs of the underground buildings being constructed in 2002, and more of the tunnel entrance concealed within a larger rectangular building in 2004. Why did the above-ground buildings now not relate to the underground buildings? Was it to deceive?

Here at this uranium enrichment plant, which was expected to be able to produce enough enriched uranium for 15 to 20 nuclear weapons each year, President Ahmadinejad had announced, 3,000 centrifuges were being installed underground in defiance of the UN and there was to be a drive for uranium enrichment. Three hundred had already been installed. The underground chambers were reputedly very deep – more than 18 metres under concrete –

and could withstand conventional bombs. Only tactical nuclear weapons could destroy their subterranean strongholds.

According to reports, Russia had dispatched crucial ores which would take another two or three months to arrive. Blowing up the underground bunkers would be more dangerous once these ores had been installed so action could be expected before the end of April. The US was furious with Russia for helping Iran to nuclear-powerdom. President Putin of Russia had rather disingenuously said that he failed to understand why Iran had not answered all the International Atomic Energy Authority's questions about its nuclear programme.

I imagined the Israeli planes – or would they be US planes? – screaming over the snowy mountains and strafing the anti-aircraft guns, and more planes coming in behind, perhaps high up, and lasering in tactical nuclear bunker-busters to explode underground. The tiny figures I had seen might soon be dead, and this site might

be the first place since Hiroshima to have nuclear weapons dropped on it (albeit, tactical ones). There could be nuclear fall-out from the attack, a wide area round it might be uninhabitable. The elders in the *Husaynieh* might have to abandon their homes. Natanz could become a ghost town like Chernobyl.

I knew that it was my role as a writer to reflect the Age. I had written about Hiroshima and Auschwitz in a verse play and an epic poem, and had visited

Kashan. Merchant's house, one of five courtyards.

both. I gave a lecture to 300 girls at Hiroshima and afterwards walked round the mangled dome in the Peace Garden. Now I was reflecting where the next nuclear strike could be. I supposed I had taken a risk: the Israelis could have attacked that afternoon. But I had calculated that the 21,500 troops Bush Jr had sent to Iraq were to hold down Iraq's Shias while Israel wiped out the nuclear sites, and I had reasoned that there would be no attack until the new troops were in place. To attack earlier than that would be to make a mockery of the new plan.

I thought back to the elders of Natanz, who were reliving the past, preparing their passion plays for *Moharram*, dwelling on the martyrdom of Husayn. And here, 17 miles north-west of them, was a nuclear site like a military base, ringed with long-barrelled anti-aircraft guns, and machine-guns were trained on passing cars. And somehow, the juxtaposition of the 7th century and the 21st century summed up the contradictions in the Arab world and in Iran: the blend of archaism and futurism, looking back to a time long past while looking ahead and seeking to become a nuclear power. Husayn and nuclear Natanz had taken me deep into the Iranian soul.

8

WITH THE QAJARS IN DESERT KASHAN

Soon, from our car, I saw the whole of Kashan spread out as an oasis on flat desert, the Dasht-e Kavir. Now I could understand why it was known for its poisonous scorpions. The story ran that the Arabs, finding Kashan's walls unassailable in the 7th century, collected thousands of scorpions from the desert and lobbed them over the walls – and in dismay and terror the inhabitants immediately opened their gates and surrendered.

Kashan has been occupied for 6,000 years, and it was 4,000 years old when according to local tradition the Three Wise Men – Zoroastrian *Magi* – set out from it with gold, frankincense and myrrh for their "adoration" of the baby Jesus. (Another tradition states that they were the kings of Persia, Arabia and India, and that only Melchior of Persia set out from there. Another view is that the Three Kings left Saveh.) Nothing remains from that time. Known in Seljuq times for its ceramics – the Persian *kashi* meaning "glazed tiles" comes from the name Kashan – it was popular with the Safavid Shah Abbas I, who created a garden there. Most of the traditional houses are from the 19th century, and belong to the time of the Turkmen Qajars, which began in 1796 with Agha Mohammad Khan.

We drove under a mourning arch decked with a large picture of Husayn by red and green flags, and headed for Tabatabei House, Khan-e Tabatabei, which was built in 1834 by a rich carpet merchant. It was like a small palace. It was on many levels and had five courtyards, which were revealed one by one, each one a surprise. From the entrance corridor we passed through an octagonal vestibule with gates to the servants' quarters and the garden. There was a latticed dome shaped like the sun. There were stables for camels and an open courtyard, a flight of steps to a basement and another courtyard. We went up two or three floors with two-foot-thick walls to keep out heat, and saw another courtyard surrounded by high walls with trees for shade. The living- and sitting-room had two doors, while the rooms for guests had an incredible five doors with arched windows over each. We looked down on another courtyard.

In one room there was a well 50 metres deep and water was pulled up by a water-wheel and emptied into an indoor pool that held a week's supply. There was an afternoon sitting-area and place of rest that looked out on a cool, paradisal garden: a courtyard with arches at each end with reliefs and stucco work carved on stone, and a rectangular fish-pond and plants so if it was 40C outside it would be 20C here. There was cool storage in the cellar, and an open-air courtyard round a fountain.

This pressing need to keep cool.... My mind went back to baking June days in Baghdad with a whirring fan, and sleeping on the flat roof on truckle-beds to catch cool breezes from the desert. I was bitten by desert sandflies and had sandfly fever with a temperature of 106. And I thought of Ghadames in the Sahara desert, where Arabs still wear Roman-style togas and live underground in sandy tunnels to escape the fierce heat above. Desert living is harsh, and desert people have been endlessly enterprising in devising ways to stay cool.

We drove to Hotel Amir Kabir (which was named after the 19th-century Qajar Chief Minister, who came from Kashan). It was on the outskirts of Kashan. My room was pretty basic. The paint was peeling in places and in need of filler round the door. There was no plug in the wash-basin as at Isfahan, and the primitive electrical heater blew out heat that made the lights flicker once a minute.

I unpacked and changed my clothes and went down to meet

Farhad in the small café-like dining-room at 7. The only people there were eight students sitting by the window. I sat down to wait for Farhad, and was aware that they were staring at me and making remarks about me, and that they were not smiling. In fact, they looked very menacing – and fanatical, as if they were al-Qaeda. The men had beards, the women headscarves, and there was one big man with a Taliban-style beard, and I thought: Taliban, allies of al-Qaeda. I felt uneasy – it was the only time so far in Iran that I had felt very uneasy. I wondered what I would do if they came over to harm me or kidnap me. They would be between me and the door because there was a long table in the way, and the windows did not look as if they had opened for years.

Then Farhad arrived and I asked him, "Who are they?" He looked at them and said, "They're from Afghanistan. They may be students in Kashan, perhaps at the *madraseh,* the theological school. "And now I was convinced that they *were* Taliban. They were still talking and looking menacingly in my direction and I again felt very uneasy. Suddenly they all stood up and I thought, 'Here we go, get ready to vault the table and run for the door.' With one final long look of disapproval in my direction they swaggered out of the door and I felt relieved. Farhad did not appear to have noticed their aggressiveness. I reflected that I had put myself in this position in the interests of my literary research, and told myself that it was beyond the call and bounds of literary duty to be cornered as an obvious Westerner by a group of Taliban recently out of Afghanistan.

Over dinner (the usual kebabs, the only practical choice) Farhad asked me about immigration in England and how the EU have allowed Romanians and Bulgarians to enter England. I answered circumspectly but said that the expansion of the EU's power over its nation-state members seemed to come from those running the world government. He did not understand, and I did not explain, aware that he might be an enemy within a matter of weeks. But I reflected that the New World Order was creating an American Union that would be supreme over the US, Canada and Mexico; an EU that with a new constitution (to be named a treaty) would be supreme over its 27 member states; and a Pacific Union. And that it would brook no opposition – it hadn't from Saddam Hussein and it wouldn't from Ahmadinejad – and that it wanted regime change in Iran so that a pipeline could carry its oil from the Caspian to the Gulf without political interference.

I wondered if Ahmadinejad knew what he was up against. I suspected he had underestimated the network of powerful families

Kashan. Intersection of *qanats* or water channels.

and corporations behind the New World Order known as the Syndicate, as had Saddam Hussein – as he had learned to his cost. They were immensely powerful. One faction was behind Bush but another faction was behind the Russian leader, who had helped Tehran and had perhaps co-created this international crisis with Iran. I wondered if, through Putin, who may have been unwitting, they had egged Ahmadinejad on, playing on his nuclear ambition, so that they could achieve their ends of owning Iran through a puppet, of being able to transport Caspian oil across Iran and of pillaging Iran's oil. I thought Ahmadinejad probably saw the conflict in terms of "Iran versus America." In fact, one faction of the Syndicate supported Iran and another faction supported America and planned to Westernize Iran.

Kashan. Safavid pavilion.

And, looking at how the EU's new constitution would attempt to shut down 1,000 years of Britain's nationhood, dismember England into eight regions and the rest of the UK and London into four more regions, I thought that Britain and Iran may actually be on the same side without realising it, just as Celtic

Kashan. Qajar pavilion.

Kashan. Qajar viewing arch.

Britain and Judea were both on the same side in the 1st century AD
when they were being absorbed into the Roman Empire. Both
Britain and Iran were in different ways under the world-

government cosh. I thought this but I could not say it as the West was already technically at war with Iran, whom it accused of arming the Shia militias in Iraq.

After dinner I went up to my room and tried to ring my wife. In this hotel I could not dial out from my room. I had to give reception the number I wanted to ring and then wait by my phone to be rung. After ten minutes the call came. The receptionist was jabbering in Persian, so I went downstairs. "Wrong number," she said, "I got wrong number." So I said I would take the call in her office and I waited while she put the call through from the counter. I made my nightly reassuring call to confirm that I had arrived where the itinerary stated and that all was well while the hotel's scanty administrative staff – of two – came in and out of the office while I talked.

I went back into my room. A bath was out of the question as there was no plug and it looked unhygienic so I put the television on to see the headlines on Sky and caught Condoleezza Rice giving a live press conference. She said, "Now's not the time to engage with Iran. Iran is in breach of a Security Council resolution. Iran has a list of questions to answer, it knows what it's got to do. Iran has not come to talk, and so must face isolation. It would be wrong to talk to Iran until it's answered the questions it's been asked." And I detected coercive diplomacy, certainly, but also early signalling (perhaps to Israel) that the US intended to strike at Iran.

*

The next day I woke with a view of low mud-walled flat-roofed houses towards mountains. I was down early. Breakfast was not ready but eventually a boiled egg arrived and I had it with coffee, orange, bread, honey and butter: the only choices.

We left the hotel at 7.55 and were in the Fin Gardens by 8. On a gate resembling the entrance to a mosque were portraits of the inseparable duo, Khomeini and Khamenei. These were the gardens designed by Shah Abbas I. Farhad said, "The Safavid buildings have partly been replaced by 19th-century Qajar ones but the trees and artesian water channels are where they were in the Safavid time 400 years ago. But it's a Qajar garden we are going to see."

We walked to a water channel in an avenue of cypresses, with an open pavilion straddling it at the end: Shah Abbas I's pavilion with a viewing area over an arch with blue decoration as in the royal palace at Isfahan. Farhad said, "Pavilions must be surrounded by water to create the idea of an earthly Paradise. In Paradise, the *Koran* tells us, there are streams of milk and honey, beautiful birds and *houri*s. Water makes a place cool, it comes from a mountain spring. See, there is water in the middle of the pavilion." There were two rectangular pools either side of the pavilion and a smaller one under the arch. The Safavid king used the building *en route* to north Iran.

We went on to a 19th-century pavilion built by the second Qajar king Fath Ali Shah. Farhad said, "There is poetry round the walls, gilded calligraphy and, look, birds and flowers. The style is more realistic because it is 19th-century, Qajar." There were magnificent suns on two pavilion ceilings. "In March and April they produce rose-water here, there is a festival. The water channels intercept and form a cross down there and irrigate fruit-trees. There are figs, pomegranates and mulberries."

We walked, passing tall cypress trees and stepping over a narrow water-runnel, to the bathhouse, which was to the far side of the site. "There was a Qajar Shah who ruled for nearly 50 years, Nasereddin Shah," said Farhad as we went through tiled rooms in the bathhouse. "At the beginning of his reign, from 1848 to 1851, his Chief Minister or Prime Minister was Amir Kabir, after whom our hotel was named. Iran was nearly bankrupt, having paid a huge war indemnity to Russia in 1828, and Amir Kabir cut the pay of the civil servants and collected tax directly, not through the court. He constructed factories, canals and bazaars and he increased customs duties to stop imports and encourage home-produced goods. He made enemies and the Shah's mother and sister were against him and plotted to get rid of him. They poisoned his reputation in the king's mind. He was exiled to Kashan. His enemies persuaded the Shah to sign his death-warrant. He was told the Shah planned to restore him, and to prepare for the ceremony. He came to the palace to bath, and here," he said, dramatically taking me into a green-tiled, vaulted room where there was a reconstruction using four waxworks, "they killed him. See, they cut his wrist. The three men were sent to do it, one wearing brown and two in red, and the kneeling man cut his wrist while he knelt, getting ready for the ceremony."

We came away. Farhad explained that in the Qajar time they had heated water by burning bushes as fuel. We came out of the gate. Farhad ran off to a nearby stall and emerged with a bottle of rose-water. "For you, as a present," he said. "This came from the festival here. It's like the rose-water in Shiraz."

We left Kashan past the last hills of the Kalkas mountains. I had seen a couple of examples of desert living under the Turkmen Qajars, two attempts to create Paradisal gardens and bring cool to desert heat in courtyards and pavilions, and I was aware of the continuity from the Turkic Safavids, whose pavilion they had taken over and adapted. Kashan had deepened my understanding of desert living in the Qajar time.

9

THE HOLY *IMAMS* OF QOM

On the road to Qom I probed Iranian democracy. Farhad said, "The Supreme Leader is nominated and appointed by the Council of Experts (or Advisers). There are 86 experts drawn from across Iran. They are elected. The Supreme Leader is not elected but appointed. He sets the spiritual course of the country but not its detail. But he is a politician. The President is elected. At the last election there were six Presidential candidates, I believe, with their followers. They do not belong to parties, they stand for themselves. Ahmadinejad selected his cabinet, 95 per cent were anti-reformist conservatives."

So was Iran democratic? To the extent that the people could choose the Council of Experts (or Advisers) and the candidates for the Presidency, yes, up to a point; but not to the extent that they could secularize the theocracy by choosing an alternative to the Supreme Leader. Iran was troubled by the secular government in Iraq, for if the 15 million Shias in Iraq could be happy with a secular government, why should not the 50 million Shias in Iran be equally happy with one – dethroning the theocracy enthroned by Ayatollah Khomeini? The true end or termination of the Revolution would involve the expulsion of the *Ayatollah*s from power.

At the core of Shia thinking was the Hidden or 12th *Imam*, who went into occultation (or hiding) in 874 AD, some said in Samarra, Iraq (where there is a cave below the mosque blocked by a gate which Shiites call Bab al-Ghayba, the "Gate of Occultation"), some believed down the Jamkaran well near Qom, Iran. The Hidden *Imam* had last been seen near the Samarra mosque in Iraq, but Iranians believed that he descended down the well at Qom.

Most Shiites believe that he was now hiding at the bottom of the Jamkaran well and that his return was believed to be imminent as there was universal chaos round Iran.

After winning power Khomeini took the title *Naebe Imam,* deputy to the (12th) *Imam,* and he had been asked by a parliamentary deputy if he was the "promised *Mahdi*" – just as Cromwell was asked if he was the promised Messiah – and he had not answered. He had been asked again and had again not answered, thus neither confirming nor denying that he was the 12th *Imam.* As Iran's Supreme Leader, Khomeini had not attended *Ashura* performances on the 10th day of *Moharram* or visited the shrine of the 8th *Imam* in Mashad, as his spiritual life was above such things.

Classical Shiism believes that all governments formed in the absence of the Hidden *Imam* are "oppressive and illegitimate". Khomeinism contradicted this by asserting that a *mullah* must rule on behalf of God, thus circumventing (while paying lip-service to) the Hidden *Imam.* Khomeini saw himself as continuing the rule of God on earth. Although outwardly supportive of the Hidden *Imam,* Khomeini took his authority from Allah (just as Darius I took his authority from Ahura Mazda). The cult of the Hidden *Imam* was therefore opposed to Khomeinism. Classical Shiism believes that there should be a separation between religion and government that is formed in the absence of the Hidden *Imam,* and since Khomeini's death there has been a shift back to a pre-Khomeinist view of Shiism.

President Ahmadinejad, however, was reputed to belong to a sect called the *Hojjatieh,* who believed that it was permissible to create chaotic conditions to accelerate the Hidden *Imam*'s return. Soon after he became president he said (on December 12, 2005) that the real ruler of Iran was the 12th *Imam,* and that government policy should hasten his return. He was reported to have made his cabinet sign a pledge of allegiance to the 12th *Imam* and to have dropped it down the Jamkaran well ("the Well of Requests"). The cabinet had reportedly spent half an hour discussing how the Hidden *Imam* would sign the contract and return it. Iranian assistance to the Shia militias in Iraq had subsequently helped spread the chaotic conditions that might trigger the Hidden *Imam*'s return.

Jamkaran. Near Qom. Entrance.

According to an article on the internet, Ahmadinejad believed that 2008 would see the Hidden *Imam*'s Second Coming, and there was a belief that this would take place up the Jamkaran well.

In 1002 AD (at midnight on 17 Ramadan 393 AH) the Hidden *Imam* had appeared to Hasan bin Muslah Jamkarani, presumably in a dream, and had asked him to build a mosque. Hasan had found

Jamkaran. Panoramic view of the well which is under arched enclosure on right.

the site marked out with chains and nails. I had read that in each generation the Hidden *Imam* had 36 "nails" (*owtad*) who served him, that their identities were kept secret and that the only known nail today was President Ahmadinejad himself, who was therefore able to communicate with the Hidden *Imam*. When he addressed the UN General Assembly in New York in September 2005, it was claimed that the President shone with the Hidden *Imam*'s Light. It was one thing for a leader to say that Israel should be wiped off the map. It was another thing for the servant of the Hidden *Imam* to say it as it implied that it was the Hidden *Imam*'s policy, which would receive uncritical acceptance among the theocracy. I knew that the President had donated $20 million to the Jamkaran mosque, and that the Supreme Leader had put his own nominee in charge of the administration of the mosque. I wondered if support for the Hidden *Imam* on this scale was an issue between the Supreme Leader and Ahmadinejad as it had been rumoured that there was tension between the two.

The Hidden *Imam* had represented a different emphasis in Shiism from Khomeini's, for Khomeini had seen himself as continuing Allah's work on earth rather than honouring *Imam*s. He was "*Faqih al-Wali*", "Custodian jurisconsult", who ruled on behalf of God, thus circumventing the Hidden *Imam*. According to local belief the Hidden *Imam* had come out of occultation to pray to Allah in the Jamkaran mosque, a story similar to that associated with Fatima in Portugal, where Catholics believe the Virgin Mary appeared six times to three children in 1917.

I knew I had to go to the Jamkaran well, which used to be an isolated well on the edge of the Dasht-e Kavir desert but had recently, following Ahmadinejad's sponsorship, increased in importance. It was not in any of the guidebooks, and I had been told that non-Muslims would not be allowed to enter the site. Jamkaran had been left off the itinerary that had been sent from

Tehran, and I had protested and had it reinstated.

We arrived in Jamkaran, flat sand with rocky hills, distant lunar mountains and low mud-walled tops and homes. Farhad said, "Many religions have a saviour figure, a Messiah. Christianity had Jesus. Zoroastrianism had a saviour. Buddhism also had a saviour. Shiism has the 12th *Imam*. Shias believe the 12th *Imam* is absent but is present at the Jamkaran well. He went down the well on a Wednesday, and so there are many services in Jamkaran on a Tuesday evening. Pilgrims come from Tehran and Isfahan to pray in the mosque. He will return, accompanied by Jesus on a mule on the Day of Judgement to save the world from cruelty and disorder. He will come on a Friday. People pray to him, 'Please come and help us, we can't wait.' Until 1970 Jamkaran used to be a tiny place, just a well in the desert with a small mosque first built over a thousand years ago and rebuilt 300 years ago, but it was extended after the Revolution."

Visible from a distance against low mountains were a blue dome, two minarets, three green domes and a lot of outbuildings with arches. We parked outside high railings, and put our hoods over our heads.

Farhad said, "Let me go first. Just walk quickly behind me, it depends on the man on the gate."

The man on the gate was in a blue padded jacket. He looked hard at me, but I kept walking and did not make eye contact. Then I was through and in the compound and hurrying across a large open space towards the distant blue dome, my hood down.

We bore left past an enormous hangar where women could wait in hot weather, shaded from the sun, and skirted the mosque with a pale blue dome. "It was built by a man to whom the *Mahdi* appeared in a dream," Farhad said, "saying, 'Build a mosque by the well.'"

Behind the mosque there was a stretch of open paved ground

Jamkaran. The well, showing its proximity to the Jamkaran mosque.

surrounded by crash barriers, like an empty car park. To the right of pine trees against the blue sky there was a small brick single-storey building with crash-barrier railings in front of it where I could see half a dozen people. "That's the well," Farhad said, and I felt a sense of disappointment. It could have been a brick bus shelter.

We hurried on and found the crash barriers had a second tier on

Jamkaran. Building in progress alongside the mosque.

Entrance to the Jamkaran mosque, with portraits of Khomeini and Khamenei.

them, bringing them up to head-height. We found a way in and stood before a grubby, much-scuffed, white, enamel-looking base ("marble," Farhad said) two feet by two feet and between knee- and waist-high, covered with a two-foot-by-two-foot green steel grille of ten bars, which brought it up to chest-height. It was made of metal, and there were ten bars on each of the four sides and on top. The bars were not wide apart but left enough room for a folded piece of paper to be pushed through so that it fell into the well below.

The well was barely wide enough to allow a well-built man to descend. Even a thin man might have got stuck, though in the 9th century it would have been a two-foot-by-two-foot opening in the ground without the chest-high appendage. The whole thing looked like an air-vent for an underground bunker.

Yet this barred-off area was where the Shia Second Coming would take place, where the world would be saved. It was all so ordinary. There was a very worn green metal table next to the well where messages could be written, the green paint on the surface having been rubbed away long ago by hordes of hands writing messages.

Farhad gave me a message sheet with green writing on it. He said, "It's in Arabic, not Persian. Arabic is the language of prayer. It's like Catholics having prayers in Latin. The language of the *Koran* and prayers is Arabic."

I asked, "What does the text say, does it say, 'Come quickly?'"

He scanned the prayer. "It says to the Hidden *Imam*, 'You are very generous, give us grace.' There is nothing about 'Come quickly'."

I watched half a dozen students in jeans and padded jackets post their messages through to the Hidden *Imam* below. Our driver had somehow appeared wearing a woollen hat. He was writing a message on his message sheet.

What happened to all the messages? Did they just accumulate down there? Were there years and years of soggy messages clogging the bottom of the well? Or was a receptacle, a tray, suspended across the well to catch the messages and was it lifted up and emptied each night? I inspected the white base for signs of a door. I could not bring myself to ask.

"Does our driver believe that his prayer will be answered?" I asked Farhad.

"Of course," Farhad replied. "All Shias believe that."

I stood and gazed on where the Hidden *Imam* and Jesus would emerge for their Second Coming, and then the half-dozen students and our driver moved away and I had the well all to myself. I had been told that non-Muslims would not be allowed into the compound, let alone near the well, yet here I was, on my own by the top of the well. I peered down between the top bars to see if there was any sign of life down the well, but it was all pitch black.

I thought of what the woman on the plane had said: "The Hidden *Imam* is everywhere." And I thought of the Iranian cabinet standing where I was standing and President Ahmadinejad stuffing his pledge and contract between the slats, localising the Hidden *Imam* to the bottom of the well. It is the mystery of divinity in all cultures that it – He – can appear in a particular place and time and yet also be everywhere. Both localisation and ubiquity – universality – are attributes of deity.

*

Aware that the chaos in Iraq was linked to the need to create the right conditions for an imminent divine event to happen here, I tore myself away from the well very reluctantly and walked back round the rear side of the mosque, past building work – rows of columns with bent iron rods poking out of their open tops, surrounded by low scaffolding.

I judged the blue-tiled entrance and its domed stalactites under a sun to be 300 years old. Khomeini and Khamenei peered down from either side of the arch. The pale-blue, bulbous, onion-shaped dome above it looked very beautiful.

"Come on," Farhad said. "We'll take our shoes off."

We entered in our socks, our driver as well. We padded through to a large hall with columns where about 50 Iranians were praying: standing, sitting or kneeling with their foreheads to the earth. They were all praying in the direction of Mecca, of course, and the well was at a slight angle, beyond the right-hand corner of the mosque. They all ignored me.

"Look, there are several *mullah*s," Farhad said. "The ones with the black turban are descendants from the Prophet. Not the white-turban ones, the black-turban. Let's sit down. Look, silk carpets, Tabriz motif, all the same. These are very expensive carpets." (He seemed to have no problem in talking while his neighbours were praying. In a church this would be unacceptable, but in a mosque it seemed to be in order.)

So I sat, shoeless, a stone's-throw from the well which was just beyond the right-hand corner wall, and, with *mullah*s before me and on either side of me, closed my eyes and went to the Light. Quietly I offered myself as a means to defuse the international crisis if the Light so willed, to act as a messenger if it was God's will.

I asked the Light to descend into human intransigence and sort out the situation short of war, and to leave it so there was no threat to mankind from nuclear weapons, and then I asked the Light to shine down the well and cleanse it and purify all hostility and aggressiveness and make it a place of peace. I asked the Light to stop a nuclear conflict involving Iran if it was its wish. Then I said to the Light, 'Here I am, sitting in pre-war Iran by the well, please guide me in my coming literary work about the clash between civilizations.' And the Light shone brightly into my soul. But I came to with a sense of foreboding, a renewed conviction that it was inevitable that Iran will be attacked. It was a poignant meditation, so near the holy well with the international crisis outside Iran so intense.

I looked round me. I had gone deep and had been oblivious of time. Farhad had his eyes open. He said, "Our driver is talking to the *mullah*." I looked and saw our driver sitting on carpet, talking, listening, nodding and talking again to a lithe *mullah* in a white turban who spoke vigorously, also sitting under his brown robes.

"He has been talking a long time," Farhad said. What was the driver discussing? We stood up and waited nearby, not interrupting but hoping to catch our driver's attention and signal it was time to go. And now I was standing near the front, the only Westerner on the site, let alone in the building, men were giving me looks as if to say, 'What is this Westerner doing here? Get him out at once.'

As something to do, I suspect, Farhad took me to the side wall and showed me rosaries of beads which some of those praying were holding and telling, moving beads forward with their thumbs. "Look," he said, holding beads he had picked up and handing a set to me, "You do 33, then 32, then 32. The first time you say '*Allahu Akbar*', 'God is great' 33 times, moving a bead each time. The second time you say '*Sobhan Allah*', 'God be praised' 32 times. The third time you say '*Al-Hamdullilah Allah*', 'Thanks be to God' or 'God be thanked' 32 times. And it was as if I were hearing a call back to universal or universalist religion among 17th-century people.

At last the driver saw us and said goodbye to the *mullah*, who gave me a sharp look and then returned to his devotions.

Outside the driver said, Farhad told me, that he had asked how many had been healed by the Hidden *Imam* at the well. The *mullah* had told him of many cases of people who had been healed since the Hidden *Imam* appeared in a dream to the builder of the mosque, so many that it seemed to have become the Shia Lourdes. Which is why the well had come to be known as the "Well of Requests".

As we walked back to the car I commented on the amount of building work that was evident. There seemed to be at least four new large buildings going up. They looked like grandstands. Perhaps the government was building grandstands so that the Second Coming of the Hidden *Imam* and of Jesus could be witnessed by vast crowds?

"They are to receive pilgrims," Farhad said. "The present government has expanded this site, and is catering for increased pilgrims."

I could see that President Ahmadinejad, who was reported on the internet as saying that 2008 will see the return of the Hidden *Imam*, was pouring government money into the site so that when the great event happened the infrastructure would be able to cope with the many thousands of pilgrims who would descend on Jamkaran. In the 17th century there had been a belief that the Messiah would come in 1656 – Menasseh ben Israel, the Jewish leader, had believed the Messiah was Cromwell – and again I was struck by the parallel between contemporary Iran and the fervour of the 17th century.

*

We drove on to Qom, a crowded, congested town of mud-walls mixed with Western buildings. From the 7th century it was a Shia centre, and became a major pilgrimage site after the death and burial in 816 of Fatima, the sister of the 8th *Imam* (who was buried in Mashad). Her caravan had been attacked at Saveh, near Qom *en route* to Mashad, and her brothers had been killed. She had been ill there, had entered Qom to be among Shiites and had died seventeen days later, aged about 27. Farhad said, "The shrine was modest until the Safavids came in 1501. They made Shiism the State religion. Before the Safavids the majority of Iranians were not Shiites."

Farhad continued, "Under the Safavids Iran adopted Arab culture and religion as State policy. They were very devout, they supported *Ithna Ashari* Shiism ('Twelver' Shiism affirming 12 rather than 7 *Imam*s), and they reconstructed the shrine – and also the shrines of Ardabil (the burial place of Sheikh Safi al-Din, the founder of the Safavids), Kerbala and Mashad (where *Imam*s were buried) – in the hope that Iranians and other Shiites would make their *Haj* pilgrimage to these sites rather than to Mecca and Medina. As Fatima was the sister of the 8th *Imam*, she was a little bit lower than the 8th *Imam*.

"The main Shiite theological schools were at Najaf and Kerbala in Iraq, but in the early 20th century a new theological school or *madraseh* was started at Qom by Ayatollah Haeri-Yazdi, one of Ayatollah Khomeini's teachers who died in 1935. Qom became even more of a teaching centre and place of pilgrimage. There was now a Najaf school of Shiism and a Qom school of Shiism.

Khomeini studied at Qom and then at Najaf. He believed the State and religion were not separate, he spoke out against the Shah's reduction of religious estates, the emancipation of women and the sending back of Americans who committed crimes in Iran to face a court in the States. The Shah sent his police against Khomeini's theological school in Qom in 1963, and killed some *mullahs*. Khomeini was arrested and imprisoned, and there were anti-government riots."

Qom. Khomeini's living-room (the room to the right of the entrance) with two *mullahs*.

Farhad continued: "The theological school where Khomeini used to teach was Faydiyeh (or Feyzie) *madraseh*. In November 1964 Khomeini was exiled by the Shah to Turkey and eventually to Najaf in Iraq. Saddam Hussein forced him to leave Iraq in 1978, and he went to Neauphle-le-Château, a suburb of Paris which was socialist and free, and acted as his centre of journalism in Europe. Paris was safe and people would hear his tape-recorded voice. His followers lived with him in France. In 1979 he was seventy-nine and was a father-figure of the nation, people loved him, they followed him because they loved him. He was neither charismatic nor sacred, he was not like the 12th *Imam*, nor like Hitler or Stalin. He was still ruling in his late eighties.

"There was not much corruption under Khomeini, people believed in the ideas of the Revolution. Those ordered to be executed carried placards saying 'Corrupters of the earth' (*mofsidin fil-arz*). Many government officials were executed for 'fighting against the Twelfth *Imam*', suggesting that he was the 12th *Imam* returning through the Revolution. People wondered if he was the 12th *Imam* returned before these executions as the overthrow of the Pahlavis and the founding of the Islamic Republic seemed divinely ordered, and he took the title '*Imam* Khomeini'. When he died his mausoleum reflected the shrine of the 8th *Imam* in Mashad, but he wasn't the 12th, or 13th, *Imam*."

We left the car and walked on sandy paths past mud-walls until we came to a yellow hoarding showing the stylized character for "Allah" (the image on the Iranian flag) shining like a sun in the direction of Ayatollah Khomeini on the right and the Supreme Leader Ali Khamenei on the left, both wearing black turbans to denote that they were descended from the Prophet. At the end of the mud-walled lane there was a blue sign with a picture of Khomeini and a notice in Persian and English: "The *Imam* Khomeini's House, Date: Present Century. Historic Records: 1745." We went down the sandy lane with a 12-foot high brick-and-mud wall on our left until we encountered a revolutionary guard in a small glass sentry-box. We went through the gate and saw the 80-year-old brick entrance, basement and white-plastered upper walls of Khomeini's flat-roofed house beyond a small garden with some shrubs.

"When Khomeini was exiled," Farhad said, "on November 4 1964, troops landed on the roof and besieged him. He was praying within. He immediately dressed and tried to open an inner door near the front door, but it was locked. The troops outside broke the door down. Khomeini found the key and left the building by another door. He gave the seal of his signatures to his wife and said to her, 'I entrust you to Allah.'"

I went in the entrance and up a few steps, took my shoes off before a cabinet which held opened books with pictures of Khomeini prominently displayed, turned right and was standing in a bare room with a green carpet whose design showed five horizontal rows of ladder-like rungs or balustrade columns. There was a desk with a sloping top with books and papers on it, at which sat reading a bespectacled *mullah* in a white turban, and beside him, on a rug, sat another *mullah*, also in a white turban, holding a glass of tea. There was a picture of Khomeini and Khamenei on the wall and a small wall-mounted bookcase with four short rows of books. That was all.

"This was Ayatollah Khomeini's living-room and office," Farhad said. "This is where he received people until his expulsion in 1964. This is where he was seized and taken into exile in a car waiting by the gate, driven straight to Mehrabad airport and put on a plane. His family – his wife and two sons – remained here while he was in exile. This is where he returned in February 1979 and lived until

Qom. Golden Shrine of Fatima.

he moved to Tehran in 1980."

The two *mullah*s looked aghast that I should be there. The expression on their faces was so disapproving I had to do something. "May I take their photos?" I asked, and I produced my camera, which flashed at them as the sitting *mullah* dived back into his reading and the tea-drinking *mullah* turned his head away.

Having defused the atmosphere, I stood and soaked in the ambience of the situation. The last Shah had exiled Khomeini for life in 1964, and in 1979 the Shah had fled and Khomeini had returned and exiled *him* for life – and a year later the Shah died. This was where Khomeini became a Philosopher Ruler or Philosopher King, living in austere simplicity. This was where the decision was taken to execute the many "corrupters of the earth" who had fought against the 12th *Imam*, and where Platonic Goodness was compromised – some would say "corrupted" – by firing-squads, as happened in all revolutions.

We left the room without going to the smaller room visible at the back, and looked through the open door into the room the other side of the steps and cabinet. A black-turbaned man was sitting grimly behind a desk, and two women in *chador*s entered and sat in front of him. He glared at me.

"He is a famous *Ayatollah*, and he is giving them advice," Farhad said, "we can't go in as they are being given advice. But that was where Ayatollah Khomeini's family lived. That was where his wife and children would have been while he was working and living in the room we have just left, receiving conservative clerics and building his powerbase. Look, these steps continue down into the basement, for cool living in hot weather."

I was struck by the simplicity of the rooms and of the life-style of Khomeini. I looked back at the room with the two *mullah*s. So this was where the hardliner composed his 1963 speech against the Shah and where he left to deliver it, a cleric of sixty-three linked to the opposition without much of a political future except behind bars. And this was where he built an old man's theocratic paradise and ruled with his Guardians as an octogenarian.

*

We returned to the lane outside and walked through a poor quarter, a network of narrow sandy lanes, mud walls and small brick houses with flat roofs. There were many Iranians going our way or squeezing past us, women in black head-to-foot *chador*s – no one wore the headscarf here – and *mullah*s with white turbans. "Those two are from Afghanistan," Farhad said. "I can tell by their look and their dress."

I was walking among *mullah*s in the most fanatical place in Iran – I wouldn't have ventured here on my own although when I worked in Baghdad 45 years previously in pre-terrorist days I used to do the equivalent every day on my own and think nothing of it – but by and large, except for a few unwelcoming stares I was ignored.

Eventually we came out near the shrine of Fatima, Hazrat-e Masumeh, whose golden dome I could see behind two minarets across a traffic jam of hooting cars. As we squeezed between cars Farhad said, "The entrance to the Faydiyeh *madraseh* is over there. We can't go in without a permit."

We crossed the road and looked up at the tiled entrance and minarets. Beyond this point non-Muslims were not allowed.

"Come on," said Farhad.

We went into the spacious courtyard of the dome with arches all round and four *iwan*s and tiled entrances to the nearby Safavid Friday mosque, whose blue dome was under scaffolding.

"Most of what you see was built by Shah Abbas I to counter-balance the Shiite shrines at Kerbala and Najaf," Farhad said. "The gold cupola was built by Fath Ali Shah. Four Safavid Shahs are buried under the golden dome: Safi I, Abbas II, Soleiman I and Sultan Husayn. Also two Qajar rulers: Fath Ali Shah and Mohammad Shah. The shrine of Fatima is like the shrine we saw in Shiraz, a cenotaph, only it is silver, dating from 1814 and renewed in 1863, with five arches and mesh grilles on each side. The dome and drum over it were gilded in the late 19th century, and mirrorwork was added. The tomb inside had tiles in 1216 that were renewed in 1998. Unfortunately I am not allowed to take you in."

At that moment a young man in a smart blue uniform with a peaked cap, carrying what looked liked a yellow fluffy duster on a stick (one of those dusters that look like candy floss) approached and spoke to us. He looked like a policeman but I read "*Masoumeh*" on his badge and grasped that he was from the shrine's International Affairs section, a kind of shrine policeman. 'Oh no,' I thought, 'I'm going to be arrested for being inside the compound.'

Farhad translated: "He says we have done wrong. We should have reported to the office of International Affairs and filled in a questionnaire. We have to do that now."

After days of scanning faces he had at last found a Westerner! So I trooped after him to a dark room out of the sunlight and Farhad asked me some questions and completed a form in a lever-arch folder, which I signed.

I saw a *mullah* watching me through a glass window. He was sitting cross-legged on a raised floor that was waist-high, and I asked if there was a book in English about the shrine.

The young man in the peaked cap, still holding his fluffy duster, went and spoke to the *mullah* behind the glass and returned with a visitors pack that included a book in English about the shrine. I offered to pay but the *mullah* was shaking his head and beaming from where he sat, cross-legged, and I thanked him.

After that the guard was devoted to us. Farhad translated: "I would have offered you tea if I'd known you were coming. Yes, do take photos."

Farhad tried to give him 20,000 *rials*.

"No money, it's my pleasure, please come again with your relatives, I look forward to seeing you again."

I said to Farhad, "Can I ask him to take me into the shrine?"

Farhad said, looking at the guard, "No, that's definitely not allowed, I'm afraid. Non-Muslims are not allowed into the shrine as they won't have abluted. They're considered unclean. Muslims must make ablutions first before they go in." I sensed it might be more than his job was worth to ask.

The courtyard was very crowded now – the contrast with the relatively deserted site of the Hidden *Imam*'s well could not have been greater – but I was still the only Westerner in the throng of pilgrims. Farhad pointed to a few more architectural details and the young man in the peaked cap hovered near us, policing us off the premises with great courtesy and charm. It had been a pleasure to be apprehended, if not arrested, by such a polite and considerate young man, even if the episode did mean that I could not enter the shrine itself.

We returned to the car across a bridge over the dried-up river. The wide street had a line of battered old crocks of cars which passed as group taxis, and Iranians were shouting out the number of vacancies. It was just as 45 years ago when, in the pre-terrorist age, making ends meet and with the trust of youth, each day I heard a shouter in Baghdad call "*Wahed, Bab* Sherge" ("one to Sherge gate") and I would climb into the back of an antiquated estate car (a *baz* or group taxi) and sit with my knees under my chin with six Arabs in *kuffeia w'agal*s and sometimes a sheep or two or a goat, and ride back from work. Pilgrims to the shrine were getting into these cars for their journey home.

*

We set off for Hamadan. Farhad told me, "Saddam Hussein fought four wars: two Gulf wars, the Kurds and Iran. The towns that were bombed during the Iran-Iraq war were: Tehran, Isfahan, Ahwaz, Tabriz, Hamadan, Kermanshah, Shiraz and smaller towns. It was like your *Blitz*, against civilians. It lasted five years. People went to safe areas. Iran did not bomb civilian targets, only military areas: oilfields, barracks. Iraq bombed bazaars where there were many civilians, and there was collateral damage to mosques."

I moved the conversation on, or rather back, to what we had been discussing before we reached the well: Iran's democracy. I asked: "Who is supporting the Shias in Iraq, Hamas in Palestine and Nasrallah in Lebanon? The Supreme Leader or the President? In Afghanistan the spiritual leadership of *Mullah* Omar was also political. Is it the same in Iran with the spiritual Supreme Leader – is he also political?" Farhad was very quiet so I went on: "There are options: (a) the spiritual leadership does nothing, and the President and government give political support to Iraq, Palestine and Lebanon; (b) both the Supreme Leader and the President and government give political support; (c) both the Supreme Leader and President and government are doing nothing; (d) the Supreme Leader is giving political support and the President and government are doing nothing."

Farhad said slowly, "I think the Supreme Leader sets a spiritual direction and the President and government reflect his thinking in action. But the Supreme Leader is a politician with a clerical background, not a religious authority who has no dealings with politics. Iran is helping Hamas and Hizbollah, but Iraq.... Perhaps al-Hakim. It's (a) or (b), I don't know which."

I said, "If there are 25 people round the Supreme Leader including 12 Guardian Council and the most influential of the Council of Experts and 25 people round the President including his Cabinet, then 50 people are dictating Iran's foreign policy towards Iraq, Palestine and Lebanon. And if Bush were to change the regime – change those 50 people – then Iran's foreign policy could be different, more pro-Western."

Farhad said, "No, the Supreme Leader and President are supported by the people, the people watch what they're saying and doing and support them. The key fact is Israel, which wants war. So regime change can't succeed. If you take out the top 50, then 50 more people will step up to take their places, and they will be just as anti-Israel. So the American policy of regime change won't work."

I had got as far as I could go with the Supreme Leader and the President. I had got to grips with the 12th *Imam*, the Hidden *Imam*, whose only known "nail" was the President. I had stood in the living-room of the titular *Imam*, Ayatollah Khomeini. And I had been in the courtyard of the shrine of the 8th *Imam*'s sister. These three *Imam*s gave Qom a special authority in influencing the Supreme Leader, the spiritual director of Iran, and the spiritual direction Khomeini had charted while Supreme Leader was anti-Pahlavi, anti-Israeli, anti-American, pro-Palestinian and anti-everything that was opposed to Shiite Islam.

Khomeini's life and sayings showed that option (a) was the one that fitted Iran best: both the Supreme Leader and President and government gave political support to Israel's and America's enemies. The Holy *Imam*s of Qom were supposed to stay apart from everyday politics, but the Hidden *Imam* was involved at every level, including healing and answering prayers, and *Imam* Khomeini had been even more practically involved while retaining some spiritual detachment and power. Khomeini had been above the worship of other *Imam*s – he had never been to Mashad and had nothing to do with *Ashura* – and the high tide of the Shia revival may have ended with him, leaving the Islamic Republic of Ali Khamenei a pale shadow of his predecessor's regime.

It remained to be seen whether Iran's nuclear defiance would be punished or prove successful, and therefore whether the Islamic Republic in Iran was already a spent force or still had life left in it. But what was certain was that judging by the visits to shrines connected with the *Imam*s the Shia revival was still strong in Iran.

10

AMONG THE MEDES AND PERSIANS

OF HAMADAN

My itinerary had stated that we would go to Hamadan via Arak, another nuclear site. I was therefore put out when I could see that we were heading north rather than west along a fast road.

"Why are we on this road?" I asked.

Farhad said, "It's faster, it's a better road. The other road is not as good."

"But we're supposed to be going to Arak."

"There's nothing there and this way there's a beautiful mosque."

"But I want to see the villages in the Zagros mountains."

"You will see them this way," Farhad said.

"But," I said, casting around for new reasons, "I want to go through Orphic villages."

"We will go past an Orphic village. There is an Orphic temple in the mountains above it."

"Why aren't we going via Arak, is the road closed?"

"No, it's not closed, but there is an obstacle."

"So I'm being prevented from going?"

"No, it's just that this way is better. The other way is more kilometres and will take longer."

In the end I played my trump card. "It's on my itinerary, and I've paid for it. Look."

Farhad looked and conferred with the driver who became heated, shrugging and waving his hands about. He snatched his woollen hat from his head and flung it down beside him. I had clearly caused a problem. It would be too far for him to go in one day, it would take too long, he might be driving after dark – perhaps these were the considerations that bugged him. I let them deliberate and then Farhad turned and said, "I have a compromise. We will continue on this road and go to Hamadan this way today. Tomorrow we will return on the other road. Do you want to go into Arak?"

"No," I said, "I want to get the feel for the nuclear site there, like the one we went past after Natanz."

"There's nothing to see."

"That's all right. I just want to see what scenery there is, how close the mountains are, so if Israel attacks – "

"Israel wouldn't dare. Their defence minister has just resigned because he could not defeat Hizbollah." Farhad added, "I didn't realise that going that way was so important to you."

He conferred again. The driver was still clearly unhappy.

"It's all right," Farhad said. "That's what we'll do. But we may go without lunch tomorrow."

But I was cross because I knew the nuclear site was 32 miles – 51.2 kilometres – after Arak, but I did not know how many miles or kilometres it was from Hamadan. So I would not be able to anticipate our approach. But there was nothing for it but to accept the situation.

We stopped in Saveh. We looked at the earliest double-spiral-staircase minaret in Iran of c. 1062, and another minaret of 1111, and lunched at the Akbar restaurant. We sat on waist-high carpeted wooden "beds" with rolled cushions like round pillows, and I ate cross-legged, awkwardly reaching for kebabs, rice and yoghurt while a noisy television blared comedy and the waiter sauntered to and fro, half-watching and half-laughing. On other "beds" sat bearded groups, some of whom glared at me. As usual I was the only Westerner there.

We resumed our journey with the Zagros mountains rising a

mile or more on our left. Very soon Farhad said, "On the left is the village of Akala. Up in the mountains behind it there is an Orphic temple. The cult of Orpheus was practised here." I nodded.

"Over there is an electrical power station," Farhad said later, "polluting the air with its white smoke." There was certainly a lot of white smoke pouring from its chimney.

I asked, " Why does Iran wants nuclear power, to stop the pollution?"

Farhad replied, "Yes."

Farhad had warned that it would be cold in Hamadan. "It was minus 25C two weeks ago, the coldest place in Iran." Mid-afternoon the sun was glistening in snow on both sides of the car, and half an hour later it was −4C with snowclad mountains on either side. Soon it was −6C as we drove into the Zagros mountains.

We approached Hamadan in the Alvand mountains in the Zagros, where Ecbatana linked Iran to Mesopotamia. Ecbatana

Hamadan. Tomb of Esther and Mordecai, outside.

was the 7th-century-BC capital of the Medes and the summer capital of the Achaemenians after the Persian Cyrus defeated the Medes in 550 BC. Herodotus said that Ecbatana was defended by seven concentric walls, the inner two of which were coated with silver and gold (perhaps an indication of the city's commercial wealth), the outer one being as long as the wall round Athens:

"The city now known as Ecbatana was built, a place of great

size and strength fortified by concentric walls, these so planned that each successive circle was higher than the one below it by the height of the battlements. The fact that it was built on a hill helped to bring about this effect, but still more was done by deliberate contrivance. The circles are seven in number, and the innermost contains the royal palace and treasury. The circuit of the outer wall is much the same in extent as at Athens. The battlements of the five outer rings are painted in different colours, the first white, the second black, the third crimson, the fourth blue, the fifth orange; the battlements of the two inner rings are plated with silver and gold respectively. These fortifications were to protect the king and his palace; the people had to build their houses outside the circuit of the walls."

Hamadan. Granite door thought to be Achaemenian.

Hamadan. Escort from one of the ten surviving Jewish families in Hamadan.

Farhad said, "There were two groups of Indo-European migrants – Aryans – from the land between the Oxus and Jaxartes (now the Amu Darya and Syr Darya) to the north of India. They called the place 'Aryanem-Vaejo'. They left probably because of climate change from about 2000 BC. The first group arrived in north-west Iran around Lake Urmia (or Urumiyeh) about 1500 BC, and they became the Kassites who were in Southern Mesopotamia until about 1100 BC and they settled as the Medes in the 9th century BC, the Parthians, the Persians and went down to Elamite Susa. The second group left the same area also about 1500 BC. They split into two groups. One group went through Afghanistan into India. The other group proceeded westwards into the Iranian plateau, the Alborz and Zagros mountains. The Medes fought wars with the Assyrians and ended Ashurbanipal's dynasty. The Medes built walls round Ecbatana about 650 BC and lost it to Cyrus in 550 BC. Cyrus used Ecbatana as an important staging-post on the road to Babylon. In 521 the Medes captured Ecbatana back, but lost it six months later to Darius. It became the capital under the Seljuqs."

*

We started in the Seljuq time. We stopped at the 12th-century Alavyn Tower, the mausoleum of the family that ruled Hamadan. It was originally a mosque before it became a mausoleum. The original dome was missing. The outside walls and *mihrab* were in stucco carved with geometric and floral designs added in the Mongol (Ilkhanid) era, which Farhad said was similar to a Sasanian design. The tomb itself was in a crypt downstairs.

All roads in Hamadan end in *Imam* Khomeini Square. We drove up to the square and back down another road to the Tomb of Esther and Mordecai, a round brick – probably 14th-century – building over, according to local tradition, the graves of the heroine of the

Book of Esther in the *Old Testament*, and her cousin and guardian Mordecai (who may have written the *Book of Esther*).

The story is that Esther, the Jewish orphan who became wife (or possibly concubine) to Ahasuerus (Xerxes I, or possibly his successor Artaxerxes) saved the Jewish community in Ecbatana from extermination by Haman, the king's commander, when she was alerted to the plan by Mordecai. She also intrigued Jewish colonies throughout the Persian Empire. Her tomb is also attributed to a Jewish queen, Shushan-Dokht, who persuaded her Sasanian husband Yazdgerd I to permit a new Jewish colony in Hamadan and may be 5th-century AD. An inscription has been found referring to the tombs of Elias and Samuel, sons of an Ismail Karlan, and it is possible that these two tombs were theirs.

There was a large block of granite that acted as a door, and this was thought to be Achaemenian, Farhad said. This was open, and as I crouched to enter I was reminded of the stone that blocked the entrance to the Garden tomb of Christ.

A suave Jewish gentleman profusely welcomed me, looking dapper in a fashionable coat and scarf. He spoke to me very fast in French. He said he was from one of the ten surviving Jewish families in Hamadan. He took me from a small ante-room down steps to the tomb-room, where there were two large decorated wooden cases that housed the coffins, one labelled 'Esther' and the other 'Mordecai'. He kissed Esther's coffin several times and went into a swoon, and I was reminded of the fervour at the Shiraz shrine. He clearly believed that this was the tomb of Esther and not the tomb of a later defender of the Jews.

There were Hebrew inscriptions on the walls, and I was struck by the very existence of the place although the President had declared his intention to wipe Israel off the map. I wanted to ask my Jewish escort what he would do if Israel bombed the nuclear sites, but at that moment he floored me by asking for my pen.

Farhad translated: "He collects pens. He would like the one you are writing with."

I said apologetically that if he had the pen I was writing with, I would not be able to make any more notes, and I tipped him generously instead.

He smiled sadly, a good tip was not as good as a Western biro. I had an image of a collection of hundreds of pens at his home which he had asked tourists to give him, and I had a vision of him taking fingerprints from them and sending the fingerprints to Israel. Why else would he make such an extraordinary request?

We left and went to a market and I looked in on a shop with awnings where every kind of spice was for sale on plates and in open jars, and Farhad bought some dried apricots.

*

It was getting dark as we drove on up snow-covered roads to the cuneiform rock carvings of Darius I and Xerxes I, called "*Ganjnameh*", "Treasure Book", because, not knowing about the Achaemenians, the memory of whom was lost at the end of the Parthian or beginning of the Sasanian time, Iranians thought the inscriptions were clues to hidden Median treasure. We parked in quite deep snow and got out in a temperature of −8C as dusk turned to dark, and climbed up steps slippery under impacted snow and ice, past stalls lit with faint lanterns and on up into the foothills of a mountain, a steep slope covered with ankle-deep snow, and to the two rock inscriptions in Old Persian, Elamite and Babylonian which hung above deep snow with mountains all round and a gorge. Farhad said, "This was on the Royal Achaemenian Road from western Turkey across the Zagros mountains to Ecbatana and via Persepolis to Susa, the winter capital, and then to Babylon."

There was a translation of the two inscriptions on a board, so

Farhad did not have to translate. The inscription of Darius I said: "A Great God (is) Ahura Mazda, who created this earth, who created that heaven, who created man, who created happiness for man, who made Darius king, the one King of many (kings), the one Commander of many (commanders). I (am) Darius the great King, the King of kings, the King of countries having many (kinds of) human beings, the King in this great earth far and wide, the son of Hystaspes, an Achaemenian." The inscription of Xerxes I was identical except that it replaced "Darius" with "Xerxes", and "Hystaspes" with "Darius".

Why are these inscriptions there? Probably to reinforce their right to rule Ecbatana after the Medes had recaptured Ecbatana for six months in 521 BC. Ahura Mazda was produced to give legitimacy to their rule. At nearby Biston (or Behistan) towards Kermanshah there is a rock-face recording Darius's victory over the rebel Gaumata, who had claimed the Achaemenian throne. The panel was begun in 521 BC and related that Gaumata was killed near there at the battle of Kundurush on September 29, 522 BC (in our dating), asserting the legitimacy of Darius' rule. Alexander the Great must have passed along this road and read this inscription and also the one at the Biston. In short, the inscription justified the subjugation of the Medes by the Persians.

We returned to our car in the dark, lit by the white glare of the snow. Some hardy Iranian youths were preparing to spend a night under a flimsy tent. Farhad said "There are wild animals in the mountains, they can come down here in the night and savage them. And it's going to be minus 20 C tonight. They're mad."

We drove to our hotel, Hotel Bu-Ali (a shortened form of Abu Ali, meaning Avicenna) and arrived at 7.15.

Over dinner, which we ate by ourselves without the driver, Farhad asked me, "Do you believe we're getting more than nuclear energy?"

I said, "In my view, and I'm not an expert, you can't have one without the other. If you know how to produce nuclear energy you know how to produce a nuclear bomb."

Farhad mused. He did not disagree.

I rang my wife and then had a final look outside. It did not feel bitingly cold. "Minus 20?" I asked the receptionist. He nodded and indicated that it would soon be –20.

*

The next morning I was up early. My room was on the ground floor and I had a sliding window, so I slid it sideways and was able to stand and have a clear view of the garden, which was covered in snow. Icicles hung from the roof of a neighbour's shed, but it did not feel very cold. I was in for breakfast at 7.10 as we had a long day ahead of us. Farhad joined me and said there was no breakfast until 8. We went to the kitchen and he negotiated. Breakfast came in dribs and drabs: first bread, honey, butter, orange and eventually coffee, and then two fried eggs; breakfast in reverse order.

In a temperature of –12C we went straight to the tomb of Avicenna (c. 980-1037), or Ibn al-Sina, a Muslim scientist and many-sided man, author of 130 books who was mentioned in Chaucer's *Prologue*. The tomb was sunk in the floor of a 1950s mausoleum surrounded by 80 of the herbs he identified, samples of which were on glass shelves. He died in Hamadan while on tour, travelling by camel.

I bowed to his knowledge of philosophy, poetry, music, economics, physics, mathematics, astronomy, medicine and law. His book on medicine was called *Law*, and his book on law was called *Healing*. He knew more in his time than perhaps anyone else. In beautiful calligraphy was written on his tombstone, Farhad translated: "Only God is the possessor of the world." This came from his original 11th-century tombstone (which was displayed under glass in the foyer). There was a picture on the wall of Avicenna with Galen and Hippocrates, for he was one of the first to apply herbs to healing. Looking at the 80 herbs and his application of each, I was uplifted and glad I had visited.

We left and drove past the tomb of the Sufi poet and *dervish* Baba Tahir, whose mystical, metaphysical poetic quatrains were written some time between 900 and 1300.

We drove on to the excavated site of Ecbatana, which was under snow and still −12C. Its brown enclosure was surrounded by distant snowy mountains and similarly shaped foreground snowdrifts. The dig area had been filled in so we trod carefully up a tree-lined icy path and spent our time in the warm museum. Farhad said, "Nothing Median has been discovered, which has been a disappointment. There are some Achaemenian post-Darius columns. They've looked for the walls but they haven't found them. They've found a lot of houses in this pattern." He pointed to a plan in a glass case showing interlocked Ts, Ls and Hs.

I saw the column bases. A soldier sat near them, holding a formidable gun worn from a strap over his shoulder. There was a Parthian skeleton, and a skeleton of 1200-900 BC, perhaps from the time of Troy. Although they had found little of ancient Media, the descendants of the Medes were all about me: the people in the market shops, the people I had passed on my way to the rock-carvings, and the hotel and museum staff.

*

We now set off for Arak, near where there was an underground nuclear site that would be a bombing target: a heavy-water plant needed for the production of enriched uranium at Natanz. We travelled through a Swiss landscape of many-humped mountains and surprisingly, an excellent road. There was snow on either side but the road was completely clear and we seemed to be driving along the top of the Zagros mountains. We passed through Luristan – the towns of Malayer (which had Orphic links, Farhad said, and was known for its walnuts) and Zanganeh – which I had always wanted to do, having seen Lurs bent double carrying furniture on their backs in Baghdad, where the vanless removal men were always Lurs. There were beautiful frost patterns on the outside of the car's side windows. I kept opening a side window to prevent the inside glass from misting over.

I knew that the nuclear site was about 32 miles north-west of Arak. I said, "The road turns left to Arak. The nuclear site is 51 kilometres this side of it."

Farhad said, studying his map, "We will join the road, it is more than 50 kilometres from the join to Arak, for sure."

But I was on my guard and looked out of the car window at the scenery, noting the sweep down of mountains ahead to a long plain covered with snow and what seemed to be distant huts over to the right with only a snowscape to the left.

Then suddenly Farhad said, "Police checkpoint," and I saw a sign in English: "Arak 45 kms."

"This is the turn-off to Arak," Farhad said. The road intersection was on a plain with Zagros mountains to the left and ahead.

The policeman looked hard at us and then waved us through. We drove off.

"Stop," I said.

The driver stopped a hundred yards from the checkpoint.

"We've passed it," I said, "it was six kilometres back there. Can we do a U-turn and go back six kilometres and look, then return?"

Farhad became agitated. He said, "We've passed through the police checkpoint, they recorded our number-plate, we can't turn back without making them suspicious. They'd be suspicious of us, and with you a foreigner.... And we're not supposed to be here. I have a letter from the police about your route, giving your itinerary to protect security. It goes to Saveh and avoids Arak. If they ask to see my letter we will all be in trouble."

Under the circumstances I could not argue.

Now I understood why we had come via Saveh the previous day. We had been conforming to a police letter, which stated our route. I had posed a problem by insisting, and was fortunate that they had accommodated me. I did not want to get them into trouble. Perhaps his eagerness to please, a charming Iranian characteristic, had been stronger than his eagerness to obey the letter. I did not like to ask what he would have said if the police

Two views of Arak.

checkpoint had asked to see his letter.

In fact, I later found out that they had brought me along the wrong road. There was a parallel route to the east, not such a good road, which came via Milajerd and Khondab. The nuclear site was just beyond Khondab. I had not appreciated that the nuclear site was 32 miles north-west of Arak on the minor road to Khondab. They had covered themselves by making sure that I had not taken the road that led past the nuclear site while allowing me to see the Zagros mountains at close quarters, as I had requested.

We drove past a restaurant on the right. It was in a complex of low white buildings with blue, green and red roofs. A workman was outside, dressed in yellow and wearing a white hat, and I had the same feeling about him, and about the policeman at the check-point, that I had had about the elders in the Natanz *Husaynieh*. Planes would sweep out of the sky and drop bombs on the nuclear site near Arak and change these people's lives perhaps for ever. Of course, this would be the other side of the mountain range but although the site near Arak was to be attacked with conventional bombs rather than tactical nuclear weapons (the fate of Natanz), there could be a release of radioactive particles into the atmosphere that would make these buildings as uninhabitable as those in the town of Natanz.

I had deepened my understanding of Iran by visiting Hamadan. I had seen Ecbatana from the Medes' point of view, and grasped that they felt occupied by Cyrus's and Darius's Persians, who had had to carve inscriptions in rock to justify their presence. The Jewish community felt doubly oppressed, by both the Medes and by the Persians. But by the Seljuq time, the Medes had lost their sense of being dominated by Persians. And now the two rubbed shoulders without realising they had once been enemies. And today, they were both committed to guarding the secrecy of Arak and making sure that it contributed to the national effort at Natanz.

Today they felt good about the country's rise to Great-Powerdom in the Middle East.

Now I was returning to Tehran, I wanted to get closer to the Revolution.

11

WITH THE SHAH AND KHOMEINI

IN TEHRAN

The excellent road from Tehran had snowy mountains on either side. We passed another electrical power station with two plumes of smoke creating clouds in the sky. "More pollution," Farhad said, perhaps making the point that Iran needed nuclear power. The conversation returned to the nuclear crisis. "The Shias in Iraq are a long way from the Shias in Iran," Farhad said. "They are cousins, not brothers. The journalists have made it so big, Israel definitely won't strike at Iran."

We passed Arak, tiny brown houses on the right under large mountains, and slowly we descended into a plain. The side wall of a whole house was covered by a poster with heads of nine martyrs from the Iran-Iraq war. We stopped to have tea and sweetmeats. "The home town of Khomeini is near here," Farhad said. "Khomein. He was too humble to have a statue while he was alive. At Qom there was just a raised copper carving, remember? Not a statue."

We drove on towards Tehran without stopping. There was a clear blue sky and Farhad said, "Oh look, there's Mount Damarvand (or Demavend), that cone-shaped peak. It's the highest mountain in Iran. 5,671 metres, 18,600 feet, Iran's Mount Fuji." It was distant, conical and high in the blue sky.

"In the *Shahnameh*," Farhad said, "a cruel ruler, Zahak (in modern Persian; Azhidihag in Old Persian) had two snakes on his shoulder. He fed them with the brains of young people. The father of a son who had been fed to the snakes imprisoned the cruel ruler in Damarvand." And I thought of Khomeini feeding the young martyrs to the two snakes of the Iran-Iraq war, like the nine martyrs I had just seen; and of the Shah before him, feeding Iran's funds to his celebration of 2,500 years of kingship and in doing so bringing the whole institution down. I wondered which had been imprisoned in the mountain.

We also had a very good view of the Alborz mountain range which is to the north of Tehran, a long white mountain range that filled the entire width of the car windscreen. Farhad said, "Tehran has a plain to the west and a desert to the south, the Dasht-e Kavir we are crossing now. Normally we can't see the mountains and now it's blue sky."

We talked about the Shah and Khomeini. I said, "I can't get it out of my mind that the Shah met Kermit Roosevelt at midnight in the Sadabad Palace in 1953 and let the Americans into Iran, and that Khomeini left that house in Qom to give his lecture against the Shah at the Theological School in 1963, and returned to that house, and then left that house to go into permanent exile, not allowed to return, and his family remained there, he vowing to return. And then that the Shah, who had the box Mohammad now has on his desk, went into permanent exile like Khomeini, and Kissinger tried to get him to Mexico but he went to Egypt and died there."

"And," Farhad said, "Khomeini had little relationship with Egypt for taking in the Shah. Iran has no relations with Israel and America, and Egypt was nearly as bad, but is slowly improving now."

I said, "The Shah sent Khomeini into permanent exile, and then Khomeini returned and imposed permanent exile on the Shah. The Shah suffered a karmic boomerang."

I widened our discussion to the War on Terror. I said, "And now bin Laden wants to do to King Abdullah of Saudi Arabia what Khomeini did to the Shah. Bin Laden opposed the puritanical Wahhabi Sunni rule of the House of Saud, which was supported by

Tehran. The Shah's White Palace, the Alborz mountains behind.

the US, as was the Shah. He struck against the US on 9/11 claiming to be more Wahhabi than the House of Saud, and decided to make common cause with Saudi Arabia's biggest rival and adversary, Shiite Iran. So bin Laden is modelling himself on Khomeini."

"But," Farhad said, "Khomeini and the present Supreme Leader are totally against the theology of bin Laden, and the Supreme Leader said after 9/11 that bin Laden had given a bad impression of the Muslims to the outside world."

"Perhaps they were public words," I said. "There are reports that bin Laden wrote to the Supreme Leader and offered him control of al-Qaeda in return for being harboured in Iran. The Sunni Zarqawi operated out of Iran, and went back to Iran when he was wounded. It's possible that al-Qaeda are now the military arm of the theocratic Iranian leadership. Think it through. The Supreme Leader is angry that the land where *Imam*s are buried, Iraq, which used to be one with Iran, has been bombed and occupied. Bin Laden is angry that the land where *Imam*s are buried has been ruled by the House of Saud, and has attacked America and the West. So it's the Saudis, America, Israel and Britain against bin Laden, Sunni al-Qaeda and Shiite Iran, all of whom are anti-American."

"Yes," Farhad said. "In Saudi Arabia there was Black Friday in July 1987 when Saudi police shot at anti-US Iranian demonstrators in Mecca so the relationship between Ayatollah Khomeini and the Saudis was not good, but it got better through Khatami and is now improving. There are theological differences."

"At the bottom of it all," I said, "is Palestine's loss of land to Israel and the Shah's pro-Israeli luxury. Khomeini got the Shah out and bin Laden wants to get the House of Saud out. The House of Saud supports the US and so he struck the US on 9/11. The US saw him coming, and, wanting a pretext to go into Afghanistan and Iraq, let him attack. The US want to get out the man who captured the US hostages in 1980, nine months after Khomeini's return: your President Ahmadinejad, who's been recognised by hostages."

"But," Farhad said, "they made a mistake. The President was a marginal figure in the hostage-taking, he wasn't a student-leader."

I said, "So it's about the US getting even for 1980, settling scores from the Carter time, and it's about bin Laden attacking the House of Saud. He wants it to become the House of bin Laden."

We had made good time, and Farhad said, perhaps still aware that he had not delivered the Arak nuclear site, "I would like to take you to the Shah's White Palace. This is not on the itinerary. It closes at 4. I will ask the driver if we can get there in time, depending on the traffic, for it is in the north of Tehran. First we have to collect the carpets from Mehrabad Airport. Mohammad rang me from Isfahan, he's done leather edges and put them on a plane last night, they're waiting for us."

So we turned off the road and parked outside the Domestic Flights terminal at Mehrabad Airport. Farhad left and returned with a taped-up cardboard box that had begun to split under his arm.

We left the airport and saw the mausoleum of Ayatollah Khomeini: four tall towers and a gold dome adorned with 72 tulips to represent Husayn's 72 followers who died with him in Kerbala. Ten million attended Khomeini's funeral and some of the crowd took his coffin from the hearse and passed it on over their heads.

*

We drove on and entered Tehran from the western side and proceeded through light traffic to Sadabad Palace, a 297-acre closed site in extensive grounds where there were 18 palaces dating from the 1930s, including the last Shah's and his father's palaces. The White Palace, now the Palace of the Nations, was built by the last Shah's father, Reza Shah, with additions by the last Shah.

We were dropped off in late afternoon sunshine outside a small arched gateway from which there was an avenue of trees. Farhad led me across a lawn covered with snow and there, in the foothills of the white Alborz mountains that were quite close behind it, set in trees, was the flat-roofed White Palace with a five-columned open terrace on the ground floor and matching balcony above.

"This was the Shah's summer palace," Farhad said. "He stayed here three months every year. Here he met J. F. Kennedy, Nixon and Elizabeth II." There were two huge sculptured bronze boots outside, and I asked what they were. "They're a symbol of power," Farhad said. But there is another view, that they belonged to a huge statue of Reza Shah that was cut down after the Khomeini revolution.

We went up a couple of dozen steps at the side to the large entrance hall of grey walls, marble columns, chandeliers and marble floors from which a grand staircase led upstairs. "The tone is French," Farhad said, "luxurious. The Persian carpets in every room are of the highest quality." There were reception areas in each corner of the large entrance hall, so that eight people could sit in comfort and confer in each quarter.

The rooms were roped off, and we looked in at each and Farhad told me what each was called. There was a waiting hall with carpets suggesting the eyes on a peacock's tail and six heavy curtains tied back, before which were two long sofas and many comfortable chairs lit by a chandelier. "The furniture by the wall is French," Farhad said. Then there was a dining-room with a long table formally laid for 16 on another peacock-eye Persian carpet, long curtains closed, Czech chandelier lit. "The ceramics are from East Germany, the carpets are to the size of the room, they fit exactly. See the tusks by the wall." We looked into the Shah's office of green gilded chairs, settees, and walls, and a gilded vase and horseman. The Persian carpet was wall-to-wall.

We went up the marble servants' staircase – the main staircase from the entrance hall was roped off – and looked in at a first-floor reception room, the Queen's bedroom with draped silk behind the bed; a first-floor dining-room with round tables (less formal than the one downstairs) and long curtains tied back to reveal the windows; and then a magnificent reception area in gold with columns and a marble floor. "You see the waves in the marble?" Farhad said. "Each square block is different, but they have matched the waves to give the effect of long wavy lines, flowing marble. It is very difficult to find enough wavy lines in the quarry to achieve this effect."

We passed to the main reception area with green walls, gold curtains, gilded ceiling and doors and three chandeliers. There were three elegant settees. "They're Louis XVI," Farhad said. "Very expensive. That middle one, I am sure, is where the last Shah met Kermit Roosevelt of the CIA at midnight in 1953 and agreed to overthrow his Prime Minister, Mohammad Mossadeq. There is too much of a foreign influence in this room. It's like Versailles. I think that is the reason for the revolution. The people wanted the Head of State to be more Iranian, less French."

We looked in on a small private sitting-room with leaf motifs on curtains and chairs. "Look at that translucent screen at the end," Farhad said. "You can see curtains through it." Through a door we could see the top of a staircase. "Look at the Shah's staircase. It was gilded, too luxurious, and the people had rough roads." We looked in at a small private sitting-room. "Look at the sofa. It is a Marie-Antoinette. All the *décor* is of the 1950s and 1960s. The telephone on the small table is 1960s. This was the Shah's Day Room." We passed a window with a view of the snowy grounds and bare trees. We looked in on a billiards room, and then we were back down in the entrance hall with its columns and marble floor that reflected the chandeliers and looked like the foyer of a hotel.

In a corner we found some equipment. "Look typewriters from the 1960s. And this is the telephone exchange from the 1950s. Look, here are the Shah's telephone numbers. Look, all these foreign entries on cards and the telephone numbers to reach each city beside each."

We emerged from the White Palace and Farhad drew my attention to the brass handle on the white front door. "Look at the handle. It has a crown and rosette in the style of the Achaemenian period, put here by the last Shah's father, Reza Shah. And look, it's also on the brass below the handle: a crown above the lock." As we came away Farhad said, "The Shah was close to Israel. In the 1973 Asian Games Iran and Israel both took part. That closeness to Israel was another cause of the Revolution."

We walked back across the snow-covered grass to the bookshop by the gate, and I bought some books in English and paid for them in dollars. Then we went in search of our driver, and Farhad said, "It would be good for you to contrast the Shah's palace with where

Ayatollah Khomeini lived in Tehran. It closes at 4.30, and it's not far from here, in Jamaran village. I will ask the driver if he will go. We may just see it from the outside."

And so we set off for nearby Jamaran.

*

"When he returned," Farhad said, "Ayatollah Khomeini lived in Qom. In the early months he ruled from there. But in 1980 his advisers said, "No, you must rule from Tehran." So he kept on the house we visited in Qom, but looked for a place in Tehran. He said, 'I don't want to own, I want to rent.' And he rented this house we are going to in a poor district. He wanted to live humbly among the poor. Hundreds came to him here. He lived like Gandhi."

We left our car by a small lane between low shops in the foothills of the Alborz mountains, which were streaked with snow. We walked down a road between small houses with mud-walls and then up past a very old plane-tree and a sentry-box until we came to an enclosed slope with shuttered shops that looked like a closed market. (It was a Friday.) Here there was another sentry-box manned by several armed revolutionary guards whose uniforms suggested they were soldiers.

We were searched by the main revolutionary guard, who looked at me with some astonishment when I appeared. I raised my hands and he patted my sides and my legs, and did the same to Farhad, and waved us through. We climbed the slope beside gushing water down a runnel in the middle. At the top of the slope there was a gate under a Persian inscription beside a modern flat-roofed two-storey house next to a three-storey house, both of which were screened by high barriers with closed doors. We came out in a small paved courtyard with a raised, railed walkway that ran from a waist-high terrace by a room with four long windows, two of which were doors, to a grey door into a concrete wall on our left.

Farhad said, "After 1980 Ayatollah Khomeini lived in that room behind those windows, and he walked along this walkway through that grey door straight onto the high-up platform of the *Husaynieh* in there, which he used as his media centre."

We went through a gap in the walkway that had been made for visitors and went up some steps and looked through the four windows at Khomeini's room. "See," Farhad said, "that settee with the white covering. There are so many photos of him sitting on that white covering. This was his living-room. Look how small it is. The settee takes up more than half of the width, there was a carpet in the middle and nothing up the other end, just that framed picture of him now propped on the floor there. All his possessions are round the settee. See, there's a thin table behind the settee with a mirror on it, three books, another book and two more, and three more on that shelf, ten in all: the *Koran* and similar books. See, his slippers are on the carpet by a small footstool. See his furled umbrella propped up on the shelf.

"There's nothing on the small table beside the settee except for a picture of his son Ahmad. There's another one of Ahmad on the wall the other side, cradling Ayatollah Khomeini's head after he died. He had two sons, both *mullah*s, and a daughter who was a university professor of philosophy. Both sons were killed in mysterious circumstances. The first one, Mustafa, was a genius who was martyred – murdered – just before the Revolution. The *mujaheddin* supported Khomeini before the Revolution, but as the revolution began to happen they felt pushed aside. "*Mujaheddin* means 'those who are fighting for God', the revolutionaries. They realised Khomeini was all-powerful and that they had little power. They were supported by the US against Russia in Afghanistan, and the US was behind their terrorist acts. Mustafa Khomeini was killed, some say by the *mujaheddin* in mysterious circumstances. We are not sure who was behind it, but many can guess. According to some books, SAVAK the Shah's secret police, may have been behind the attack. Both the *mujaheddin* and SAVAK had America behind them.

"Here he met Gorbachev before 1989 and told him Communism would collapse. Hundreds would come here to greet him. He would raise his hand, which meant 'I respect you'. Ten million came to his funeral. Here he lived very simply, with no possessions, like Gandhi, in less than one room. All his possessions could be put in a small box and carried under one arm. It was the opposite of the Shah's French luxury. Look at the simple spotlight there and think of the Shah's opulent chandeliers. This is Iranian simplicity, among the poor."

I could not help but admire the man's austerity. I stood and gazed through the glass at the man's scorn of possessions. He had learned the entire *Koran* by the time he was seven. He was as austere as the *dervish* who had hung around the tomb of Hafez –

who in the 14th century had also learned the *Koran* by heart. His devoutness and spiritual strength came with inflexibility. Here he decided to impose a *fatwa* on an infidel author, Rushdie, on Valentine's Day in 1989, shortly before he died. Here he sent a generation of young men to become martyrs in the Iran-Iraq war, and be on posters by roads.

I had read that the son of Haeri, who founded his theological school at Qom, came to plead for these young men – "It

Khomeini sitting under the apple tree at Neauphle-le-Château, Paris; picture in the Khomeini museum.

is not right for Muslims to kill Muslims, hundreds of thousands are dying in a war that has no end and no good purpose" – and Khomeini had replied reproachfully, without looking at him, "Do you also criticise God when he sends an earthquake?" Shocked that Khomeini had compared himself to God, Haeri left and never spoke to him again.

Khomeini had set a standard in inflexibility, I thought, and the inflexibility of the present leadership on the nuclear issue was in the tradition of Khomeini's inflexibility, which derived its unchallengeability from the simplicity of this living-room.

"Now, we are going into the *Husaynieh*. Ayatollah Khomeini only had to walk – at the end of his life, shuffle – ten yards from the settee, along the walkway, through the grey door. We're going round, we'll go in by another entrance."

*

We left the compound, returned down the slope and turned right through a door. I found myself in a building that felt like a gym that was about to close. No one else was there. There were functional green columns that supported a green-railed first floor round the edge of the *Husaynieh*, and on a raised platform with green backing over head-high to anyone standing on the strips of matting-like carpet below, was a chair draped in a white cover before a microphone.

"That's where Khomeini sat," Farhad said. "The grey door we saw is that green door on this side. So he walked three more paces and sat on the chair to speak. You see this jutting-out platform opposite where he sat? That is for television cameras. This was his media centre.

"Here he said, 'America is nothing, has no power.' 'If the hundred million Arabs unite America cannot do anything.' People would gather here before he appeared, men downstairs, ladies upstairs. They chanted, 'We support you Khomeini,' and 'Ruhallah' ('spirit of God', his first name), you are my spirit, you are my spirit, Khomeini.' The air-force officers met him here immediately after the Revolution. The army had not submitted. The air-force officers joined the Revolution."

I stood and surveyed the scene. The humble *Ayatollah* who lived so simply was raised above his followers in this *Husaynieh* and, drawing on the setting of the passion plays at *Moharram*, spoke sternly out to implement his policies that were – staunchly, inflexibly – pro-Palestine, anti-Israel, anti-American, pro-Islam, anti-Shah (who was pro-Western) and anti-luxury.

We went next door to the Khomeini museum, which the curator opened specially for me and which we had to ourselves. It was a basement room with two rows of glass cases filled with photos. There was the house of his birth in Khomein, a flat-roofed white bungalow with a garden full of colourful flowers. There was Khomeini as a young student and then as a young man with an intense look, suggesting a Russian Nihilist. There was Khomeini making his speech at Qom in 1963. There was Khomeini in Najaf and sitting cross-legged under an apple tree with his followers in exile in the Paris surburb. There was Khomeini during the Iran-Iraq war.

Farhad said, "His followers said to him, 'You must go to a safe place,' and he said, 'Is my blood redder than other people's?' Saddam sent missiles on Tehran in the Iran-Iraq war. Saddam was supported by all countries – the Russians gave him missiles, the Americans gave him fighter planes, the British him gave him tanks. The Germans gave him chemical weapons."

Here was the boy, the exile, the return. And finally in a glass by themselves there were postage stamps bearing the face of Khomeini, his first passport open at the page bearing his photo, and his spectacles.

The curator wanted to close the museum.

"Very interesting," I said. "Is there a book in English?"

And the curator went off and returned with a book of Khomeini's speeches on Palestine.

I flipped through it. There were four sections: 'The Nature of Israel'; 'The Relationship Between Iran and Israel and the Shah's Regime'; 'The *Imam* and the Islamic Revolution, Bastions of the Resistance to Israel'; and 'The Enemies' Efforts to Prevent the Islamic Republic of Iran from Leading the Struggle'. I found the speech about America being unable to do anything if the Arabs unite.

"How much is this?" I asked.

Farhad translated the curator's reply: "No, it is my gift to you."

I thanked him, and he smiled at me, a Khomeini loyalist and supporter, and I was aware again of the immense Iranian kindness to foreigners.

*

I came away with Khomeini's challenge to the Shah clear in my mind. At its origin was Palestine being occupied by Israel, following the British Foreign Secretary Lord Balfour's 1917 letter to Lord Rothschild promising a state of Israel, which was implemented after the Second World War. The Shah supported Israel, according to Khomeini. Khomeini was expelled by the Shah and exiled for life, and then the Shah was expelled and exiled for life. Khomeini allowed the students to hold the US hostages for 444 days. Ahmadinejad had been "recognised" as one of the students' leaders, and he had threatened to wipe Israel off the map.

Meanwhile bin Laden had wanted to do to the House of Saud what Khomeini had done to the Shah, and had attacked the House of Saud's ally, the US, on 9/11. If the US had been tipped off by Israel, the US let it happen. The attack on the US had served as a

Pearl-Harbour outrage to rally America behind invasions – and oil-seizing – in Afghanistan, Iraq and soon Iran, when Ahmadinejad would be punished for holding the hostages. The successors of Khomeini, the Shiite who had no time for *Imam*s, and bin Laden, the Sunni, had made common cause, and for all I knew bin Laden had been sheltered by Tehran and had brought al-Qaeda with him. For all I knew bin Laden was in Iran now, although press reports confidently placed him in north Waziristan, on the Pakistan-Afghanistan border.

Khomeini's Revolution had been based on the *Koran* just as bin Laden's revolution against the House of Saud would be, if it happened. Khomeini felt all Muslims should give their wealth to the poor, and he had lived among the poor without possessions. Ahmadinejad had come from a modest house in east Tehran, and had an outlook similar to Khomeini's. It all came down to pro-Israelis and pro-Americans on the one hand, and anti-Israelis and anti-Americans on the other hand, and the countries of the world fell into two groups. Khomeini had said "America is nothing." It was all so clear. I understood the War on Terror with a new clarity following my visit to Khomeini's living-room in Qom and now Tehran.

We drove back and passed stalls selling lanterns. Farhad said, "Forty lanterns for *Moharram*. 'Forty' means 'a lot'. 'Ali Baba and the forty thieves' means 'Ali Baba and a lot of thieves' not exactly forty. So there are a lot of lanterns for *Moharram*. Ali is going back to his home town, Semman in north-east Iran, to take part in the *Moharram* procession. *Moharram* begins tomorrow."

Suddenly Farhad turned and asked me, "Can you delay your departure by a day?"

I replied, "Not really. Why?"

He said, "Today is Friday, and it's impossible for you to see anybody. But tomorrow you could see someone and take back a message."

"Who would I be seeing?" I asked.

"The Deputy Minister of Tourism."

I said, "My flight's booked and it might be difficult to get on another flight. If it were the Supreme Leader or the President, I would stay. But the Deputy Minister of Tourism isn't going to give me much of a message about the nuclear crisis. His message will be of a tourist nature. Thank you for pursuing the idea of obtaining a message, but as it's the Deputy Minister of Tourism I should decline and stick to my plan of leaving early tomorrow morning."

Farhad said, "The Minister of Tourism will be visiting London in the autumn of this year, and we can arrange for you to meet him then."

I said, "That will be too late. The bombing will have happened long before then."

He said, "There will be no bombing – they wouldn't dare. Iran is too powerful now."

*

We checked in at the Laleh Hotel in the centre of Tehran, a very modern hotel. There were several gift shops on the ground floor, including a "coffee-shop" separated from the huge foyer by a waist-high rail. Farhad said to me, "I am torn. I have been invited to a small party by two of my old schoolfriends, and I have accepted but I feel I should cancel as it is your last night."

I encouraged him to go, wondering if he had to report on me. I had read an article in a Sunday supplement about tours in Syria and Jordan where a national guide is a secret police escort and has to report on the questions he is asked. I had asked so many questions and discussed politics on so many occasions that if the same were true of Iran it would take my escort longer than an evening to cover all that I had asked and said.

He had been truly wonderful in sharing his knowledge of Iran so enthusiastically, and I had probably gone in search of old Persia more enthusiastically than his usual clients, or so he had told me. Regardless of whatever Iranian allegiance he had, which was par for the system in the Middle East, I regarded him as something of a friend.

Because it was a Friday, Farhad explained, two of the four restaurants in the Laleh were closed, but there was a very full menu in the downstairs coffee-shop. I said I had to pack for my early flight the next morning, and that would suit me fine. I was actually quite pleased to have an evening to myself to make a few purchases. I arranged to meet him and the driver at 4.50am, and ate a solitary meal watching the goings-on in the foyer at 6.30pm before a party came in at 7pm.

When I had finished I wandered round the shops. I went into a jewellers and looked at some little boxes, which, not being hand-painted, were cheaper than the ones I had bought in Isfahan. The fellow behind the counter had an interesting, creased face, grey hair and a sympathetic look, and I asked him if he had any stamps.

"Yes," he said, producing two albums, "look, this page the Shah. And Revolution too, look *Ayatollah*s."

I pored over the stamps of the Shah.

"Did you meet him?" I asked.

"Sure. Shah was a good man, he liked the people. We were one of the richest families in Iran, Shah was always in our shops and we went to the palace."

"The White Palace?"

"Once, 50 years ago, for two days. After that, another palace, the New Palace."

"Which room in the White Palace?"

"A downstairs room. The dining-room. I had to fix jewels. I was in the dining-room for two days."

"You didn't go upstairs?"

He looked at me in astonishment. How could I have asked such a thing? "No, not upstairs. Downstairs in the dining-room. Then Revolution happened."

"You suffered."

"Yes. They crazy. They put my father in prison, aged seventy-three, for three months. I said, 'I will get you out.' I went to the *mullah*s. 'How much?' 'Seventy dialysis machines to the hospital.' I paid for 70 dialysis machines and they let him out. I paid it to the hospital, I didn't give a penny to the *mullah*s. To the hospital, yes. They said, '*Koran* says you must give your riches to the poor.' So I gave to the hospital. Some of our family were killed. We suffered very bad time."

I said, "There may be a change soon, Israel may bomb the nuclear sites."

"I hope. They're crazy. Of course I want a change. We have no customers."

I bought the two stamp albums and some boxes and paid him in dollars, and as we completed the transaction two men in leather jackets came and stood near me. I thought of the Shia militiamen wearing leather jackets while they hanged Saddam Hussein. They did not say anything to the shopkeeper, and I sensed it was time to stop the conversation and I left with my purchases.

I took my purchases up to my room and then returned to go to the bookshop where I bought some books. I looked in again at the creased man's shop. He was alone. I asked him if he had a card so I could tell people to visit his shop, and he smiled and produced one and asked if he could write my name in his little book. I shook him by his hand. Then two more men in leather jackets came in, not the same as the other two, and they stood silently observing quite blatantly and again I sensed it was time to leave, and went up to my room and packed.

My meeting with the shopkeeper had put the Islamic Revolution in perspective. I could see how it had appealed to Iranians after nearly 40 years of the last Shah's extravagance and luxurious living, but it had imposed poverty on this shopkeeper by forcing him to give his riches to the State and had made war on a class of non-devout Muslims to Islamicize Iran. Like Cromwell's, Khomeini's puritanism had been detested by Royalists such as this creased fellow. The Islamic Revolution was like Cromwell's Commonwealth of Saints, the *mullah*s on the Council of 86 Experts being the saints.

In Britain, the Commonwealth had come to an end in the late 1650s and the monarchy had been restored. The Shah had a son who, I believed, was living in America. Would he too be restored one day?

12

THE PATTERN IN THE PERSIAN CARPET

On my last morning in contradictory Iran I woke at 3.45am and had an early breakfast of coffee and cake in the coffee-shop. Farhad came at 4.50am and oversaw the removal of my luggage and carpets from my room.

I discussed the tips I would be giving him and the driver. He said they should be more than I was proposing as I was the sole client; the tour company's guidelines applied to groups rather than sole clients. I paid up and added on without hesitation in a mixture of dollars and pounds as he had been excellent and had put himself out for me in so many ways, as had our driver, and as he had no clients booked for at least two months.

"How did your party go?" I asked.

"I didn't go," he said. "I went back to my family and fell asleep at 10."

Had I worn him out?

Ali came for us soon afterwards, and we drove through a dark and deserted central Tehran. As we approached Mehrabad Airport I took him Farhad into my confidence and said, "I can now reveal that I am an author."

He went very quiet. Did he already know? How could the visa authorities not have known after their search of the internet?

At the barrier I said goodbye to Ali and wished him a happy *Moharram* passion play, and Farhad said, "I am going to say goodbye Iranian-style." He kissed me three times on my cheeks. I believe he really was sorry to see me go. His last words were, "I will wait here for half an hour in case anything goes wrong." I wondered if he meant, 'In case you are taken away to a VIP lounge and have your passport confiscated.'

*

In fact, my hold luggage was confiscated. I checked in and the Iranian girl said, "You are five kilos over, you have to make payment over there. We will keep your hold luggage here." She gave me a piece of paper in Persian.

There was a long queue behind me and I could not get her to be more specific, so, taking my hand luggage I went and joined a queue "over there" and after several minutes of not advancing in the queue at all eventually showed the Iranian behind me my piece of paper.

"No," he said, "this is Cashiers, you have to go to Excess Baggage first. Come with me." And he quite unnecessarily forfeited his place in the queue and helpfully took me on a long walk round to another area of the airport which was out of sight and left me at the right window.

There, after two separate Iranians pushed in before me, both in a highly worked-up state, I was given another piece of paper and told to go back to the Cashiers queue I had come from, where, after a long wait, I paid for my excess baggage. I took evidence of my payment back to Excess Baggage and, after queuing again, received authorization to have a boarding pass.

I went back to the check-in and queued to present it to the girl who had identified my excess baggage. She nodded and gave me a boarding pass. There was no sign of my luggage. "Gone," she said, "gone through there."

I could now proceed to the departure gate. Two other flights were leaving by that same gate, one for Stockholm at exactly the same time as the London flight, 7.45am, and one to for Frankfurt about the same time. There was one queue for all three flights and no separation at the end. There were no announcements. Rumour had it that the Stockholm flight was going first so I maintained my place in the queue.

In the event, the London flight was delayed half an hour. When I finally boarded the captain of the British Airways plane said over the intercom, "I'm sorry for the late departure, but we have had issues involving paperwork which have delayed our flight." Had the Iranians been searching all the luggage, or at any rate *my* luggage, and used "paperwork" as an excuse?

The captain then announced that due to strong head winds we might not have enough fuel to reach London in a direct flight and so it had been agreed that we would be landing in Prague to refuel, and there would be a further delay of 45 minutes which he would try to cut to 25 minutes. This announcement was received with some dismay and not a little consternation among the passengers.

The plane was not full and the seat next to mine was not taken. Beyond it, in the aisle seat, was an Iranian man of about 30 in a Western suit, who took a number of sleeping-tablets, dropped the plastic wrapper in the gangway and went into a deep sleep during which he somehow managed to kick off first his shoes, then his socks. His head rolled sideways and he began to collapse onto me.

Drinks were brought and the steward picked up the sleeping-pill wrapper, tapped him on his shoulder and asked, "Is this yours?"

The Iranian forced open one eye and stared blearily, too glazed and befuddled to reply.

"Drink, sir?" the steward persisted.

The Iranian made a huge effort and forced out, "Whisky," defying the prohibition at home. And he then promptly closed his eyes and went into a coma.

Barmily the steward put a glass of whisky into his sleeping hand, which kept tilting in my direction, slopping and pouring neat whisky near my leg as he slept. I took the glass out of his hand and stood it on a flat table between us, which I had pulled down.

The steward came and put the drink back in his hand.

I explained he had taken a lot of sleeping-pills and was in no fit state to be holding a drink, which he was about to slop and spill over my hand luggage, which was near my feet on the floor.

"Shall I put your hand-luggage in the overhead rack?" the steward asked aggressively as a threat, meaning 'Put up with having neat whisky spilled over your trousers or I'll take away the source of your work.' He went off leaving the Iranian asleep, slopping the whisky now into the seat next to me.

I took the glass of whisky from his hand and this time called a stewardess and handed her the drink, explaining he was too drugged to hold it. She understood. "We'll let him sleep it off," she said, taking the whisky.

I looked at the comatose Iranian whose behaviour had literally spilled over onto his neighbours. He symbolized a state of mind I had encountered that assumed no one would dare attack Iran, and so it did not matter if Iranians sprawled and spilled over their neighbours (Iraq, Lebanon, Palestine). Looking at his comatose form, checking that he was still breathing and had not died of an overdose, I now saw him as a symbol of the excessive Thermidorian reaction and pleasure-making that would surely follow the ousting of the *mullah*s. Which was preferable: the sobriety, restraint and dignified behaviour of the teetotal, ascetically austere *mullah*s and their followers, or this abandon and binge-drinking-like loss of self-control? I had to admit, I preferred the *mullah*s' sobriety to the Iranian's embracing of the abandoned West with its tarnished image of nonentity "celebrities" staggering off the stage into rehab for their own pathetic indiscipline.

*

In the air, I looked back on contradictory Iran, and thought that the contradiction was how it superficially appeared. Zoroastrianism had contained the contradiction of dualism between light and darkness, and this had found its way into Sasanian thinking and Manichaeism. Yet the contradiction had an underlying unity like two identical motifs on one of the Persian carpets I had bought.

On the one hand was the old Persian consciousness: the Shah's pride in the 2,500-year-old tradition of kingship, the reverence for Cyrus, Darius, Xerxes and the Achaemenians whose culture had inspired Greek art and philosophy and for the Sasanians after them, the Persian pride in the epic deeds of the kings in Ferdowsi's *Shahnameh* whose exploits were shown in paintings on walls – pride in the long independence of the Iranian civilization until it was occupied by the Arabs yet still retained in its indigenous Persian culture and in the feeling that the Persians are superior to the Arabs by virtue of their aesthetic tradition.

And on the other hand was the Islamic consciousness: pride in the *Koran,* which was superimposed on the traditional Persian culture, and in the Shiite tradition of the 12 *Imam*s, in the fervour at the shrines and in the beliefs about the Hidden *Imam*, in the Sufi mystical union with God, in the Safavid devoutness and fervour which culminated in the Islamic Republic set up by Ayatollah Khomeini as a province within the Arab civilization that Persian Royalist Iranians secretly despised but which Islamic Iranians publicly adored.

These two motifs, the Persian and the Islamic, looked like contradictions but within the Persian carpet of the Iranian tradition they were woven into an underlying unity, held in balance by their background. It was possible to be *both* Persian and aware of the Iranian tradition and now defunct civilization following its passage into the Arab civilization around 1511 AD and the subordination of the Safavid kings to the Islamic tradition which they expressed in the mosques of Isfahan; *and* to be a devout Muslim and be enthusiastic about the Islamic tradition of the *Imam*s. It was not either-

or, it was dualistically both-and, and behind the dualism there was a unity.

But in the centre, holding these two apparent contradictions in balance, was the Western way of freedom and democracy imposed by bomb and gun, and of the limitation of nuclear weapons – indeed, the determination to avoid nuclear weapons falling into the hands of terrorist states. And as a reaction to the West there was nuclear defiance, support for Palestine, Lebanon and Iraqi Shias – and Iran's reputed support for a terrorist international network under which, since 1989 (the year the Berlin wall and Communism fell, and Khomeini died) 90 per cent of all terrorist acts can, it is claimed (for example in Ilan Berman's *Tehran Rising*) be laid at Iran's door. (I saw no evidence to indicate that Iran sponsors terrorism, but I was not allowed to investigate this and having been excluded from the Susa/Ahwaz region as al-Qaeda were there, I can imagine that it might be.) This anti-Western outlook was more to do with the Islamic than the Persian consciousness. The Shah, a Persian, had been very pro-West, an outlook reflected in his preference for European furniture.

I reviewed the Revolution in my mind. The Revolution had been a blend of Western and Islamic thinking. I recalled showing in my study of the Western revolutions that revolutions begin with a heretical occult inspiration which is given intellectual expression. There is then a political expression and finally a physical consolidation. In the companion volume to that work, I had stated the four stages of the Iranian Revolution:

Occult Inspiration	Marx
Intellectual Expression	Rafsanjani
Political Expression	Khomeini
Physical Consolidation	Khamenei

Marx had been the inspirer via the Marxist intellectual Ali Shariati, who had written of Shiism in Marxist terms before he died in 1977. He had translated Marxist ideas into cultural symbols that Shias could grasp, seeing Husayn as a Guevara figure. He more than anyone else had given intellectual expression to the Marxist basis of the Iranian revolution, and Shariati should have been before Rafsanjani in the second column of the above table.

The Revolution had blended Western Marxism and Islamic Shiism, and the Hidden *Imam* was perceived to have made common cause with the revolutionary overthrow of the Shah. It was this mixture of Marxism and Shiism that had turned Iran from the peaceful Islam fundamentally desired by the Hidden *Imam* to revolutionary struggle against pro-Western leaders in the Middle East and into (according to Western analysts) a terror state. It was this mixture that explained the paradox that the representative of the just and peaceful Hidden *Imam* could condone acts of terror and support the nuclear annihilation of the Israeli nation-state.

I thought of Khomeini, the Philosopher Ruler or Philosopher King, and his attempt to recreate Plato's Republic in Islamic terms with Guardians as devout as Cromwell's "Parliament of Saints".

I thought of the nobility of the concept of the Philosopher Ruler who knew transcendent truth and of the concept of the Guardians living saintly lives of austere simplicity while serving their country as expert jurists, as plain and pure as Cromwell's puritans (the Shah, unlike Charles I, escaping execution by going into exile). Yet, with revolutionary severity they meted out cruel executions and were dangerously bent on acquiring nuclear weapons covertly in order to threaten Israel and expand Shiism and the sway of the Hidden *Imam* into a Shia Crescent that would extend from the Mediterranean coast to India, an empire with the reach of mighty Alexander's.

I thought of the nobility of the world-government idea and the cruelty of the way the Syndicate (the network behind the New World Order) implemented it, sacrificing hundreds of thousands of Middle-Easterners to the acquisition of oil under the guise of spreading freedom and democracy. I thought of its support (in the tradition of the 1776 Bavarian Illuminati) for Lucifer, god of wealth and worldly power, as it went about its business of spreading its New World Order by the use of American planes and troops, bombing those who defied it even if they had noble visions of living by truth and spreading the justice of the Hidden *Imam*.

I shook my head at the contradictions on both sides: at the saintly austerity that also meant wiping Israel off the map and confronting the West with nuclear weapons; and at the spreading of Western freedom and democracy by bombing saintly *mullah*s, their cultural mourning for Husayn and their devotion to the Hidden *Imam*, in order to run an oil pipeline from the Caspian to the Gulf.

I saw that through the Revolution Iran chose the Islamic consciousness in preference to its Persian consciousness – hence the suffering of the Royalist jeweller. And now the Hidden *Imam* was the true ruler of Iran, as the President had asserted. The Supreme Leader had taken over the Jamkaran mosque and installed his own guardian there, and the President could claim that the Hidden *Imam* had told him to wipe out Israel, thus winning the support of the theocracy. And where, in this Shia revival and its archaistic imitation of an early Islamic phase embodied in its admiration for the 12 *Imam*s, was the Persian ideal? Persepolis had been cold-shouldered along with tourists, who were tolerated as necessary evils who brought in foreign currency and had to be policed and watched so that the Islamic Republic would be kept pure from corruption.

What did the future hold for Iran? The phase that all revolutions pass into when they have run their course, the Thermidorian reaction, the restoration of the ex-regime. ("Thermidorian reaction" comes from France, from the overthrow of Robespierre and the Committee of Public Safety which began on 8 Thermidor Year II – July 26 1794.) This collapse of the revolutionary outlook was inevitable – my study of revolutions had convinced me of that. The English, American, French and Russian revolutions had all ended in a reversion to their pre-existing state. In Iran, the Persian consciousness would be restored, although Iran would remain Islamic and within the Arab civilization but with less public fervour. And when the Arab civilization ended and passed into its successor civilization, Iran would pass with it. Civilizations in the last quarter of their life are conquered several times by different foreign powers, and this fate awaited the Arab civilization.

It was possible that an American or Israeli attack would accelerate a process of regime change in Iran, and that a regime with a more Persian consciousness would come to power. It was also possible that the Supreme Leader's regime would weather the international storms but find the young adopting a more Persian identity through fashion, make-up, use of the internet and reading.

Would an Islamic identity and anti-Westernism shift to a Persian identity and pro-Westernism? Would the Syndicate of world government and New World Order politicians, multinationals and billionaires succeed in changing the regime so that an oil pipeline could convey Caspian oil to the Gulf and thence by sea to India, Pakistan and China and ultimately to the Western world? Would Iran join a United States of the Middle East along with Israel, which is the New World Order's immediate goal?

Universalist historians plot similar courses of events in different civilizations and make a comparative study between civilizations, which allows for predictions. Certainly, that is what I had done. Sitting in the plane by the unconscious Iranian, I thought I could see the future of Iran. I was awake, Iran was asleep.

Looking back over my tour, I felt I had achieved my aim of

absorbing Iranian culture before the bombing began. I had not fallen ill or been ill-treated in any way and I had not given succour to a pariah state but had contested its confrontationalism at every turn while admiring its traditional culture. I had studied a civilization which began before c. 2250 BC and ended with the Safavids, who (most beautifully) imposed Arab culture on the Iranian peoples in the early 16th century and made Shiism the State religion, and which, following the Islamic Revolution, continues to be part of the Arab civilization. I had had a very compact tour, the most compact Farhad had known in ten years of touring Iran. If I had read more widely or deeply before I left England I would have insisted on seeing inside the Seljuq Friday mosque in Isfahan. I had done the research I wanted to and had got to grips with the Shia Arab culture.

*

After a long flight, and a stop in Prague of 25 minutes and circling for half an hour, we landed at Heathrow, London, and we all stood up. Half an hour later we were still standing. "Unfortunately as it's a Saturday we have had difficulty in finding a qualified driver to drive the steps," the captain announced. (A few days later British Airways were briefly on strike, and the delays I had encountered were probably a work-to-rule.)

When I had left the plane and collected my luggage, which did not look as if it had been opened, I pushed it through to Arrivals and saw my English driver, the ex-Falklands soldier, waving at me. He then said, "I've been watching the Iranians coming through from your flight. They've been heading for the cars with diplomatic number-plates where I'm parked." He said, "I've been watching television expecting to see you paraded like Ken Bigley. After I dropped you off I went back and put your name into my computer and it came up so many times as author. You said they were doing a search on you to give you a visa. If I could find it so easily, they certainly would have found it. There's no way they could not have known you're an author. Thirty-eight weapons inspectors have been refused visas. They gave you a visa because they were happy for you to go in."

Was he right? Who knows – probably not even Farhad. I rang my wife on his phone and an hour later she was standing beaming at our front door. "It sounds as though you achieved all you set out to do," she said after I had greeted her warmly.

"Yes," I said. "I've understood Iran. I've got a balanced view of it all. I did the literary research I had in mind. I can write my long poem about the Islamic world now."

"Look," she said as I sat down to a light omelette she had made, "three goldfinches on the niger seed."

And the little life of England had taken over and I was looking at goldfinches with red heads and gold wings, and the Persian, Islamic and Western consciousnesses receded and seemed a long way away. Then I unrolled the Persian carpets on the floor for her to approve, and as she enthused they were back, in balance, two motifs held in place by a third and neither dominating over the other. A dualism within a unity.

*

I wrote this account quickly in 25 days (from January 23 to February 16) to get my memories out of my head and on paper before they faded. I learned on the day of my return that America had begun to ratchet up its threats against Iran while I was touring there, and that the tour operator had become so alarmed that she rang Tehran to seek an assurance that I was safe.

While I wrote an American armada built up outside the straits of Hormuz, and the Americans ratcheted up the nuclear issue into a crisis, accusing Iran of supplying arms to Shia militias in Iraq and therefore of causing the carnage in Baghdad. There were daily car bombs and death tolls of approaching 100, sometimes more, and the great majority of the explosions were in Shia areas, suggesting Sunni involvement, perhaps in response to the hanging of Saddam Hussein by Shia militias. (Saddam had been in Iraqi custody for less than an hour before his execution, which meant he was unable to reveal the full extent of how he had been supported by the CIA and armed by the West throughout the 1980s.)

On February 21 the 60 days of diplomacy announced by the UN expired. Iran failed to respond to the deadline it had been set to stop enriching uranium. It was clear that Israel would not tolerate Iran's developing a nuclear weapon and was not prepared to risk delaying decisive action in case Iran suddenly announced it had tested a nuclear bomb. Articles appeared in the Western press claiming that the Council on Foreign Relations (CFR) wanted to extend the war to Iran, and that the decision had been taken. It was predicted that there would be a new terrorist attack in the style of Pearl Harbour and 9/11, perhaps on an American battleship, which would be blamed on Iran and trigger an American response.

It was announced that the Americans were setting up a defence system against rogue states, particularly Iran: specific countries including Britain, Poland and Czechoslovakia would permit a silo of 10 anti-ballistic missiles to be installed at their American bases as an insurance policy, and these would be fired to intercept long-range weapons from the Middle East, particularly Iran. The first silo to be installed in Europe would be in use in Poland by 2012 and would knock out North Korean or Iranian missiles in mid-course, as they entered space. Missiles travel more slowly during their ascent than when they emerge from space and descend on their target at eight miles per second.

It was then announced that Iran had successfully launched its first rocket into space, raising the spectre of Iranian inter-continental ballistic missiles tipped with nuclear bombs being fired into space and diving down at the United States and Britain at eight miles per second. This news was accompanied by a statement that Iran would not retreat on its nuclear plans and did not believe that America was in a position to attack Iran.

Was the Supreme Leader aware that the network of multinational oil companies and political internationalists known collectively as the Syndicate planned to install a pipeline across Iran to carry Caspian oil to tankers in the Gulf, and that this commercial ambition would require a regime more stable than Ahmadinejad's? Was he aware that the Council on Foreign Relations would find a pretext for wiping out Iran's nuclear bunkers which had been dispersed under ground and in more than 20 sites to avoid a repetition of Israel's bombing of Iraq's Osirak nuclear reactor in 1981? Had Iran miscalculated?

The Syrian President visited Tehran for talks, and Moqtada al-Sadr, Iraq's Shia militia leader, coincidentally "fled" to Iran for a few days, presumably to attend a summit meeting. This raised the prospect that if Iran was attacked, Iran and Syria would invade Iraq, having co-ordinated a plan with al-Sadr. Ahmadinejad visited King Abdullah of Saudi Arabia, his major Sunni rival now that Saddam was no longer alive.

Following North Korea's agreement to give up nuclear weapons in return for cash, which she had brokered, Condoleezza Rice, the US Secretary of State, was given free rein to conduct a new round of diplomacy in accordance with the wishes of the US Iraq Study Group and the now dominant Democrats, and for a while diplomacy seemed to be triumphing over belligerency throughout the Middle East. Or was it a form of deception, lulling Iran into a false sense of security to restore an element of surprise to a coming attack?

There were reports that US special forces were inside Iran, identifying and preparing targets for an attack. America, Israel and Iran all looked ready for war, and there were fears that Iran's intransigence would lead to a Middle-Eastern arms race. At the same time articles appeared suggesting that an attack on Iran would trigger a Third World War. An article in the British newspaper, *The Guardian,* contained a warning by the British Museum that raids on the Iranian nuclear sites would damage the mosques of Isfahan and Natanz and the ruins of Persepolis and Pasargadae, which would all suffer the same way as Iraq, where the US troops turned Babylon into a military base.

On March 23 the commander of the British Forces in Basra city told his troops that Iran had armed Shia militias in Iraq with sophisticated new weapons and was paying fighters in Iraq $500 (£275) per month to attack British forces. He said that 90 per cent of all attacks on British forces in Iraq stemmed from Iran.

The same day Iran captured eight British sailors and seven Marines in what the British claimed were Iraqi waters on the Shatt al-Arab, took them to Tehran for questioning and held them hostage. It was swiftly announced by Iran's Gen. Afshar that the 15 Britons had "confessed" to knowing they were inside Iranian waters, and a website run by associates of President Ahmadinejad referred to them as "insurgents" and "spies" and said they would be charged with espionage – for which the penalty in Iran is death. It was reported that the Supreme Leader Khamenei had personally approved the plan to abduct the Britons, and that they were to be held against five Iranians seized by the Americans in Iraq. It was revealed that the CIA had warned the British in January – the month of my visit – that Iran might abduct hostages to be held against the five Americans.

In this confused and confusing atmosphere, the next day the UN

Security Council voted unanimously, 15-0, to impose further sanctions on Iran (a ban on arms exports and a freeze of nuclear industry assets) with the prospect of more sanctions to follow if Iran did not suspend uranium enrichment within 60 days. The Iranian Foreign Minister, speaking at the UN in place of President Ahmadinejad who had planned to speak but did not appear because he had not been granted a visa, issued a defiant response.

Britain banned bilateral business contacts with Iran. Both sides publicised technical information, Britain demonstrating that GPS (Global Positioning System) co-ordinates proved the sailors and Marines were in Iraqi waters, Iran demonstrating that GPS co-ordinates proved they were in Iranian waters. Iran paraded the hostages on TV and publicised letters from the only female hostage "admitting" to straying into Iranian waters and urging Britain to withdraw from Iraq. The UN Security Council urged Iran to release the hostages in a watered-down resolution that was not as strong as the UK hoped, bearing in mind that the sailors and Marines were doing UN business in Iraqi waters under a UN resolution. The operation to capture the hostages now looked premeditated.

The situation of the hostages seemed to get worse. All the 15 Britons were reported as admitting to be in Iranian waters in statements that appeared to be written in Iranian English. Two hundred bearded Iranian "students" close to the President demonstrated violently outside the British Embassy, which they pelted with rocks and exploding fireworks, chanted "Death to the British" and called for the execution of the hostages. One placard said, "15 British agressors (*sic*) must be executed." They called for the British Embassy to be closed, for the Ambassador to be deported, for diplomatic ties to be severed and for the 15 Britons to be put on trial.

Following Foreign Office diplomacy – being quiet but firm, making no concessions or admissions of guilt and no deals, making a veiled threat and calmly persuading Arab countries within the region to bring pressure to bear on Iran – the Supreme Leader seems to have reined back Ahmadinejad and ordered him to release the hostages. At a press conference Ahmadinejad criticised the injustice of the world order and Britain's role in Iraq, decorated the naval commander of the unit that arrested the Britons and, in an act of political theatre, announced that the 15 Britons would be immediately freed without any punishment as a "gift to Britain on the birthday of the Prophet" and on the "passing of Christ."

The announcement shocked Iranian hardliners and stunned and delighted the West. The 15 Britons, watching the press conference on TV in captivity in the room next door, shouted with joy. They were later filmed wearing suits rather than uniform and individually thanking the President. Many British people were shocked at the spectacle of young sailors and Marines cravenly co-operating with their captors. The next day they were released to the British Embassy.

To many it seemed that Iran had pulled off a media masterstroke. By capturing the 15 Britons, ratcheting up the tension and then releasing them within a fortnight they had replaced the negative image of Iran with the image of Iran as kind, generous and compassionate, of "good guys" hard-done-by in the nuclear crisis, wanting nuclear energy and not nuclear bombs and ready to come in from the cold to avoid being bombed by the US and Israel. At the same time the Iranian action said to the Arab world, "Look how powerful we are, we can do this to one of the two members of the Coalition in Iraq, take them out of uniform and send them home in new civilian suits and shoes. We can humiliate the UK and get away with it." Iran had sent out a message to the West: "Iran can be reasonable and does not want a war with the West. You can trust us to have nuclear bombs and we will treat the world as responsibly and kindly as we have treated these hostages. Don't attack our nuclear program. We respond to negotiation. Stand down your aircraft and return to diplomacy. At the same time, do not search ships for arms in the Shatt al-Arab."

Just before the 15 Britons landed in London, four British servicemen and women were killed by a sophisticated EFP (Explosively Formed Projectile). The roadside bomb with a shaped charge had been detonated by remote control and penetrated the armour of their Warrior. Prime Minister Blair made a statement. He pointed out that elements of the Iranian regime were actively arming Iraqi insurgents with weapons, including sophisticated road bombs, and financing terrorism against British troops, who were in Iraq at the request of the democratically elected Iraqi government. He said that although there were now new channels of communication with Iran, which would be pursued, the world would have to oppose its support for terrorism and restrict its nuclear programme to civilian use.

The day after their return, six of the captured Britons gave a press conference at which they repeated they had been seized 1.7 miles within Iraqi waters. They had been taken to a detention centre, blindfolded and had their hands bound. They were lined up against a wall and heard weapons being cocked, and some feared they would be executed. They were held in solitary confinement and suffered random interrogations at night, depriving them of sleep. They were told that if they admitted to being in Iranian waters, they would be home within three days, but if they did not admit this they would be in prison for several years. Their "confessions" had been edited to convey the story the Iranians wanted to convey, presumably to distract attention from the intensification of UN sanctions.

The British Navy called off searches of ships in the Shatt al-Arab while they conducted an investigation. Iran formally requested that Britain should return Iran's "gift" by urging the US to release the five Iranian detainees. It now seemed that the British sailors and Marines had been captured "to order" to stop the searches of arms-bearing ships heading for Iraq and to secure the release of Iranian detainees. When Britain, outraged at the treatment of the hostages, did not respond Iran warned that there might be more kidnappings. There was a fear that tourists might be kidnapped.

Despite the UN Security Council's new 60-day deadline for Iran to suspend uranium enrichment and begin negotiations, on 9 April Ahmadinejad announced that Iran now had 3,000 centrifuges at Natanz and was therefore capable of enriching uranium at an industrial level of production. The millions of Iranian citizens who owned mobiles received texted messages of congratulation from the regime, suggesting that an event of great significance had taken place. The development of an Iranian nuclear bomb might now be unstoppable.

The White House was very concerned. A spokesman said that Iran must begin negotiating before the end of the current 60-day period. There was now considerable feeling in the region that Iran was too unpredictable to be trusted with nuclear weapons, one day calling for the hostages to be executed, the next day releasing them – and that Iran's propaganda stunt had backfired. Would Iran comply with the UN? If not, what would the American response be?

At the same time the American General in charge of US troops in Baghdad announced on television that he had found in a house in north Baghdad sophisticated shaped armour-penetrating roadside bombs (EFPs), rockets and mortars which had clearly been made in Iran. He said that Iranians had trained Iraqi Shias in how to use them as recently as the previous month (March). There was now Western acceptance that a proxy war was taking place between Iran and its Shia proxies in Iraq on the one hand, and the

US, aided by Britain, and its proxies in Iraq on the other hand.

Meanwhile, in March, fares in Iran, including those of shared taxis, rose by 50 per cent. It was announced that on May 21 petrol rationing would be introduced. Regime-subsidised petrol would rise by 20 per cent, and only 3 litres per day would be available at the subsidised price. Ration cards would be issued, and any purchase of petrol over that limit would be at a non-subsidised rate.

Drivers were soon rationed to 5 gallons of petrol a week. Riots broke out and at least 12, some reports said 20, petrol stations were set on fire. The cost of driving round Iran, as I had just done, had gone up and would involve grappling with ration cards.

With dilapidated refineries despite having the second-largest oil reserves in the world, Iran imported 40-50 per cent of its petrol for domestic consumption, and its large budget deficit was caused by generous fuel subsidies. Iran needed £6 billion of foreign investment to become self-sufficient in petrol by upgrading refineries and another £46 billion to produce its full potential of oil – at a time when its policies were alienating the West and triggering UN sanctions.

In May the British Ministry of Defence warned that Iran was supplying weapons to insurgents fighting Western forces in Afghanistan as well as in Iraq. Vice-President Dick Cheney visited the aircraft carrier USS John C Stennis and told the crew: "With two carrier strike groups in the Gulf, we're sending clear messages to friends and adversaries alike. We'll stand with others to prevent Iran from gaining nuclear weapons and dominating the region." Iran immediately offered talks with the US in Iraq.

On May 28 the US Ambassador to Iraq met an Iranian envoy in Baghdad for four hours in the presence of the Iraqi Prime Minister, to discuss Iraq. The Iranian envoy described the meeting as "shaking hands with the Devil".

The US Ambassador laid on the table a sample of Iranian-made explosives seized on their way to Iraq. He demanded that Iran should stop sending projectile bombs to Iraq.

Iran denied doing this and said that the US was using Iraq as a base from which to send spying missions into Iran. Iran proposed a trilateral commission on Iraqi security, comprising the US, Iran and Iraq.

The US Ambassador said that on paper the two sides had similar aims on Iraq, but that Iran must deliver in practice what it says in principle – and stop sending projectile bombs to militias to destabilise Iraq. He said there would be a further meeting within weeks, by when it would be possible to say whether the flow of projectile bombs had stopped. The success of the May 28 meeting would be measured in terms of the cessation of EFPs.

The same day a pro-Iranian Shiite group of 40 disguised as police with correct documentation kidnapped five Britons in Baghdad, and in Tehran a number of Iranian Americans were seized and imprisoned as spies.

All the indications were that Bush Jr was trying what the Democrats and Iraq Study Group had advocated, without too much hope that anything would actually change. Diplomacy had to be exhausted before there was conflict.

Such a view seemed to be confirmed when the Bilderberg Group (whose resolutions tend to be implemented in the coming year) resolved at their annual meeting in Istanbul in early June that they were troubled by Iran's ambitions but more concerned about its oil, and that any US military action must be limited to strategic air strikes with no attacks by land (or "boots on the ground").

The summer saw a wave of public executions and floggings conducted by hooded policemen in Iran, many shown live on Iranian television. The punishments, part of the government's "Plan to Enforce Moral Behaviour", came from the same thinking that immediately succeeded the 1979 Revolution. A young man received 80 lashes on his bare back for abusing alcohol (like my neighbour on the return flight). This brutal purge was aimed at intimidating the regime's opponents. It had been reported that a third of Iran's petrol stations had now been destroyed by protesters against fuel rationing. In mid-August the White House classified the 125,000 Revolutionary Guards (some of whom had amassed secret fortunes) as a "terrorist organisation". In a speech President Ahmadinejad vowed to fill a "power vaccum" in Iraq. President Bush, believing Iran was already fighting a "proxy war" against the US in Iraq, accused Tehran of putting the Middle East "under the shadow of a nuclear holocaust" and thundered, "We will confront the danger of Iran before it is too late."

In early September it was widely reported that the Pentagon had drawn up a plan for massive airstrikes by B2 bombers and cruise missiles against 1,200 targets in Iran. It would annihilate Iranian military capability within three days, and B61-11 bunker-busting tactical nuclear weapons would disable heavily fortified installations such as Natanz. Was the plan a bluff to force Iran to abandon its nuclear programme? Supreme Leader Ayatollah Khamenei retaliated by appointing as new head of the Revolutionary Guards an anti-US hardliner who had criticised the release of the British hostages and taken part in clandestine operations in Iraq. The hardliner had already announced that 50,000 volunteers were being trained in Iran for "martyrdom-seeking operations", and he now said that if America attacked Iran "we will set fire to its interests all over the world".

A further report stated that Bush was placing America on a path to war with Iran, and that the Pentagon had a list of 2,000 bombing targets in Iran to ensure that Iran was not capable of developing a nuclear weapon. A senior commander of the Revolutionary Guard replied by saying that Iran's Shahab-3 rockets had a range of 1,250 miles and could strike an array of US targets across the Middle

East, including US bases in Iraq, if Iran were attacked. A Persian-language website asserted that Iran had 600 Shahab-3 missiles, which it would launch at Israel, including its nuclear reactor in the south, on the day Iran or Syria was attacked.

Iran was now a country in crisis, threatened from without and defiantly confrontational from within. The world had moved on, things had changed and I could not have embarked on my tour now. A few months had, indeed, made a tremendous difference. It now seemed that I had, indeed, been the last tourist in Iran before the bombing began.

But nations are resilient, and even in the darkest hours a seemingly unrelated news item can reveal an attitude that, when read between the lines, offers a glimmer of hope. In the second week of June the American plan to site a missile defence shield in Poland and Czechoslovakia had been opposed by Russia. America reiterated that the shield was to intercept missiles from North Korea and Iran, not Russia, and offered Russia the chance to share in it. At the G8 meeting the Russian president proposed that if it was designed to shield from Iran it should be sited in Azerbaijan. The assumption behind the joint proposal was that despite all the American talk of attacking Iran, in the American view Iran would become a nuclear power with nuclear missiles – hence the joint missile defence shield.

It looked as if there might be light at the end of the tunnel. Having toured Iran under the storm clouds of an imminent American-Israeli attack on the Natanz enrichment site and elsewhere, when it seemed possible that I would be the last tourist in Iran before the bombing began, there was now a hope that the prevailing mood of foreboding might be lifting and that a new generation of tourists would be able to tread in my footsteps and savour the splendours that I had found so thrilling.

APPENDIX

IRANIAN DYNASTIES

I. 2,500 YEARS OF KINGSHIP
539 BC – AD 1971

(Dates indicate period of reign, not life)

A. Within Iranian Civilization

1. Pre-Islamic Persia

Achaemenians
(See family tree in Appendix II)

Cyrus II the Great (Kurosh)	559-529 BC
Cambyses II (Kambujiyeh)	529-522 BC
Bardia (Smerdis)	522-522 BC
Darius the Great (Dariush)	522-486 BC
Xerxes I (Khashayarsha)	486-465 BC
Artaxerxes I (Ardashir)	465-424 BC
Xerxes II (Khashayarsha II)	424-423 BC
Darius II (Dariush II)	423-404 BC
Artaxerxes II (Ardashir II)	404-359 BC
Cyrus the Younger (Kurosh)	401-401 BC
Artaxerxes III (Ardashir III)	359-338 BC
Arses	338-336 BC
Darius III (Dariush III)	336-330 BC
Alexander's occupation	
Alexander (Eskandar)	334-330 BC

Seleucids

Seleucus I (Nicator)	312-281 BC
Antiochus I (Soter)	281-261 BC
Antiochus II (Theos)	261-246 BC
Seleucus II (Callinicus)	246-226 BC
Seleucus III (Sotor) Antiochus III (the Great)	226-223 BC
Antiochus III (the Great)	223-187 BC
Seleucus IV (Philopator)	187-175 BC
Antiochus IV (Epiphanes)	175-163 BC
Antiochus V (Eupator)	163-162 BC
Demetrius I (Soter)	162-150 BC
Alexander I (Balas)	150-145 BC
Antiochus VI (Epiphanes)	145-142 BC
Demitrius II (Nicator)	142-138 BC
Tryphon (Usurper)	142-138 BC
Antiochus VII (Sidetes)	139-129 BC

Parthian domination

Parthians

Arsaces (Arashk)	247-211 BC
Tiridates I (Tirdad)	?-211 BC
Artabanus I (Arsaces II)	211-191 BC
Priapatius	191-176 BC
Phraates I (Farhad I)	176-171 BC
Mithradates (Mehrdad)	171-138 BC
Phraates II (Farhad II)	138-128 BC
Artabanus II (Ardavan II)	128-123 BC
Mithradates II (Mehrdad II)	123-87 BC
Gotarzes (Gudarz)	90-80 BC
Orodes (Orod)	80-77 BC
Sinartukes	77-70 BC
Phraates III (Farhad III)	70-57 BC

Mithradates III (Mehrdad III)	57-54 BC
Orodes II (Orod II)	57-38 BC
Phraates IV (Farhad IV)	38-2 BC
Tiridates II (pretender to the throne)	30-25 BC
Phraates V (Farhad V)	2 BC-4 AD
Orodes III (Orod III)	4-7
Vonones I (Vonon I)	7-12
Artabanus III (Ardavan III)	12-38
Gotarzes II (Gudarz II)	38-51
Vardanes I	39-45
Vonones II (Vonon II)	51-51
Vologeses I	51-78
Vardanes II	55-58
Vologeses II	77-80
Artabanus IV (Ardavan IV)	80-81
Pacorus I	78-105
Vologeses III	105-147
Osroes	109-129
Mithradates IV (Mehrdad IV)	129-147
Vologeses IV	147-191
Vologeses V	191-208
Vologeses VI	208-222
Artabanus V (Ardavan V)	213-224

Sasanian conquest

Sasanians

Ardashir I	224-240
Shapur I	240-272
Hormizd I	272-273
Bahram I	273-276
Bahram II	276-293
Bahram III	293-293

Narseh	293-302
Hormizd II	302-309
Shapur II	309-379
Ardashir II	379-383
Shapur III	383-388
Bahram IV	388-399
Yazdgerd I	399-421
Bahram V	421-439
Yazdgerd II	439-457
Hormizd III	457-459
Piruz	459-484
Balash	484-488
Kavad I, first reign	488-496
Zamasp	496-498
Kavad I, second reign	498-531
Khosrow Anushirvan	531-579
Hormizd IV	579-590
Bahram Chubin	590-591
Khosrow II (Khosrow Parvis)	591-628
Kavad II	628-628
Ardashir III	628-630
Boran (Daughter of Khosrow Parviz)	630-631
Azarmedukht (Sister)	631-632
Khosrow III	630-632
Yazdgerd III	632-651

Muslim conquest

2. Islamic
(See Early Islamic Leaders in Appendix III)

Umayyads of Syria
Muawiya I Ibn Abu Sifyan	661-680

Yazid I Ibn Muawiya	680-683
Muawiya II Ibn Yazid	683-684
Marwan Ibn al-Hakam	684-684
Abdul Malik Ibn Marvan	684-705
Al-Walid I Ibn Abdul Malik	705-715
Sulaiman Ibn Abdul Malik	715-717
Umar II Ibn Abdul Azis Ibn Marwan	717-720
Yazid II Ibn Abdul Malik	720-724
Hisham Ibn Abdul Malik	724-743
Al-Walid II Ibn Yazid II	743-744
Yazid III Ibn al-Walid	744-744
Ibrahim Ibn al-Walid	744-744
Marwan II Ibn Muhammad Ibn al-Hamar	744-750

Abbasids of Iran and Baghdad

As-Saffah	749-754
Al-Mansur	754-775
Al-Mahdi	775-785
Al-Hadi	785-786
Harun ar-Rashid	786-809
Al-Amin	809-813
Al-Mamun	813-817
Ibrahim Ibn al-Mahdi	817-819
Al-Mutasim	833-842
Al-Wathiq	842-847
Al-Mutawakkil	847-861
Al-Muntasir	861-862
Al-Mustain	862-866
Al-Mutazz	866-869
Al-Muhtadi	869-870
Al-Mutamid	870-892
Al-Mutadid	892-902

Al-Muktafi	902-908
Al-Mugtadir	908-932
Al-Qahir	932-934
Ar-Radi	934-940
Al-Muttaqi	940-944
Al-Mustakfi	944-946
Al-Muti	946-974
At-Ta'I	974-991
Al-Qadir	991-1031
Al-Qaim	1031-1075
Al-Muqtadi	1075-1094
Al-Mustazhir	1094-1118
Al-Mustarshid	1118-1135
Ar-Rashid	1135-1136
Al-Muqtafi	1136-1160
Al-Mustanjid	1160-1170
Al-Mustadi	1170-1180
An-Nasir	1180-1225
Az-Zahir	1225-1226
Al-Mustansir	1226-1242
Al-Mustasim	1242-1258
Mongol sack of Baghdad	

Saffarids of Sistan

Yaqub Leis Saffar	867-879
Amr Ibn Leis	879-901
Tahir Ibn Mohammad	901-908
Leis Ibn Ali	908-910
Mohammad Ibn Ali	910-911
First Samanid Occupation	911-912
Amr Ibn Yaqub	912-913
Second Samanid Occupation	913-922

| Ahmad Ibn Mohammad | 922-963 |
| Khalaf Ibn Ahmad (Vali od-Dowleh) | 963-971 |

Samanids of Khorasan and Transoxiana

Ahmad I Ibn Asad Ibn Saman	819-864
Nasr I Ibn Ahmad I	864-892
Ismail I Ibn Ahmad	892-907
Ahmad II Ibn Ismail	907-914
Nasr II Ibn Ahmad II	914-943
Nuh Ibn Nasr II	943-954
Abdul Malik Ibn Nuh I	954-961
Mansur I Ibn Nuh	961-976
Nuh II Ibn Mansur	976-997
Mansur II Ibn Nuh II	997-999
Abdol Malik II Ibn Nuh II	999-1000
Ismail II (al-Muntasir)	1000-1005

Tahirids of Khorasan

Tahir I Ibn Husayn (Zol-Yaninayn)	821-822
Talheh	822-828
Abdollah	828-845
Tahir II	845-862
Mohammad	862-873

Ziyarids of Tabarestan and Gorgan

Mardavij Ibn Ziyar	927-935
Voshmgir (Zahir od-Dowleh)	935-967
Behsotun (Zahir od-Dowleh)	967-978
Qabus (Shams ol-Maali)	978-1012
Manuchehr (Falak ol-Maali)	1012-1029
Anushirvan	1029-1049
Key Kavus (Onsur ol-Maali)	1049-?

Gilan Shah	?-1090

Buyids of Iran and Iraq
Buyids of Fars & Khuzestan

Ali (Emad od-Dowleh)	934-949
Fana Khosrow (Azod od-Dowleh)	949-983
Shirzil (Sharaf od-Dowleh)	983-990
Marzban (Samsaam od-Dowleh)	990-998
Firuz (Baha od-Dowleh)	998-1012
Soltan od-Dowleh	1012-1021
Hasan (Mosharraf od-Dowleh)	1021-1024
Marzban (Emad od-Din)	1024-1048
Khosrow Firuz (Malik or-Rahim)	1048-1055
Fulad Soltan (In Fars only)	1055-1062

Fars occupation by the Kurdish Chief Fazluya

Buyids of Kerman

Ahmad (Moez od-Dowleh)	936-949
Fana Khosrow (Azod od-Dowleh)	949-983
Marzban (Samsaam od-Dowleh)	983-998
Firuz (Baha od-Dowleh)	998-1012
Qavam od-Dowleh	1012-1028
Marzban (Emad od-Din)	1028-1048

Seljuq line of Qawurd

Buyids of Jebal

Ali (Emad od-Dowleh)	932-947
Hasan (Rokn od-Dowleh)	947-977

Buyids of Hamadan and Isfahan

Buya (Moayyed od-Dowleh)	977-983
Ali (Fakhr od-Dowleh)	983-997

| Shams od-Dowleh | 997-1021 |
| Samad od-Dowleh | 1021-1028 |

Buyids of Reyy
| Ali (Fakhr od-Dowleh) | 977-997 |
| Rostam (Majd od-Dowleh) | 997-1029 |

Ghaznavid conquest

Buyids of Iraq
Ahmad (Moez od-Dowleh)	945-967
Bakhtiar (Ez od-Dowleh)	967-978
Fana Khosrow (Azod od-Dowleh)	978-983
Marzban (Samsaam od-Dowleh)	983-987
Shirzil (Sharaf od-Dowleh)	987-989
Soltan od-Dowleh	1012-1021
Hassan (Mosharraf od-Dowleh)	1021-1025
Shirzil (Jalal od-Din)	1025-1044
Marzban Emad od-Din	1044-1048
Khosrow Firus (Malik or-Rahim)	1048-1055

Saljuq occupation of Baghdad

Ghaznavids of Khorasan, Afghanistan and N India
Sebuktigin (Nasir od-Dowleh)	971-977
Ismail	977-998
Mahmud (Yamin od-Dowleh)	998-1030
Mohammad (Jalal od Dowleh) 1st reign	1030-1031
Masud (Shihab od-Dowleh)	1031-1041
Mohammad (Jalal od-Dowleh), 2nd reign	1041-1041
Mowdud (Shahab od-Dowleh)	1041-1050
Masud II	1050-1050
Ali (Baha od-Dowleh)	1050-1050
Abd or-Rashid (Ez od-Dowleh)	1050-1053

Toghril (Qavam od-Dowleh)	1053-1053
Farrokhzad (Jamal od-Dowleh)	1053-1059
Ebrahim (Zahir od-Dowleh)	1059-1099
Masud III (Ala od-Dowleh)	1099-1115
Shirzad (Kamal od-Dowleh)	1115-1115
Arsalan Shah (Soltan od-Dowleh)	1115-1118
Bahram Shah (Yamin od-Dowleh)	1118-1152
Khosrow Shah (Moez od-Dowleh)	1152-1160
Khosrow Malik (Taj od-Dowleh)	1160-1186

Seljuqs

Toghril I (Rokn od-Donya va ad-Din)	1037-1063
Alp Arsalan (Azod od-Dowleh)	1063-1072
Malik Shah (Jalal od-Dowleh)	1072-1092
Mahmud (Nasir od-Din)	1092-1094
Berk Yaruq (Rokn od-Din)	1094-1105
Malik Shah II (Moez od-Din)	1105-1105
Mohammad (Ghias od-Din)	1105-1118
Sanjar (Moez od-Din)	1118-1157

Seljuqs of Western Persia

Mahmud II (Moghis od Din)	1118-1131
Davud (Ghias od-Din)	1131-1132
Toghril II (Rokn od-Din)	1132-1134
Masud (Ghias od-Din	1134-1153
Mohammad II (Rokn od-Din)	1153-1160
Solayman Shah (Ghias od-Din)	1160-1161
Arsalan (Moez od-Din)	1161-1176
Toghril III (Rokn od-Din)	1176-1194

Khawrazm-Shahs domination

Seljuqs of Kerman

Qavurd (Imad od-Din)	1041-1073
Kermanshah	1073-1074
Husayn	1074-1074
Soltanshah (Rokn od-Dawla)	1074-1085
Turanshah (Mohy od-Din)	1085-1097
Iranshah (Baha od-Din)	1097-1101
Arsalan Shah (Mohy od-Din)	1101-1142
Mohammad I (Moghith od-Din)	1142-1156
Toghril Shah (Mohy od-Din)	1156-1170
Bahram Shah	1170-1175
Mohammad II	1183-1186

Oghuz occupation

Khwarazm-Shahs

Anushtegin	1077-1098
Qutb od-Din Mohammad	1098-1128
Alaeddin Atsiz Ibn Qotb od-Din	1128-1156
Il-Arsalan	1156-1172
Mohammad Sultanshah Ibn Ilarsalan	1172-1193
Tekish Ibn Ilarsalan (Ala od-Din)	1172-1200
Ala od-Din Mohammad	1200-1220
Jalal od-Din	1220-1231

Atabegs of Fars

Sonqor	1148-1162
Zangi	1162-1175
Takla	1175-1195
Sad	1195-1226
Abu Bakr	1226-1260
Mohammad	1260-1262
Mohammad Shah	1262-1262

Seljuq Shah	1262-1263
Abish	1263-1287

Mongols

Hulagu	1256-1265
Abaqa	1265-1282
Ahmad Tiguder	1282-1284
Arghun	1284-1291
Gaykhatu	1291-1295
Baydu	?-1295
Mahmud Ghazan	1295-1304
Oljeitu (Mohammad Khodabanda)	1304-1316
Abu Said	1316-1335
Arpa	1335-1336
Musa	1336-1353

Muzaffirids of Southern Iran

Mohammad Ibn Muzafar (Mobariz od-Din)	1314-1358
Shah Mahmud (Qotb od-Din)	1358-1364
Shah Shoja (Jalal od-Din)	1364-1384
Zayn ol-Abidin Ali (Mojahid od-Din)	1384-1387
Yaya (Nosrat od-Din) of Yazd	1387-1393
Mansur of Isfahan, Fars & Iraq	1387-1393

Jalalirids of Azerbaijan, Kurdestan and Iraq

Hassan Bozorg (Taj od-Din)	1336-1356
Oways I	1356-1374
Husayn I (Jalal od-Din)	1374-1382
Ahmad (Ghias od-Din)	1382-1410
Bayazid of Kurdistan	1382-1383
Shah Walad	1410-1411
Mahmud, 1st reign	1411-1415

Oways II	1415-1421
Mohammad	1421-1422
Mahmud, 2nd reign	1422-1424
Husayn II	1424-1432

Timurids of Transoxiana and Iran
Timurids of Samarqand

Timur (Tamburlaine)	1370-1405
Khalil	1370-1409
Shahrokh	1405-1447
Ulugh Beg	1447-1449
Abdul Latif	1449-1450
Abdollah Mirza	1450-1451
Abu Said	1451-1469
Ahmad	1469-1494
Mahmud Ibn Abu Said	1494-1500

Timurids of Western Iran after Timur

Miranshah	1404-1409
Khalil	1409-1414
Ayyal	1414-1414
Aylankar	1414-1415

Timurids of Khorasan after Ulugh Beg

Babur	1449-1457
Mahmud Ibn Babur	1457-1459
Abu Said	1459-1469
Yadegar Mohammad	1469-1470
Husayn Baqara	1470-1506
Badi oz-Zaman	1506-

Qara Quyunlu of Azerbaijan and Iraq

Qara Mohammad Turmush	1380-1389
Qara Yusof	1389-1400
Timurid invasion	
Qara Yusof, reinstated	1406-1420
Iskandar	1420-1438
Jahan Shah	1438-1467
Hassan Ali	1467-1468

Aq Quyunlu of Diyarbakir, E. Anatolia and Azerbaijan

Qara Othman (Yuluk)	1378-1435
Hamza	1435-1438
Jahangir	1444-1453
Uzaun Hassan	1453-1478
Khalil	1478-1490
Yaqub	1478-1490
Baysonqor	1490-1493
Rostam	1493-1497
Ahmad Govde	1497-1497
Morad of Qom	1497-1498
Alvand of Azerbaijan	1498-1504
Mohammad Mirza of Rars	1498-1500
Morad	1502-1508

B. Within Arab Civilization
(Islamic Shiism as State Religion)

Safavids

Ismail I	1502-1524
Tahmasp I	1524-1576
Ismail II	1576-1578
Mohammad Khoda-Banda	1578-1587

Abbas I	1588-1629
Safi I	1629-1642
Abbas II	1642-1667
Soleiman (Safi II)	1667-1694
Sultan Husayn	1694-1722
Tahmasp II	1722-1732

Afsharids

Nadir Shah	1736-1747
Adel Shah	1747-1748
Ebrahim	1748-1748
Shahrokh of Khorasan	1748-1796
Nadir Mirza of Khorasan	1797-1802

Zands

Mohammad Karim Khan	1750-1779
Abol Fath and Mohammad Ali	1779-1779
Sadiq of Shiraz	1779-1781
Ali Morad of Isfahan	1779-1785
Jafar	1785-1785
Lotf Ali Khan	1789-1794

Qajars

Aga Mohammad Khan	1779-1797
Fath Ali Shah	1797-1834
Mohammad Shah	1834-1848
Nasereddin Shah	1848-1896
Mozafareddin Shah	1896-1907
Mohammad Ali Shah	1907-1909
Ahmad Shah	1909-1924

Pahlavis

Reza Shah	1925-1941
Mohammad Reza Shah	1941-1979
Islamic Revolution	*1979-*

II. THE ACHAEMENIAN FAMILY TREE

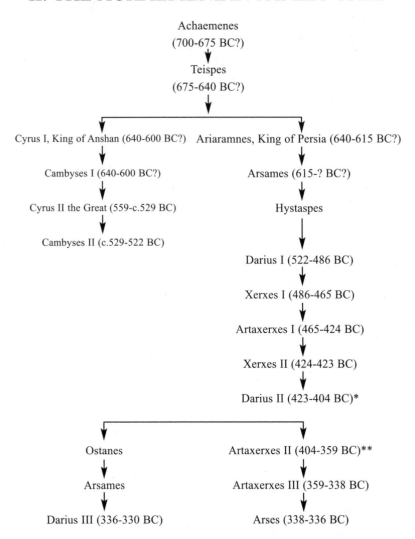

*Artaxerxes I died soon after December 24, 424 BC and was succeeded by his son Xerxes II. After a month and a half Xerxes II was murdered by his brother Secydianus (or Sogdianus). He was in turn killed by his illegitimate brother, Ochus, the son of Artaxerxes I by a Babylonian concubine, who took the name Darius and ruled as Darius II.

**Cyrus the Younger, younger son of Darius II, challenged his brother Artaxerxes II for the throne in 401 BC but did not succeed him.

III. EARLY ISLAMIC LEADERS

Prophet Mohammad (al-Mostafa)   570-632

Rashidin ("Orthodox") Sunni *Caliphs* ("Successors")

Abu Bakr as-Siddiq	632-634
Umar Ibn al-Khattab	634-644
Uthman Ibn Affan	644-656
Ali Ibn Abu Talib*	656-661

(*Mohammad's cousin and son-in-law, married to Mohammad's daughter Fatima)

Then see Ummayads and Abbasids in Appendix I

Shia *Imam*s

(Dates of lifespan)

1. Ali Ibn Abu Talib (al-Morteza)	597-661
2. Hassan Ibn Ali (al-Mojtaba)*	625-680
3. Husayn Ibn Ali (Aba-Abdullah)*	626-680
4. Ali Ibn al-Husayn (Zein ol-Abedin)	657-715
5. Mohammad Ibn Ali (al-Baqir)	676-733
6. Jafar Ibn Mohammad (al-Sadiq)	703-765
7. Musa Ibn Jafar (al-Kazim)	747-800
8. Ali Ibn Musa (ar-Reza)	765-818
9. Mohammad Ibn Ali (at-Taqi)	812-836
10. Ali Ibn Mohammad (an-Naqi)	828-869
11. Hassan Ibn Ali (al-Asgari)	839-875
12. Mohammad Ibn Hassan (al-Mahdi)	870-

(*Sons of Ali and grandsons of Mohammad)

MAP OF IRAN SHOWING
NICHOLAS HAGGER'S ROUTE

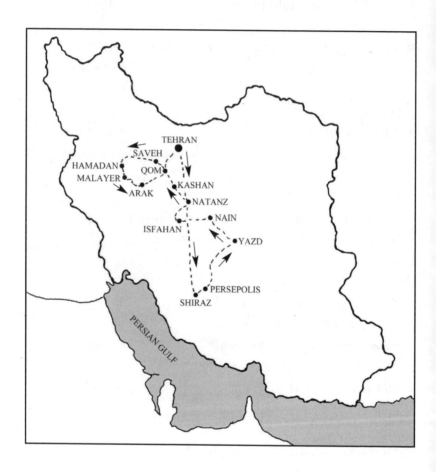

MAP OF SHIA POPULATIONS

(Percentages are of Shias in each country)

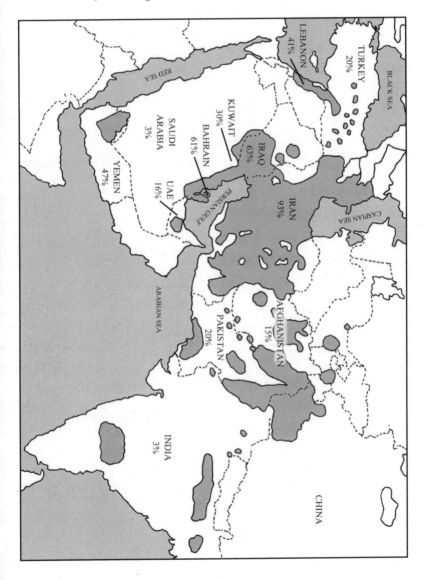

BIBLIOGRAPHY

Arnold, Matthew, 'Sohrab and Rustam' in '*A Selection*', ed. Kenneth Allott, Penguin Poets, 1954.

Berman, Ilan, *Tehran Rising*, Roman and Littlefield, 2005.

Bury, J. B., *History of Greece*, Macmillan, 1929.

Byron, Robert, *The Road to Oxiana*, Oxford University Press, 1937, 1966, 1982.

Ferdowsi's, *Shahnameh*, The Epic of the Kings, trans. by Reuben Levy, Routledge and Kegan Paul, 1967/Yassavoli Publications, Tehran, 2003.

Ghomshei, Dr Hossein Elahi, A Study *of Islamic Texts in English Translation (II)*, Tehran, n. d.

Hicks, Jim, *The Persians,* The Emergence of Man Series, Time-Life Books, 1976.

Houghton, Lord, The *Life and Letters of John Keats*, Everyman, J. M. Dent, 1954.

Khorshidian, Dr Ardeshir, A New Look at Persepolis, Makan Publications, 2004.

Marlowe, Christopher, *Tamburlaine the Great* in *Marlowe, Plays and Poems*, ed. M. R. Ridley, Everyman, J. M. Dent, 1955.

Nafisi, Nadereh*, Persepolis, Pearl of Persia*, Gooya Art House, Tehran, n. d.

Sharp, The Rev Ralph Norman, *The Inscriptions in old Persian Cuneiform of the Achaemenian Emperors*, no publisher or date on title page.

Wiesehöfer, Josef, *Ancient Persia*, I. B. Tauris, 2006.

Books by Nicholas Hagger referred to in the text:
The Light of Civilization (p64)
The Rise and Fall of Civilizations (pp4, 83, 84, 222)

BOOKS

O books
O is a symbol of the world, of oneness and unity. In different cultures it also means the "eye", symbolizing knowledge and insight, and in Old English it means "place of love or home". O books explores the many paths of understanding which different traditions have developed down the ages, particularly those today that express respect for the planet and all of life.

For more information on the full list of over 300 titles please visit our website
www.O-books.net

Created in the Image of God
A foundational course in the Kabbalah
Esther Ben-Toviya

This book provides a foundational course in the Kabbalah which speaks to the universal truths of the human experience, and is relevant to people of all backgrounds. It is a life changing, interactive course using the ancient tenets of the Kabbalah to pass on to you the experience of your unique place in the Eternal Worlds and to open your pathways of conscious conversation with the Higher Dimensions for everyday living.
1846940079 272pp **£11.99 $21.95**

Son of Karbala
The spiritual journey of an Iraqi Muslim
Shaykh Haeri

A new dawn has appeared in spiritual travelogue with the publication of Son of Karbala. It deserves a place among the great spiritual odysseys of our time, right next to Gurdjieff's Meetings with Remarkable Men, which it at once resembles and exceeds in its honesty and clarity. **Professor Bruce B. Lawrence**, Duke University, Durham NC
1905047517 240pp **£14.99 $29.95**

The Thoughtful Guide to Islam
Shaykh Haeri

About as timely as any book can be, should be read, and re-read, not only by so-called Christians but by many Muslims too. **The Guardian**
   Thoughtful without being an academic textbook, Shaykh Haeri shows

us the completeness of Islam and gives many insights. The scope of this
Thoughtful Guide is impressive. **Sangha**
1903816629 176pp **£7.99 $12.95**

The Thoughtful Guide to Sufism

Shaykh Haeri

A Sufi is a whole human being, primarily concerned with the "heart" that
reflects the truth that exists within it beyojnd time and in time. The aim is
to reach the pinnacle of "his" self by achieving physical silence. The Sufi
path is one of self denial. I found this book an absorbing and heartfelt
source of information. **Sangha**
1903816637 128pp **£9.99 $14.95**

You Called My Name
The hidden treasures of your Hebrew heritage

Esther Ben-Toviya

We are entering a new era of Jewish-Christian dialogue. This offers the
reader a guided tour of Judaism, the religion of Jesus, that will enhance
the spiritual lives of all who follow the religion about Jesus, Christianity.
This is more than a book. It is a cherished resource. **Rabbi Rami**
Shapiro, author of *The Divine Feminine.*
1905047797 272pp **£11.99 $19.95**